Developing Competencies to Teach Music
in the Elementary Classroom

Developing Competencies to Teach Music in the Elementary Classroom

Dennis M. Holt
University of North Florida

Keith P. Thompson
Pennsylvania State University

CHARLES E. MERRILL PUBLISHING COMPANY
A Bell & Howell Company
Columbus   Toronto   London   Sydney

Published by
CHARLES E. MERRILL PUBLISHING CO.
A Bell & Howell Company
Columbus, Ohio 43216

This book was set in Helvetica and Souvenir.
Production Coordination: Judith Rose Sacks
Cover Design Coordination: Will Chenoweth
Cover Photo: Larry Hamill

Photo Credits

pp. 15, 233, 283—Keith Thompson   *pp. 57, 93, 135*—Charles J.
Quinlan   *pp. 79, 145, 297*—Music Educators' National Conference
pp. 111, 247, 267—David S. Strickler   *p. 116*—Student at the
National Music Camp, Interlochen, MI. Interlochen photo by Brill

Library of Congress Catalog Card Number: 79–92853
International Standard Book Number: 0–675–08135–1
Printed in the United States of America
1 2 3 4 5 6 7 8 9 10—85 84 83 82 81 80

Contents

Acknowledgments

We wish to recognize the help of many people who have in ways great and small contributed to this book. Our students, who over the years have worked with us testing ideas and techniques. Our colleagues, who have acted as a "sounding board" making numerous suggestions. Beyond these professionals, the many people who reviewed the manuscript merit recognition. Six educators, Joan Lehr at Ohio State University, Barbara Bair at University of North Carolina–Greensboro, Sharon Mitchell at Conservatory of Music, University of Cincinnati, Sheila Brown at University of Nebraska–Lincoln, Joan Haines at Southern Connecticut State College, and Linda Gerber, Public School Music Specialist. And finally, deep appreciation is expressed to our wives and children, who understood our need to complete this book.

Preface

The elementary classroom should be a place where children learn about life by living. As a teacher, you are responsible for ensuring that your classroom is full of lifelike experiences especially structured for your particular group of students. We are aware of the awesome implications of this responsibility, but we also have known a great many elementary teachers who were extremely competent. It is our hope that this book will help you develop some of those competencies that we have observed in successful elementary teachers.

We believe that the basic purpose of education is learning to live life to its fullest extent. This is an ultimate goal for the kindergartener, the sixth grader, the high school senior, or, for that matter, the graduate student. Whatever the level, *total living* requires knowledge and skill. One must have knowledge of the people, places, events, and things that exist in the world. Of at least equal importance are a knowledge of the feelings that exist within each of us, a sensitivity to the feelings of those around us, and a knowledge of the total range of possible human feelings. *Total living* requires skill in perceiving and communicating. It also requires social and physical skill.

This book is primarily concerned with a relatively narrow segment of the knowledge and skill that are required for total living. Music is a source of knowledge of both facts and feelings. Because of its unique ability to symbolize human feelings, music provides one of the few ways through which we can share the essence of humanness with people of other times and other places. Through music we can learn what they saw and what they heard in their world—we can share their thoughts and their feelings. Through music we can also learn a great deal about our present world and about ourselves, particularly our own feelings. And through music we can share the joy of living with all humanity.

The process of developing musical skill is similar to the process of developing general skill. The skills needed to perceive the subtleties of sound in a musical composition are similar to the general skills of perception. Learning to perform and to read musical notation have some things in common with learning to communicate through the language arts. Musical experiences also provide a means for the development of social and physical skill.

Music is basic to life and therefore a part of basic education. If it is to serve this function, however, there is specific and specialized knowledge about music that one must acquire. There are specific musical skills that must be developed. The elementary years are ones in which this knowledge and this skill can most effectively be acquired by students if their teachers have the necessary competencies and if music is a part of their daily life in the school.

It is important to point out that music is an integral part of life in our society. Music sells products on television and in the shopping mall, reinforces the drama in the theater and on film, relaxes the patient in the dentist chair, builds tension in the spectators at the football game, soothes the infant to sleep, releases the energy of the teenager, announces the call letters of the radio station, and provides companionship to the lonely college student in the dormitory room. Music may also be a special part of life. Concert halls can be found in most cities, and many people set aside special times for listening to music or for taking part in musical performances. The industries that produce musical instruments and recordings play an important role in our economy. While it is important that music be a part of the ongoing daily activities in school, it is essential that special times be provided when elementary school children experience music if they are to come to know the many contributions that music makes to *total living*.

Our *primary concern* in this book is to help you develop competencies in guiding activities that will enable your students to acquire specific musical knowledge and skill; it is essential that these be acquired during the elementary years if a student is to realize the full potential of music as a part of life. We will constantly remind you, however, that other kinds of knowledge and other kinds of skill can be developed through musical experience for we believe that an integrated approach to teaching is the most effective. Not only will this enable you to accomplish more in the limited amount of time you have with students each day, but it will present a more realistic view of life to your students. Life in your classroom will be more like life itself if music is an integral part of it.

We will be advocating active involvement in musical experiences because we have found that through participation in well-planned musical activities children can develop increasing depth of knowledge about what music is and what it does. With this knowledge will come the realization of the joy that music adds to human life and an increasing knowledge of the range of feelings that are expressed through music. The amount of knowledge that students can acquire through a musical experience and the amount of enjoyment that is realized from music are directly dependent on the musical skills that students have acquired. It is therefore essential that musical experiences be sequentially planned to ensure the systematic development of musical skill. The question as to whether to begin with the development of skill or the development of knowledge is much like the "chicken or the egg" question, since each is highly dependent on the other. We have decided to utilize the musical skills of performing, listening, and creating as a structure for this book because our experience in working with both children and teachers has shown that knowledge is more easily developed within the context of a specific skill and that students of all ages find the excitement of doing more motivating than the satisfaction of knowing.

We recognize that professional musicians must have a high degree of specialized knowledge and highly refined skills in music. We are also aware that some teachers have specialized musical knowledge and skill which they have acquired through years of study and practice. Such knowledge and skill will be quite helpful in developing the competencies that we have identified in this book. We believe, however, that you can become competent in guiding musical activities in the elementary classroom with minimal musical knowledge and skill. Although they are interrelated in some ways, we believe that there is a distinct difference between *musical competence* and *competency in teaching music*. We urge you to continually work toward the development of increased musical knowledge and skill because this will enable you to have more flexibility and spontaneity in your teaching. This book, however, is not intended to help you develop musical competency but, rather, competency in *teaching music*. We believe that you can become quite competent in guiding musical activities in the elementary classroom even if your own musical knowledge and skill is quite limited.

We have found that children can most effectively learn about music and learn through music by directly participating in lifelike musical experiences. In life outside of school, people perform music, they listen to music, and they create music. We recognize that these three kinds of musical activities are closely interrelated. Listening is a part of both performing and creating. Performing is a part of creating, and listening and musical performances have an element of creativeness. For the purpose of discussion, we have found it necessary to treat performing, listening, and creating as though they were discrete musical behaviors and have designed this book to help you develop competencies in guiding activities in each area.

As we began to examine the specific competencies needed by teachers in guiding performing, listening, and creating activities, we discovered that for each kind of activity teachers must be able to assess the musical needs of students, identify goals and objectives, analyze musical materials, design and manage learning environments, and select and implement specific teaching/learning strategies. It is these behaviors that provide a structure for each of our three chapters.

Each chapter contains information about, and a description of, teaching behaviors that will lead to competence. A self-check section has been provided at the end of each chapter to give you the opportunity to assess your assimilation of these ideas. At the conclusion of each chapter, we have suggested a number of activities to be carried out in the privacy of your own room, in the campus classroom, in the library, and in the elementary classroom. These activities will enable you to practice and refine the behaviors which we have suggested. We believe that it is through a combination of reading and doing that you can begin to develop the skills of teaching. By gaining knowledge and developing skill, you can move toward *competency in teaching music in the elementary classroom*.

Learning Through Performing

OBJECTIVES

After completing this chapter, you will be able to:
- *State a rationale for performing music in the elementary classroom*
- *Identify goals and objectives for performing activities*
- *Assess musical needs of students through performing activities*
- *Analyze songs and other musical compositions as to their potential for development of musical skills and knowledge*
- *Plan effective classroom environments for performing activities*
- *Demonstrate a number of strategies for guiding performing activities*

KINDS OF PERFORMING

Musical performance is the means through which ideas and feelings are brought to life in sound. Anything that makes a sound has the potential for becoming a musical instrument. The voice is probably the oldest means of musical performance and is still the most widely used musical sound source. For this reason, and because almost everyone is capable of vocal performance, singing is the basic performance medium in the classroom. Competencies in providing opportunities for musical performance through singing are therefore considered essential for all teachers.

Because musical expression has been so important to humans, we have created many sound-producing instruments for the sole purpose of performing music. Keyboard and orchestral instruments, and more recently electronic instruments, have evolved through years of redesign and refinement and are capable of producing an endless variety of subtle variations of sound. In recent years, environmental sounds and sounds produced by machines and other objects from everyday life have also become a part of musical performances.

There are many instruments that can be played with a minimum of skill. Some instruments have even been specially designed for use in the classroom so that children (and teachers) who have not yet developed a high degree of performing skill can express ideas and feelings through musical performance. Competency in providing opportunities for musical performance through the use of classroom instruments is considered essential for teachers.

Physical movement is another means of performance to be considered in this chapter. While movement is not a means of musical performance, there is a long-established relationship between music and dance. In addition to being its own means of expression, movement, or dance, is an especially effective way to learn about music because movement can be seen and felt through space and time. Movement is an excellent way to objectify the abstract qualities of music. Competency in guiding movement activities as a means for developing musical knowledge and skill is considered essential for teachers. For this reason, performance through movement will be considered in this chapter along with performance through singing and playing instruments.

WHY PERFORM IN THE CLASSROOM?

Educators have long recognized the value of "learning by doing." Singing, playing instruments, and moving to music are ways of "doing music." This makes them effective ways for developing musical knowledge and skills. The more young children know about music and the more musical skills they develop, the more they will find that music is a meaningful and enjoyable part of their life. Later you will learn more about specific goals for musical learning, but let us point out here that singing, playing, and moving to melodies are very good ways to help your children learn about melodic movement. Also, singing, playing, and moving to rhythm patterns are very good ways to learn about rhythmic relationships that exist within music. Therefore, we consider performing music to be an important activity for elementary school children; *we have found musical performance to be an effective—perhaps the most effective—way of developing specific knowledge about music.*

Musical performance is an effective way to develop musical skills, too. Many musical skills can be ends in themselves. Millions of people have found a lifetime of enjoyment in playing musical instruments and singing. It goes without saying that one learns to play by *playing,* and one learns to sing by *singing.* We must point out, however, that merely providing the opportunity for children to perform will not necessarily ensure the development of performance skill. You should realize that sequentially planned performing activities will result in the most effective skill development.

In addition to being ends in themselves, musical skills are necessary if one is to develop musical knowledge by "doing music." Singing, playing instruments, and moving to music are practical applications of musical knowledge. The acquisition and retention of knowledge are usually more efficient when that knowledge can be *applied.* Many children are capable of understanding much more musical knowledge than they now possess. In the past, they have been limited because they lacked the musical skills through which to develop their musical knowledge. Please do not limit your students' musical knowledge by not helping them develop the performing skills that have been found to be important ways for acquiring knowledge. So, a second reason that we consider performing music to be important in the elementary classroom is that *it provides the opportunity to develop musical skills.*

A musical performance can also provide the opportunity to develop more general knowledge. The text of a song or the circumstances in which a particular composition was created may provide important facts about the world, people, or events. The way in which the various parts or sections of a composition are combined may provide a source of knowledge about relationships that exist not only in the music but also in the world. Perhaps the most unique contribution of music is that it is a source of knowledge about feelings. While children are singing, playing, or moving to music, they can learn how it feels to be part of a group working for a common goal; how it feels to be a special soloist; how it feels to help someone else on a part; and, perhaps, how it feels to have a friend help them. Because musical performance requires skill and knowledge quite different from many other school activities, performing may be the only opportunity for success that some students find in school. The entire range of human feelings from extreme joy to deep sadness, from lonely tranquility to exuberant excitement, has been expressed through music. A carefully executed musical performance can recreate these feelings in the classroom, permitting your students to experience feelings that may be outside of their usual emotional experiences. In summary, a third reason for performing music in the elementary classroom is that *it provides the opportunity to develop knowledge about the world, about people, about events, and about emotion and feelings.*

A final reason for performing in the classroom is that a musical performance can be a way of developing general skills. Performing through singing, playing instruments, or moving to music requires perception of the sounds being produced; it requires interaction with others in the group; and it requires a communication of the intent of the composer and of the leader of the performing group. Many performing activities require reading of both musical notation and the text of songs. Performing is an expression of ideas and feelings of both the composer and the performer. Reading and expressing are both important aspects of communication. Playing instruments and moving to music provide the opportunity for children to develop physical skills. Since most classroom performances are group performances, they afford students the opportunity to develop important social skills.

We are not suggesting that musical experiences could provide total learning experiences in schools. We recognize that learning to read the texts of songs may not be the most efficient way to learn to read and that developing physical skills through moving to music may not provide for total physical development. What we are suggesting is that many of the skills that are to be developed during the school years are utilized in performing experiences. It is our belief that *performing music provides an opportunity for children to practice, refine, and develop those general skills.*

COMPETENCIES FOR GUIDING PERFORMANCE

If musical knowledge and skills and general knowledge and skills are to be developed through performance activities, there must be daily opportunities to perform in the elementary classroom. In many instances, a music specialist will be available to provide some assistance, but the major responsibility for guiding performance activities rests with the classroom teacher. Many classroom teachers can sing, play instruments, and move to music with a high degree of skill. Others have not had the opportunity to develop these skills.

While there is some advantage for the teacher who has performing skills, we have seen many teachers with limited musical skills who are highly competent in guiding the classroom performances of their students. As stated earlier, we urge all of our readers to work toward the development and further refinement of performing skills. The intent of this chapter, however, is to help you develop competencies in guiding the musical performances of students in your classroom. Many of these competencies are independent of your own skills of musical performance.

The effective guidance of musical performance is a cluster of interrelated behaviors, many of which must occur simultaneously. These include the identification of goals, assessment of student needs, identification of instructional objectives, analysis of musical materials, designing and managing learning environments, and selecting teaching/learning strategies and the development of classroom procedures.

For the purposes of our discussion, we have dissected the process of guiding performing activities so that we can examine each of the behaviors listed. Please remember, however, that to be a competent teacher you must not only be able to carry out each of the steps independently, but you must also be able to combine them in a variety of ways within the context of musical performance in the elementary classroom.

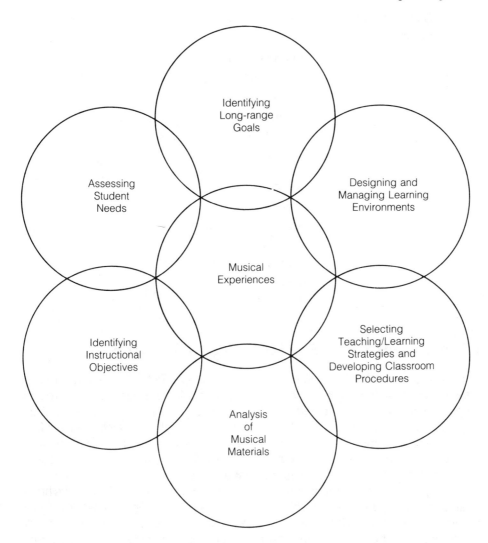

The specific competencies that we believe are necessary for all teachers in guiding performing activities are found in the following list. The intent of this chapter is to help you develop these competencies. The competent teacher can

- Identify musical and general goals that can be achieved through performing experiences
- Assess students' musical knowledge and skill through performing activities
- Identify instructional objectives for performing activities
- Analyze musical material, identifying goals that may be achieved through musical performance
- Design and manage teaching/learning enviroments appropriate for performing activities

• Select and carry out specific strategies and procedures for guiding performing activities:

> Call and response
> Echo phrase
> Play along
> What's it about
> Listen to a record
> Reading from notation
> Ostinato
> Rounds
> Partner songs
> Performing in harmony
> Free movement
> Accompanied movement
> Feeling the sound
> Folk dance

IDENTIFYING GOALS FOR PERFORMING ACTIVITIES

In the section, "Why Perform in the Classroom?" we indicated that the reason for including performing activities in the school curriculum was that they provide opportunities for the development of musical knowledge and skills as well as general knowledge and skill. As you continue through this book, you will find that the development of knowledge and skill is the ultimate goal for all musical activities in the classroom. This is a rather broad goal, and it will provide some guidance as you plan classroom musical activities.

We have found, however, that the more competent teachers have rather specific goals toward which to work. (It is rather difficult to get anywhere if you don't know where you are going.) Specific goals for any classroom activity should be based on the identified needs of the students. The students' backgrounds, present levels of achievement, and interests, as well as the specific goals in other curricula areas, should all influence the specific goals set for classroom performing activities. We can, however, provide a few general performing activity goals that have been identified by music educators based on a number of years of research and experience with elementary school students. We recognize that there are a great many other goals that could be met through performing activities. Our list is intended to represent minimal goals and to provide a basis from which you can identify more specific performing goals for your students. Classroom performing activities should provide students opportunities to

1. Experience the joy and satisfaction that comes from performing music

2. Experience a wide variety of music through singing, playing instruments, and moving to music alone and with others

3. Develop increased understanding of melody, rhythm, harmony, dynamics, timbre, and form

4. Develop skill in performing music accurately

5. Develop increasing awareness of the ideas and feelings expressed through musical performance

6. Develop skill in performing music expressively

7. Develop skill in using musical notation

You will notice that our list has not included goals for the development of general knowledge and skill. We do not imply a lesser importance for these goals but have chosen to limit our listing to musical goals. Competent classroom teachers will be able to add specific goals for general learning to this list.

You may also notice that we have not differentiated goals for lower, middle, or upper grades. We believe the goals that we have identified are appropriate for all grade levels. Certainly we would expect a higher level of skill development and a deeper understanding in upper-grade students than in students in the lower grades. Because of the broad range in both quality and quantity of musical experiences available to elementary school students, to say nothing of the wide variation of musical experiences provided in homes, we find it impossible to identify more specific goals for developmental levels. These must be based on an assesment of student needs.

ASSESSING MUSICAL NEEDS THROUGH PERFORMANCE

The assessment of student needs is one of the most important phases of the planning process. *Assessment* is the process of collecting data about the degree to which students have met identified goals. Decisions as to which musical materials you will use and what strategies and learning environments you will employ must be based on information about the present level of musical knowledge and skill of the students.

The process of assessment will enable you to determine how well students sing, play instruments, or move to music. It can also help you decide what knowledge they have developed about music. Assessment procedures can be used to identify students' attitudes toward music or the musical values that they have developed. If used with care, assessment can be a positive force in your classroom. It can make you a better teacher and help your students become more effective learners.

Although there may be times when you will plan a particular activity to "test" the students' knowledge or skill, assessment should be an ongoing process—a part of every musical activity. At times you will be collecting data about groups of students to make decisions as to what "class needs" might be. At other times, you will be assessing the musical needs of individuals within the class. Recent legislation has required educators to consider the unique needs of handicapped and gifted learners and to design an Individualized Educational Program (IEP) for each of them. An IEP begins with an assessment of the student's present level of achievement. The aesthetic, or musical, needs of students should be considered as part of every IEP.

Even though you will not be writing an IEP for every student in your classroom, we urge you to make continual assessments of the musical needs of individual students. We have found that competent teachers recognize the individuality of every student and plan learning experiences to meet students' unique needs.

We suggest three questions as guides in the process of assessment:

1. Do the students know what I am trying to teach (or can they perform it) before I teach it?
2. Did the students learn what I tried to teach?
3. Did the students enjoy what they learned?

We urge you to keep these questions in mind as you plan and guide musical activities in your classroom.

We have found that one of the most effective procedures for assessment is the observation of students' performances. The ways in which students perform often demonstate their knowledge about music as well as their musical skills. The checklists on pages 9–10 can be used as guides for observing either individual or group performances. The "possible problems" included in each section are not intended to be all-inclusive but rather to indicate what we have found to be some of the most common problems in elementary school children's musical performances. We urge you to analyze each performance carefully and identify the positive factors of each as well as those aspects which need improvement.

There may be times when you will want to make assessments of some particular aspects of students' knowledge or performing skills. You may, for example, design a "paper and pencil test" to identify knowledge about music, skill in working with musical notation, or students' attitudes toward music. We point out, however, that assessment of musical knowledge and skill is most effectively carried out within a musical context. To make such assessments, you may design specific performance tasks through which students can demonstrate their present level of achievement. Asking students to play stepwise and skipwise melodies, for example, may demonstrate their knowledge of melodic movement. Asking students to clap duple and triple meter may demonstrate their understanding of meter. Having students walk to a recorded composition that changes tempo may reveal their perception of beat and tempo. It must be recognized, however, that poorly developed motor skills may limit a student's performing ability and that a particular performance may not adequately reveal his or her knowledge. It is for this reason that assessments should not be based on data collected on one occasion or through one type of procedure.

ASSESSMENT OF PERFORMING ACTIVITIES

Student (Class) _____ School _____ Date _____
Observer _____

A.   Accuracy of the Performance

   1. Was the performance melodically accurate?
      Possible problems
      _____ range too high (   ) too low (   )
      _____ intervals unfamiliar
      _____ did not observe key signature or accidentals
      _____ did not read notation accurately
      Did physical movement reflect melodic movement?

   2. Was the performance rhythmically accurate?
      Possible problems
      _____ unable to maintain steady beat
      _____ unable to feel metric accent
      _____ inappropriate tempo
              too fast (   ) too slow (   )
      _____ failure to observe tempo changes
      _____ inability to perform specific patterns
              dotted rhythms (   ) syncopation (   ) triplets (   )
              sixteenth notes (   ) other _____ (   )
      _____ did not read notation accurately
      Did physical movement reflect rhythm of the music?

   3. Was the performance harmonically accurate?
      Possible problems
      _____ incorrect chords
      _____ chords played at incorrect time
      _____ parts not in tune with one another
      _____ major and minor modes confused
      Did physical movement reflect harmonic changes?

B.   Expressiveness of the Performance

      Was the performance musically expressive?
      Possible problems
      _____ more attention needed to dynamics
      _____ more attention needed to phrasing
      _____ more attention needed to articulation
      _____ more attention needed to tone
      Were physical movements expressive of the feelings in the music?

ASSESSMENT OF PERFORMING ACTIVITIES

C.   Skillfulness of the Performance

Was the performance skillful?
Suggested improvements
_____ more careful listening to one another
_____ more careful watching the leader (conductor)
_____ more skillful manipulation of instruments
(need to develop more technique through practice)
_____ more careful reading of musical notation
Were physical movements free? (   ) or inhibited? (   )
Did movements reflect an awareness of body (   ) space (   ) time (   )

D.   Joyfulness of the Performance

Did students enjoy participating in the performance?
_____ facial expressions showed joy
_____ body movements indicated enjoyment
_____ positive verbal comments
_____ requested more time for activity or requested to repeat the experience

IDENTIFYING OBJECTIVES FOR PERFORMING ACTIVITIES

After long-range goals for performing in the classroom have been identified and an assessment has been made of students' musical needs, it becomes necessary to state specific objectives for performing activities. *Objectives* identify student behaviors that will occur as part of the activity. Because of the emphasis on student behavior, the term *behavioral objective* is sometimes used to describe these statements. We consider skill in writing such objectives essential for teaching in all subject areas, but the development of such skill is beyond the scope of this book.[1] We will, however, provide a brief overview of the process in a music-teaching context.

An objective must contain an *action verb*. In most instances, the verb should identify an observable student behavior. The following are some examples of objectives for performing activities:

1. Students will sing the melody of "The Elephant."
2. Students will step to the steady beat as the teacher sings the song.
3. Students will describe the melodic direction of the last phrase.
4. Students will play the notated rhythm pattern on the tambourine.
5. Students will clap the first beat of each measure while singing the song.

There are some musical behaviors that are not directly observable. Perceiving melodic direction and feeling the steady beat are musical behaviors, but observation does not always reveal what a student is perceiving or feeling. For this reason, it frequently becomes necessary to translate the covert musical behavior into some overt behavior through which the student can demonstrate a particular knowledge or skill. The following are some examples:

1. Students will demonstrate awareness of melodic direction of the last phrase by drawing lines on the chalkboard.
2. Students will demonstrate awareness of the changing tempo by moving to the beat of the music.
3. Student will demonstrate awareness of melodic skips through discussion.
4. Students will demonstrate a feeling of meter by playing percussion instruments on the first beat of each measure.
5. Students will demonstrate the enjoyment of an activity by requesting to repeat it.

---

1. If additional work is needed on writing objectives, the student is referred to Norman E. Gronlund, *Stating Objectives for Classroom Instruction*, 2nd Edition (New York: Macmillan Publishing Co., 1978).

Because the end product of musical activities is not always observable behaviors, we use the term *instructional objectives* to identify those specific objectives that are necessary for each musical activity. Table 1 may help you to formulate instructional objectives for musical activities. "Action Verbs" suggest students' behaviors, "Content" suggests knowledge that may be gained through an experience, and "Conditions" give criteria of acceptance and/or conditions under which the students will perform. If you are primarily concerned with developing skill, an action verb and statement of condition may be all you need for an objective:

1. The students will sing "The Goat" without accompaniment.
2. The students will play maracas and claves from notation.
3. The students will enjoy singing "Lame Tame Crane."

In planning classroom musical activities, you may also want to state objectives for the development of general knowledge and general skills. In most instances we have not done so, because the emphasis of this book is on teaching *music*. As you plan musical activities for children, we urge you to consider the development of general knowledge and skill and include some of these objectives in your planning.

TABLE 1 *Instructional Objectives Guide*

Action Verb	Content	Conditions
Sing	Melody upward—downward	Accurately
Play	stepwise—skipwise jagged—smooth	With 80 percent accuracy
Clap		As the teacher sings the song
Move	Rhythm beat	To a recording
Conduct	tempo meter	Without accompaniment
Describe	rhythm pattern	Without a recording
Identify		From notation
List	Dynamics loud—soft changing	While singing the song
Demonstrate		On the last phrase of the song
Explore	Timbre	While listening to
Invent		On the tambourine
Organize	Harmony unison—harmony chords	On the melody bells

Action Verb	Content	Conditions
Perceive	polyphonic	
	consonance—dissonance	
Feel		
Enjoy	Form	
	phrase	
	sections	
	contrast-repetition	
	variation	

ANALYZING MUSICAL MATERIALS FOR PERFORMANCE

One of your tasks as a teacher will be to select the music that your students will perform. Perhaps the first question you should ask yourself in choosing music is "Would I enjoy performing this music?" For, if you enjoy the particular composition, chances are very good that your enthusiasm will rub off on your students.

In addition to being an enjoyable experience, classroom performance should also be a learning experience. As a teacher you will need competency in analyzing musical materials to determine their potential for specific kinds of learning. While some knowledge of "music theory" is necessary for such analysis, a teacher with limited knowledge can easily identify some important musical aspects of every composition to point out to students as they take part in performing activities.

Since music is basically a *sound* experience, analysis of musical materials should always begin with the *sound* of a particular composition. Unless you have a good "mental image" of the sound of a particular selection, we suggest that you begin by listening to a recording, by playing the composition on piano or recorder, or by singing the song yourself. The process of analysis is essentially that of answering this question: What knowledge and skills can effectively be developed as the students perform this composition? Specifically, you should ask the following:

1. What musical knowledge can be developed?
    a) What aspects of melody are clearly illustrated in this composition?
    b) What aspects of rhythm are clearly illustrated in this composition?
    c) What aspects of harmony are clearly illustrated in this composition?
    d) What aspects of dynamics, tempo, and color are clearly illustrated in this composition?
    e) What aspects of form are clearly illustrated in this composition?

2. What musical skills can be developed?
    a) What singing skills can be developed through this composition?
    b) What playing skills can be developed through this composition?
    c) What movement skills can be developed through this composition?
    d) What listening skills can be developed through this composition?
    e) What creating skills can be developed through this composition?

3. What general knowledge can be developed?
    a) What knowledge about people, places, or events can be gained through performing this composition?
    b) What knowledge about relationships can be gained through performing this composition?
    c) What knowledge of emotions and feelings can be gained through performing this composition?

4. What general skills can be developed?
    a) What interpersonal and social skills can be developed through performing this composition?
    b) What communication skills can be gained through performing this composition?
    c) What (specify other skills that you have identified as needs of your students) can be gained through performing this composition.

It is quite unlikely that any one performing experience will accomplish all of these things. In fact, you would probably overwhelm your students if you attempted to accomplish too much at any one time. The primary interest in some musical compositions is in the melody, while in others it may be in the harmony or rhythm. Some compositions will relate very well to other aspects of the curriculum, while others will not. We urge you, however, to begin your planning of classroom performing experiences with an analysis of the musical materials to determine what knowledge and skills can be developed through performance. The following are examples of analysis made by competent teachers.

Clap Your Hands

American folk song collected by Ruth Crawford Seeger

SOURCE: From Elizabeth Crook, Bennett Reimer, and David S. Walker, *Music*, Book 1 (Morristown, N.J.: Silver Burdett Co., 1978), p. 37. Used with permission.

ANALYSIS OF MUSIC FOR PERFORMING

TITLE: "CLAP YOUR HANDS"
SOURCE: *MUSIC*, BOOK 1, p. 37

MUSICAL KNOWLEDGE THAT CAN BE DEVELOPED
    MELODY   *Low and high*
    RHYTHM   *Steady beat, slow and fast (first section slow, second
                 section fast)*
    TIMBRE   *Two contrasting sounds—one each section*
    HARMONY
    DYNAMICS
    FORM   *AB*
MUSICAL SKILLS THAT CAN BE DEVELOPED
    SINGING   *Extending range upward*
    PLAYING   *Percussion instruments*
    MOVING   *To steady beat*
    LISTENING
    CREATING
    READING
    DESCRIBING   *Difference between two sections*
GENERAL KNOWLEDGE THAT CAN BE DEVELOPED
    OF THE WORLD   *Body parts*
    OF RELATIONSHIPS   *Ways in which things contrast*
    OF FEELINGS
GENERAL SKILLS THAT CAN BE DEVELOPED
    PERCEIVING
    COMMUNICATING
    SOCIAL SKILLS   *Working as part of a group*
    PHYSICAL SKILLS   *Large- and small-muscle coordination*
    OTHER

The Death of Mister Fly

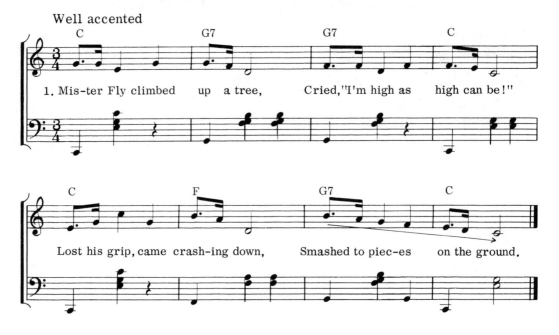

Well accented

1. Mis-ter Fly climbed   up   a tree,   Cried,"I'm high as   high can be!"

Lost his grip, came crash-ing down,   Smashed to piec-es   on the ground.

2. When the insects heard the sound
   Echoing for miles around,
   They began to buzz and cry,
   "Quick! First aid for Mister Fly!"

3. "Where's a bandage?" "Where's a splint?"
   "Get some liniment and lint!"
   "Someone, give him aspirin!"
   "Should we call the doctor in?"

4. Then a wise old flea spoke out,
   "You don't know what you're about!
   He's beyond the reach of aid,
   Get a pick and get a spade!"

5. Then at last those insects knew
   What they really had to do!
   Now his tombstone bears the scrawl:
   "He who climbs too high must fall."

Source: English words by Margaret Marks. From SILVER BURDETT MUSIC, Book 1. © 1974
General Learning Corporation. Reprinted by permission of Silver Burdett Company.

ANALYSIS OF MUSIC FOR PERFORMING

TITLE: "THE DEATH OF MR. FLY"
SOURCE: *MUSIC*, BOOK 1 P. 21

MUSICAL KNOWLEDGE THAT CAN BE DEVELOPED
    MELODY   *Downward scale line, last phrase*
    RHYTHM   *Uneven, "bouncy" rhythm of dotted notes*
    HARMONY
    TIMBRE
    DYNAMICS
    FORM

MUSICAL SKILLS THAT CAN BE DEVELOPED
    SINGING   *Small groups or solos on dialogue parts*
    PLAYING   *Tone bells on last phrase, autoharp accompaniment (C, F, G_7*
                        chords)
    MOVING
    LISTENING
    CREATING
    READING   *Line and traditional notation for last phrase*
    DESCRIBING   *Melodic direction of last phrase*

GENERAL SKILLS THAT CAN BE DEVELOPED
    OF THE WORLD   *Insects*
    OF RELATIONSHIPS
    OF FEELINGS   *All living things experience death.*

GENERAL SKILLS THAT CAN BE DEVELOPED
    SOCIAL SKILLS   *Cooperation*
    COMMUNICATION SKILLS
    PHYSICAL SKILLS   *Eye-hand coordination for playing bells*
    Other

ENVIRONMENTS FOR PERFORMING

The Human Environment

The classroom environment is a crucial element in the learning process. Just as the farmer cannot determine the amount of rain that will fall on his crops nor the temperatures during the growing season, the teacher cannot control all elements of the classroom environment. The farmer is, however, aware of the "yearly averages" for his geographical area and plans crops that will thrive in that environment. He also prepares, when necessary, to supplement the natural rainfall through irrigation. To be a competent teacher, you should be aware of the effects of various environments on the learning process and be prepared to alter environments, when necessary, for more productive learning.

The most important part of the learning environment is the human interaction which takes place during the learning process. Because of the uniqueness of individuals, this human environment is also the most difficult to predict and to control. Yet, it has often been said that a good teacher can be effective in any classroom and without a lot of "fancy" equipment and materials.

Each combination of teacher and students forms a unique human environment with many subtle interactions that defy discussion or categorization. For the purposes of this text, however, three types of human environment will be identified. You must remember that the distinctions are not absolute, nor are the categories all-inclusive. We are not implying a value ordering of environmental categories. All three may be equally valid in some circumstances. Teaching styles, learning styles, the nature of the subject matter, and the physical environment interact to determine the effectiveness of a given human environment for learning.

Autocratic Environment

An *autocratic environment* is teacher-centered and is characterized by lectures, demonstrations, presentations, and teacher-directed performances. The teacher asks closed questions which require short, direct, and precise answers from the students. In a "performing activity," some typical teacher behaviors in an autocratic environment would be

1. Providing models of the song
2. Giving countdowns and playing accompaniments
3. Instructing students to clap certain rhythmic patterns
4. Instructing students to draw melodic contours in the air
5. Asking questions such as:
   a) Does the melody in the first phrase move up or down?
   b) How many counts will the last note get?
   c) From what country did this song come?
   d) What are the letter names of the first two notes?

e) Which measure has the octave skip?

f) What chords should we use to accompany this song on the autoharp?

6. Assigning certain students accompanimental parts on percussion instruments

7. Rehearsing particular phrases until they are performed accurately

In an autocratic environment the students' attention is focused on the teacher and on the subject matter. Students answer questions rather than ask them. Interaction between students is discouraged, although cooperation and a "team spirit" is desired. The autocratic environment is characteristic of most bands, choirs, and other performing groups.

Within the autocratic environment, the teacher's role is that of leader, source of knowledge, disciplinarian, decision maker, and musical director. The student is the recipient of knowledge, the follower, and the musical performer.

Democratic Environment

The *democratic environment* is characterized by discovery learning. Teacher and students share leadership roles. The teacher at times may lecture, make presentations, demonstrate musical performance, and direct performances. The questions asked by the teacher are more open-ended, requiring exploration of the materials and thinking on the part of the students. Some typical teacher behaviors in a democratic environment would be

1. Asking students to choose music to be performed

2. Assisting students in playing accompaniments

3. Suggesting that students improvise rhythmic patterns to accompany the song

4. Asking questions such as:

   a) What do the words tell us about the people in this song?

   b) What does the tempo tell us about the people in this song?

   c) What do the instruments used in the accompaniment tell us about the place where this song was written?

   d) What do you notice about the melody of this piece?

   e) Where are the longest notes in this song?

   f) Are there any large skips in this song?

   g) Could we accompany this song on the autoharp?

5. Asking for volunteers to play accompaniments on instruments

6. Recording a performance and asking students to listen to the recording and suggest ways in which the performance might be improved

In the democratic environment, the students share the responsibility for learning. Students are encouraged to think for themselves, make evaluations, and ask questions. Interaction between students is considered a part of the learning process since one student may be able to answer another student's questions more effectively than the teacher. Students and teacher work together for a good performance although the *process* through which the performance is achieved is considered more important than the final product itself.

Open, Informal Environment

Open school environments are child-centered. The teacher is a facilitator, a provider of materials, and a diagnostician. The teacher establishes the physical environment, then observes and analyzes the student interactions within that environment. On the basis of this observation, the student's future needs are determined and a new environment planned. Throughout the process, the teacher may ask open-ended questions that cause the students to analyze the materials with which they are working and/or their own musical performances. Some typical teacher behaviors during a performance activity in an open environment might be

1. Providing recordings of songs
2. Providing time and space for students to engage in performing activities
3. Observing students as they choose songs, noting the kinds of songs they choose and the factors that influence choice
4. Observing students as they learn songs, noting the procedures they use and the difficulties they encounter
5. Intervening in the above processes when necessary with questions such as:
   a) Have you thought about learning new songs?
   b) Did you notice any songs in the book from Japan?
   c) What makes a good song?
   d) If the recording is too fast, could you learn the last phrase by playing it on the piano?
   e) Have you thought about instruments which would provide good accompaniments for this song? What would they play?
   f) Here is a tape recorder. Record your performance on tape and compare it with the phonograph recording.
   g) What does the text of this song tell you about the people of Japan?
   h) What does the melody (or rhythm) tell you about the people of Japan?
   i) What is unusual about the harmony of this song?

In an open environment, the student is responsible for learning. For the most part, student interests and needs determine the content of the curriculum. Minimal restrictions are placed on the use of time and space, and students are encouraged to freely interact with one another in the belief that students can learn much from each other. Musical performances are prepared by the students. Evaluation by the teacher is in terms of the learning that occurs in the *process* of preparing and presenting the performance rather than in the final product itself.

The Physical Environment

The human and physical environments interact to affect the learning process. Space, time, and materials available will, to some extent, influence the human environment that is created within the classroom. The human environment will, in turn, influence the way in which space, time, and materials are utilized.

Time

Singing, playing instruments, and moving to music can occur at any time in the classroom. A designated time each day for performing will ensure the daily practice necessary for building skills and will contribute to the systematic musical growth of children. Such "performing time" may be part of another classroom routine. It may, for example, mark the beginning of a "sharing circle" or follow the morning "Pledge of Allegiance."

More spontaneous performing should occur at other times to meet student needs. Time to sing "Canoe Song" during a discussion of the lifestyle of the American Indian, for example, may meet cognitive needs of the students. Likewise, singing and playing instruments to songs in duple and triple meter may help children clarify concepts of grouping in math. A lively song may help revive the class on a dreary afternoon or after they have been working for some time on a difficult project, thus meeting the students' affective needs. An action song may constructively channel physical activity while the class is waiting for the arrival of a bus or for their turn to go to the library.

Time for performing music will, in most instances, be determined by the teacher. Students may, however, suggest performing activities as part of many classroom events. For example, a student may recall the ballads of John Henry or Davy Crockett while reading these folk legends and suggest the class sing them. Or, a student may bring to school a song learned at camp or scouts and request time to share it with other students.

The amount of time devoted to performing activities will vary among classrooms. Some states require a specific number of minutes for musical activities, others recommend minimums. There is no question that time is a crucial element of the classroom environment. Students need experiences in many subject areas, all of which require the expenditure of time. Most songs performed in elementary school do not exceed two minutes in length. Even in the busiest classroom, two minutes for performing can be found several times each day.

Space

Space requirements for performing activities are quite flexible. Performing can occur in almost any classroom arrangement and with any grouping of students. There are, however, some arrangements that are more effective than others for certain performing activities.

Learning rote songs and engaging in performing activities that include physical movement are often most effective with the children seated in an informal manner on the floor. In such instances, the teacher should also sit on the floor or on a low stool so as not to appear a "giant" towering over the students.

Performance from musical notation often requires the use of music books. The management of books in an informal setting can become a problem. In such instances, it may be more advantageous to have children seated at desks. Chairs and desks are also recommended if the performing activity is to include writing or careful listening since the more informal seating arrangements encourage student interactions which distract from listening. Sitting with good posture in chairs is also more conducive to good vocal tone and improved vocal range.

There is a disadvantage to singing in the usual classroom arrangement of desks and chairs. Students are placed at some distance from one another and may be unable to hear the voices of many other children. This leads to the feeling that "I'm the only one singing" and tends to inhibit singing, particularly in older students. A solution to this problem is standing, away from desks and chairs, in a "choir" formation. This provides the posture necessary for singing as well as a more formal setting, and it permits students to hear one another as they sing.

Moving to music probably requires more careful planning of the space environment than any other musical activity. Some movements, such as clapping, toe tapping, or drawing phrases in the air with hands, can be accomplished in very limited space. Folk dances and creative movement activities require much larger space.

Some space should be provided in every classroom for students' small-group performances. We have discussed the importance of building performing skills for both enjoying music and developing greater musical knowledge. The development of skill requires practice, and it is your responsibility as a teacher to provide space in your classroom for students to practice musical skills. Unfortunately, the sounds from musical performances can be distracting to both children working at other things and to children involved in practice. One child cannot practice soft sounds on a drum if other children are singing or playing loudly on a tambourine. Ideally, a classroom should have one or two small rooms in which children can work when sound becomes a problem. Although such space is seldom available, we have seen *sound spaces* provided by competent teachers. One very satisfactory *sound house* was constructed by lining a large applicance box with carpet. While it was not soundproof, the carpet did absorb much of the sound and provided a space in which students could practice musical performing skills.

Fortunately, most classrooms now offer a great deal of flexibility in the kinds of space available. The competent teacher must carefully plan for the kind of space that will contribute to the most effective learning environment for each activity.

Materials

Classroom performing can occur without necessitating any materials other than a song. There are, however, a number of materials that will enrich the students' experiences. Instruments such as autoharp, xylophone, ukulele, guitar, or piano can be utilized by the teacher and students for accompanying singing. A good-quality record player should be available if recordings are to be utilized as models of songs for children. Excellent recordings of the songs found in current elementary music textbooks are available and can be invaluable to teachers with limited musical skills. A collection of printed song materials should also be available for both students and teacher in order to permit the constant addition of new songs to the repertoire. An overhead projector is also an excellent way to present song material to a large group of students, and a good-quality tape recorder is a valuable tool for the assessment of performing activities.

Managing the Environments

The way in which classroom environments are managed is an extremely important factor in the learning process. It is your responsibility as a teacher to manage the interaction of human and physical elements in such a way that performing activities can be effectively carried out and the learning objectives met. Our experience in working with elementary-aged children has suggested a number of specific management techniques. Effective classroom management begins with careful planning for the way in which you and your students will interact with one another and with the physical aspects of the learning environment. Such planning enables you to determine the kinds of behaviors that you will expect from your students. Planning also implies communication of these expectations to your students. When your students are clearly aware of your expectations, problem behavior will be minimal.

MANAGEMENT TECHNIQUES FOR PERFORMING ACTIVITIES

1. *Know the music well.*
    a) Memorize songs so that you can maintain eye contact with students.
    b) Be familiar enough with accompaniments so that you can look at students frequently.
    c) If performing with a recording, know what is on the record. Is there an introduction? How long? How many verses are recorded? Are there instrumental interludes between verses?

2. *Establish efficient classroom routines.*
   a) Plan procedures for passing out music books or song sheets. Could the class sing a familiar song while this is being done?
   b) Plan procedures for assigning and distributing instruments. What criteria will you use for choosing players?
   c) Plan procedures for moving from one area of the classroom to another. How will students get to the open space? Can it be done in a musical context (one row for each phrase)? How will they return to their seats?
   d) Establish a routine for what to do with instruments when they are not to be played. "Mallets on the desk" or "Place the instruments on the floor under your chair" are examples of routines that can be established.

3. *Provide clear and concise directions.*
   a) Establish a routine for starting a song. Students need to hear starting pitch and tempo and be given a starting point.
   b) When playing introductions, keep them short—one phrase. Students want to perform, not listen to you play.
   c) Musical (or movement) demonstrations are frequently more effective than verbal explanations.

4. *Help students learn the music.*
   a) Analyze music before class to anticipate problem areas.
   b) Break down difficult sections into simple patterns and plan a variety of ways to help students learn those patterns—through clapping, playing instruments, moving, or singing.
   c) Refer to notation whenever possible. Notation will help students become independent music learners, but they must be taught to read it.
   d). Return to a given musical selection on successive days. Unless children can sing a song on the school bus or at home "in the shower," they have not learned the song.
   e) Perform with the students, but do not let them become dependent on your performance. Frequently stop singing or playing and listen to their performance.
   f) When using recordings, do not let students become dependent on recordings for support. As students learn a song, decrease the volume of the record player. Remember, your goal is to help students become independent performers.

5. *Plan transitions from one activity to another.*
   a) Point out relationships between musical selections. "Here is another song about an animal." "Now let's perform a work song that also has syncopated rhythm." "Phrasing is important in singing. Let's find out if it is important in moving."
   b) Sequence activities so that the mood of the music can shape the overall mood of the class. A fast-tempo song that includes physical movement may be a good way to draw the class

together after an exciting game at recess. Follow this with a quiet song and the class is ready for a library activity.

c) Plan periods of rest within a period of strenuous activity. After working for ten minutes on a new song, sing a familiar song before moving to another new composition. After a period of working on a strenuous movement activity, have students sit on the floor and sing a quiet song before continuing the work with the movement.

6. *Reinforce good performances.*

a) Use a variety of verbal and nonverbal reinforcers for both individual and group performances.

b) Provide opportunities for the class to "show off" their performing skills for classroom guests by performing for another class or for a parents' group.

c) Tape-record students' performances on a good-quality recorder so they can hear themselves. Exchange tapes of favorite songs with a class in another school.

7. *Plan an ending for the music lessons.*

a) Whenever possible help students find a feeling of accomplishment by putting a song together with accompaniment or with movement.

b) If musical satisfaction cannot be achieved through the particular music on which the class has been working, end the music lesson with the performance of a favorite song.

c) Plan a "musical summary"—let's perform this song and notice the stepwise melody, the triple meter, the ABA form, and the other things we discovered today.

d) Plan efficient ways to return books, instruments, and other materials to storage areas.

e) Plan efficient ways to return students to their desks.

ROTE STRATEGIES

We have all learned songs by hearing them over and over again. Much of the music that children perform is learned in this way. This is not to say, however, that mere repetition of music will ensure learning. More importantly, it will not ensure the most efficient learning nor the kind of learning that will meet the total needs of the student and the goals of the teacher. The five strategies listed below and discussed on the following pages are designed to provide for the development of knowledge and skill. (Rote teaching strategies are employed most frequently with young children but, on occasion, may be utilized in the upper grades as well.)

- Call and response
- Echo phrases

- Play along
- What's it about
- Listen to a record

CALL AND RESPONSE

Call and response strategies are appropriate for a limited number of songs which have a phrase or motive that is repeated frequently throughout the song. These strategies are particularly effective for the first meeting with a group of students since they provide for immediate involvement in performance. The responses are usually quite simple, frequently consisting of only a few notes. In most cases, these will be sung, but they may also be performed on instruments or the response may be one of movement. We suggest teaching the response first by performing it yourself for the students or by helping them read the notational patterns. When students have some degree of confidence in performing the response, invite them to respond to the phrases you sing. Students will learn the "call" part of the song by hearing it repeated many times. We also point out that students may respond to a "call" on a record if you do not feel confident enough in your own performance.

Mr. Frog Went Courtin'

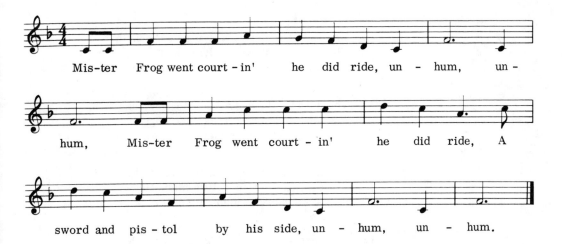

Mis-ter Frog went court - in' he did ride, un - hum, un -

hum, Mis-ter Frog went court - in' he did ride, A

sword and pis - tol by his side, un - hum, un - hum.

2. He rode up to Miss Mousey's Door, un-hum,
   He rode up to Miss Mousey's door,
   Gave three raps and a very loud roar, un-hum.

3. Said he, "Miss Mouse are you within?" un-hum,
   Said he, "Miss Mouse are you within?"
   "Yes, kind sir, I sit and spin," un-hum.

4. He took Miss Mouse upon his knee, he-he,
   He took Miss Mouse upon his knee,
   And said, "Miss Mouse will you marry me?" he-he.

5. Without my Uncle Rat's consent, oh-no,
   Without my Uncle Rat's consent,
   I would not marry the president, oh-no.

6. Well, Uncle Rat laughed and shook his fat sides, ho-ho,
   Uncle Rat laughed and shook his fat sides,
   To think that this niece would be a bride, ho-ho.

7. Where will the wedding supper be? he-he,
   Where will the wedding supper be?
   Way down yonder by the hollow tree, he-he.

8. What will the wedding supper be? be-be,
   What will the wedding supper be?
   A fried mosquito and a black-eyed pea, be-be.

9. The first one in was a flying moth, un-hum,
   The first one in was a flying moth,
   She spread out the table cloth, un-hum.

10. The next one in was a big June bug, ugh-ugh,
    The next one in was a big June bug,
    Carrying a big water jug, ugh-ugh.

11. The next one in was a little black tick, so sick,
    The next one in was a little black tick,
    He ate so much he made himself sick, so sick.

12. The next one in was a big horsefly, oh-my,
    The next one in was a big horsefly,
    He landed in the middle of a chocolate pie, oh-my.

13. The next one in was Mrs. Cow, no-how,
    The next one in was Mrs. Cow,
    She tried to dance but didn't know how, no-how.

14. The next to come in was a big black snake, hiss-hiss,
    The next to come in was a big black snake,
    Ate up all of the wedding cake, hiss-hiss.

15. The last one in was a great big cat, like that,
    The last one in was a great big cat,
    Ate up the mouse and swallowed the rat, like that.

16. And Mr. Frog went hoppin' over the brook, un-hum,
    Mr. Frog went hoppin' over the brook,
    A lilly-white duck came and swallowed him up, un-hum.

ANALYSIS OF MUSIC FOR PERFORMING

TITLE: "MR. FROG WENT COURTIN' "
SOURCE: TRADITIONAL

MUSICAL KNOWLEDGE THAT CAN BE DEVELOPED
    MELODY   *Upward skip*
    RHYTHM   *Steady beat*
    TIMBRE
    HARMONY
    DYNAMICS
    FORM   *Call and response*
MUSICAL SKILLS THAT CAN BE DEVELOPED
    SINGING   *Response at end of phrase*
    PLAYING   *Playing response at end of phrase*
    MOVING
    LISTENING   *To identify phrase ending*
    CREATING
    READING
    DESCRIBING
GENERAL KNOWLEDGE THAT CAN BE DEVELOPED
    OF THE WORLD   *American folk tales, a wedding
                        ceremony*
    OF RELATIONSHIPS
    OF FEELINGS   *Celebration*
GENERAL SKILLS THAT CAN BE DEVELOPED
    PERCEIVING
    COMMUNICATING
    SOCIAL SKILLS
    PHYSICAL SKILLS   *Physical coordination for playing bells*
    OTHER

Call and Response

"Mr. Frog Went Courtin' "
Traditional (Recording available on Folkways #EP–701)

Lower Grades

Instructional Objectives

1. Students will sing a two-tone response at the end of each phrase.
2. Students will demonstrate awareness of the upward direction of the response through discussion and by finding the pattern on melody bells.

Environment

An informal, yet teacher-centered, environment is suggested for this activity. Tone bells C, D, E, F, and G will be needed. Five to ten minutes will be needed.

Initial Procedures

1. Ask, "Can you say 'un-hum?' I'm going to sing a song that has 'un-hum' and some other things like that in special places. After I sing 'un-hum,' I'll stop just long enough for you to sing 'un-hum' too, so you sing it just after I do."
2. Sing the song with children responding at the end of each phrase.
3. Say, "I'd like you to think about the music that said 'un-hum.' Did those sounds go up or down?" (All sing them to verify the answer.)
4. "Here are some melody bells. This one (playing C) is the one that sounds like 'un.' Who can find the tone for 'hum'?"
5. Select students to explore the pitches of the bells until the C-F pattern for 'un-hum' is found. (If necessary, sing the pattern as the students hunt for the correct pitch.)
6. Repeat the song, you singing, the class responding, and student playing bells on response.

Extended Procedures

1. Provide a recording of the song in the learning center so students can respond to the recording as well as learn the song itself.
2. As students become more familiar with the main part of the song, invite them to sing along on the teacher's part.
3. Select students to be the frog, mouse, and other animals and dramatize the song while the class sings.

Modifications for Exceptional Learners

1. Low-functioning children may have difficulty responding with correct pitches. A satisfactory initial response may be at the correct time, later in correct rhythm.

2. Some children may have difficulty remembering the sequence of this rather long song. A series of pictures—a frog, a mouse, a rat, and so forth—will help them remember what comes next.

Evaluation

1. Did students accurately sing responses at the end of each phrase?
   a) Which students did not?
   b) What difficulties were apparent—rhythmic or melodic?

2. Did the discussion demonstrate an awareness of the melodic direction of the response?

3. Were students able to recognize the two pitches and play them on the bells?

Skin and Bones

1. There was an old wom-an all skin and bones, Oo - oo - oo - ooh!

2. She lived down by the old graveyard, Oo-oo-oo-ooh!

3. One night the thought she'd take a walk, Oo-oo-oo-ooh!

4. She walked down by the old graveyard, Oo-oo-oo-ooh!

5. She saw the bones a-layin' around, Oo-oo-oo-ooh!

6. She went to the closet to get a broom, Oo-oo-oo-ooh!

7. She opened the door and BOO!!

SOURCE: From *Folk Songs from Kentucky* by Jean Ritchie, © 1953 Geordie Music Publishing Company.

ANALYSIS OF MUSIC FOR PERFORMING

TITLE: "SKIN AND BONES"
SOURCE: *MAKING MUSIC YOUR OWN*, BOOK 3, P. 36

MUSICAL KNOWLEDGE THAT CAN BE DEVELOPED
    MELODY   *Downward, mostly stepwise*
    RHYTHM   *Uneven*
    TIMBRE
    HARMONY   *Minor mode*
    DYNAMICS
    FORM
MUSICAL SKILLS THAT CAN BE DEVELOPED
    SINGING   *Within a limited range*
    PLAYING   *Melody bells*
    MOVING
    LISTENING
    CREATING
    READING
    DESCRIBING   *Downward movement of melody*
GENERAL KNOWLEDGE THAT CAN BE DEVELOPED
    OF THE WORLD   *Halloween story*
    OF RELATIONSHIPS
    OF FEELINGS   *Suspense, surprise*
GENERAL SKILLS THAT CAN BE DEVELOPED
    PERCEIVING
    COMMUNICATING   *Telling a story*
    SOCIAL SKILLS
    PHYSICAL SKILLS   *Small-muscle coordination*
    OTHER

Call and Response

"Skin and Bones"
Making Music Your Own, Book 3, p. 36

Middle Grades

Instructional Objectives

1. Students will arrange melody bells in downward stepwise order.
2. Students will echo-clap the uneven rhythm pattern.
3. Selected students will play the final phrase on the melody bells.
4. The class will sing the final phrase of the song.

Environment

This activity is designed for an autocratic environment. An informal, story-telling seating arrangement is suggested, and the lights may be lowered to add to the Halloween atmosphere of this song. Melody bells B, A, G, and E will be needed. Five minutes of time should be allotted.

Initial Procedures

1. Select a student to play the four melody bells that have been placed before him or her in random order.
2. Ask the class to help find the bell with the highest tone. Through listening and discussion, help the student select the B and place it to the extreme right of the grouping.
3. Following the procedures above, have the class identify the lowest tone and place that bell to the extreme left.
4. Arrange the other two bells so the pattern is in descending order from right to left.
5. Have a student play the four-tone pattern.
6. Lead the class in echo clapping, ending with the rhythm of the last phrase of the song.
7. Have a student play the bells using the rhythm pattern just clapped. (If necessary, have the class clap while students play melody bells.)
8. Lead the class in singing the final phrase of the song while a student plays the pattern on the bells.
9. Sing the song with students singing the final phrase after each verse.

Extended Procedures

1. Students will soon learn the text of this song and then will be able to join in singing the first part.

2. Divide the class having one part sing the first phrase, the other part singing the second.

3. Select some students to dramatize the story told through this song.

4. Select rhythm instruments that will reinforce the suspense of each verse—wood block for walking, maracas for the graveyard, claves for bones, and so forth. Have a student play the rhythm of the final phrase of each verse while class sings the response.

Modifications for Exceptional Learners

In some classes, it may be better to omit the bell playing at the beginning. Teach the response by rote. During a later lesson, students may play the response on the bells.

Evaluation

1. Could students identify the proper sequence for the melody bells?

2. Did students accurately clap the uneven rhythm patterns of the response?

3. Did the student selected play the correct melody and rhythm on the melody bells?

4. Did students accurately sing the response?

5. Did students enjoy this activity?

ECHO PHRASE

Echo phrase is a strategy that can be effectively used with a limited number of songs in which identical phrases are repeated one after another. The teacher, or a recording, performs the first phrase and the students "echo" that same musical idea. As students become more familiar with the music, the class can be divided—half singing the first phrase, the other half echoing. After students know the song well, individuals can be helped to develop confidence in their own singing voices by singing the first phrase (teacher's part) as solos with the class singing the echo.

Echo clapping, echo playing, and *echo moving* are specific teaching techniques that are not necessarily musical experiences in and of themselves but that can lead to meaningful musical experiences. Echoing melodic and rhythmic patterns is one way that children can gain musical knowledge and develop musical skills. We begin this section with a description of these activities; we point out to you, however, that we do not intend them to become isolated drills but rather a means through which students may progress to musical performance.

Echo Clap, Echo Play, Echo Move

Since these activities are not considered complete musical experiences we will not discuss them in the "Lesson Plan" format of the other strategies. It is our intent that these techniques may be used as part of a variety of teaching strategies.

A great deal of learning takes place as we imitate one another. Echoing the teacher is one way students can learn about steady beat, metric patterns, rhythm patterns, and melodic patterns. We suggest beginning on most occasions with relatively simple, short patterns and progressing to longer and more complicated patterns. The teacher claps the pattern, and the students, beginning on the next beat, echo that pattern by clapping, by playing on untuned percussion, or by moving. A wide variety of movement responses are possible. Stepping the pattern, nodding the head, twisting the wrist, blinking the eyes, and using many parts of the body in a more complete dance are among the possibilities.

The patterns that you select for echo activities should always be directly related to a more complete musical experience. We suggest selecting more difficult patterns from music that the class is to perform and building up to them in the following way:

This Land Was Made for You and Me

We have found that it is essential that students be given some way to indicate the beat on rests and tones extending beyond one beat. We suggest pushing open hands apart to indicate rests and holding hands together, while bending the elbows or wrists, to show extended tones when clapping. When large body movements are used, rests and extended tones can be shown by bending the knees while standing still.

We have also found it extremely helpful to give students a non-verbal signal when they are to begin their "echo." This can be done with a nod of the head or an exaggerated movement of the arms while you continue to clap or move with the students. We also urge you to vary loudness and tempo in the echo exercises to help students develop sensitivity to these aspects of music.

Tongo

SOURCE: From Eunice Boardman and Beth Landis, *Exploring Music*, Book 3 (New York: Holt, Rinehart and Winston, 1975), p. 42. Used with permission.

ANALYSIS OF MUSIC FOR PERFORMING

TITLE: "TONGO"
SOURCE: *EXPLORING MUSIC*, BOOK 3, P. 42

MUSICAL KNOWLEDGE THAT CAN BE DEVELOPED
    MELODY
    RHYTHM   *Steady beat, quarter- and eighth-note patterns, syncopation*
    TIMBRE
    HARMONY
    DYNAMICS   *Contrasts of loudness*
    FORM   *Repeated phrase*
MUSICAL SKILLS THAT CAN BE DEVELOPED
    SINGING   *Octave range, pitch matching*
    PLAYING
    MOVING
    LISTENING   *Imitating rhythms and melodies heard*
    CREATING
    READING
    DESCRIBING
GENERAL KNOWLEDGE THAT CAN BE DEVELOPED
    OF THE WORLD   *Polynesian islands*
    OF RELATIONSHIPS   *Repetition*
    OF FEELINGS
GENERAL SKILLS THAT CAN BE DEVELOPED
    PERCEIVING
    COMMUNICATING
    SOCIAL SKILLS
    PHYSICAL SKILLS
    OTHER

Echo Phrase

"Tongo"
Exploring Music, Book 3, p. 42

Middle Grades

Instructional Objectives

1. Students will echo melodic and rhythmic patterns sung by the teacher.
2. Students will sing a song in Polynesian language.
3. Students will clap and play a steady beat throughout the song.

Environment

In an autocratic environment, students should be seated so they can clearly see you since lip reading may help them to learn the words to this song. After this song is known by the class, it can be sung in more informal settings. A large hand drum will be needed. Five minutes should be ample for this activity.

Initial Procedures

1. Lead the class in echo clapping the rhythms of the song. (Note the dotted quarter at the beginning of the seventh phrase. Slide hands together here to indicate sustained sound.)
2. Echo-sing the song. (You may need to sing with the class on their echo, but if you do, sing very softly.)
3. Discuss the Polynesian islands; locate them on a map. Discuss people that live there—what things do they like? How might they feel as they sing this song?
4. Repeat the song several times until students begin to sound confident on the echo parts.
5. Lead students in clapping a steady beat. When a beat is well established, begin singing the song with students echoing their parts.
6. Select a student(s) to play a steady beat on a hand drum while you and the class echo the song.

Extended Procedures

1. Divide the class into two groups, one singing the leader's part, the other being the echo.
2. Place a recording of the song in the learning center so that individuals and small groups can echo the record.

3. Select individuals to sing the first phrase as solos, with the rest of the class singing the echo.

Modification for Exceptional Learners

Provide a set of tone bells — C, D, E$^\flat$, F, G, A$^\flat$, B$^\flat$, C. Mark E$^\flat$ as the starting pitch and have gifted students find echo parts and play them on the bells.

Evaluation

1. Could students echo the parts?
   a) Which students had difficulty?
   b) Were the difficulties rhythmic, melodic, or both?
2. Were students able to clap and/or play the steady beat to the song?
3. Did students enjoy the experience?

2. They've plowed and fenced my cattle range,
   And the people there are all so strange.

3. I'll take my horse, I'll take my rope,
   And hit the trail upon a lope.

4. Say *adios* to the Alamo
   And turn my head toward Mexico.

SOURCE: From Elizabeth Crook, Bennett Reimer, and David S. Walker, *Music*, Book 4 (Morristown, N.J.: Silver Burdett Co., 1978), p. 89.

ANALYSIS OF MUSIC FOR PERFORMING

TITLE: "OLD TEXAS"
SOURCE: *MUSIC*, BOOK 4, P. 89

MUSICAL KNOWLEDGE THAT CAN BE DEVELOPED
    MELODY   *Phrase beginnings moving upward by skips*
    RHYTHM   *Steady beat; quarter-, eighth- and half-note relationships*
    TIMBRE
    HARMONY   *I–V^7 relationship*
    DYNAMICS
    FORM   *Two contrasting phrases*
MUSICAL SKILLS THAT CAN BE DEVELOPED
    SINGING   *Within the range of an octave*
    PLAYING   *Autoharp and wood block accompaniment*
    MOVING
    LISTENING
    CREATING
    READING   *Identifying melodic patterns that move upward and skipwise*
    DESCRIBING
GENERAL KNOWLEDGE THAT CAN BE DEVELOPED
    OF THE WORLD   *Cowboys*
    OF RELATIONSHIPS   *Repetition and contrast*
    OF FEELINGS   *Loneliness*
GENERAL SKILLS THAT CAN BE DEVELOPED
    PERCEIVING
    COMMUNICATING
    SOCIAL SKILLS
    PHYSICAL SKILLS
    OTHER

Echo Phrase

"Old Texas"
Music, Book 4, p. 89

Middle Grades

Instructional Objectives

1. Students will echo melodic phrases played by the teacher.
2. Students will sing echo phrases in the song "Old Texas."
3. Students will demonstrate awareness of melodic skips through discussion.

Environment

This activity is designed for an autocratic environment in which you lead the class in singing and playing. A xylophone or set of melody bells will be needed. Five minutes should be ample time for this activity.

Initial Procedures

1. Begin by playing patterns using the notes F, A, and C with students singing an "echo" on *la* or other neutral syllable.

2. Sing each phrase of "Old Texas" with students repeating as an echo.
3. Repeat step 2, being certain that you sustain the last tone of each phrase during the echo. Discuss this with students.
4. After singing the melody several times, discuss it using the following questions:
   a) Does this melody begin by moving up or down?
   b) Does it move in steps or skips?
5. Lead the class in singing again after discussion.

Extended Procedures

1. Divide the class, having one part sing first phrase, the other part singing the echo.
2. Using a wood block or other untuned percussion, have students play a "clip-clop" steady-beat accompaniment.
3. Select individual students to sing the first phrase as a solo while the class sings the echo.

Modifications for Exceptional Learners

1. Suggest outstanding students play echo on xylophone or melody bells. They should listen carefully and play by ear rather than read the notes from the printed page.
2. Some students may have difficulty singing the wide pitch range of the first phrase. Help them play the four notes on piano or xylophone, singing as they play.

Evaluation

1. Could students echo patterns played on tone bells?
2. Did students successfully echo your singing of the phrases of the song?
3. Did students' comments indicate an awareness of pitch movement and direction?

The Goat

1. There was   a   man, (there was a man). now please take note, (now please. etc.).
2. One day that   goat_____ felt frisk and fine,_____
3. But when the train_____ hove in - to sight_____

There was   a   man _____ who had a   goat._____
Ate three red   shirts _____ from off the line._____
That goat grew pale_____ and green with fright._____

He loved that   goat, _____ in - deed he   did,_____
The man, he   grabbed _____ him by the back _____
He heaved a   sigh _____ as if in pain,_____

He loved that   goat _____ just like a   kid._____
And tied him   to_____ a   rail- road track._____
Coughed up those shirts_____ and flagged the train._____

SOURCE: From Beatrice Landeck, et al. *Making Music Your Own*, Book 4 (Morristown, N.J.: Silver Burdett Co., 1971), p. 26.

ANALYSIS OF MUSIC FOR PERFORMING

TITLE: "THE GOAT"
SOURCE: *MAKING MUSIC YOUR OWN*, BOOK 4, P. 26

MUSICAL KNOWLEDGE THAT CAN BE DEVELOPED
    MELODY
    RHYTHM
    TIMBRE
    HARMONY   *Solo and ensemble*
    DYNAMICS
    FORM
MUSICAL SKILLS THAT CAN BE DEVELOPED
    SINGING   *Breath support for sustaining a tone, solo singing*
    PLAYING
    MOVING
    LISTENING   *And imitating another part*
    CREATING
    READING
    DESCRIBING
GENERAL KNOWLEDGE THAT CAN BE DEVELOPED
    OF THE WORLD   *Folk tales*
    OF RELATIONSHIPS   *Imitation*
    OF FEELINGS   *Humor, suspense as developed through the story line and through the sustained tones*
GENERAL SKILLS THAT CAN BE DEVELOPED
    PERCEIVING
    COMMUNICATING
    SOCIAL SKILLS
    PHYSICAL SKILLS
    OTHER

Echo Phrase

"The Goat"
Making Music Your Own, Book 4, p. 26

Middle Grades

Instructional Objectives

1. Students will listen to the teacher and imitate short phrases within the song.
2. Students will distinguish solo singing from unison ensemble.
3. Students will discuss the text as American folklore.

Environment

This song will most effectively be taught without books in a teacher-centered environment. Two to three minutes should be sufficient for initial procedures.

Initial Procedures

1. Lead the class in a period of echo clapping, ending with the rhythm of the first phrase of the song.
2. Instruct students to echo with their voices.
3. Sing through the first verse of the song, students echoing each phrase.
4. Point out to students the sustained tone as they echo phrase. Repeat the first verse and continue with the second and third.
5. Discuss the text of the song. What is it about? What happened? Is it believable? What other folk tales do you know?
6. Repeat the entire song, students echoing you.
7. How is the teacher's part the same as the students' part? (It has the same rhythm, the same melody, and the same words.) How are the two parts different? (The teacher's part is solo and the students sing in ensemble, but everyone sings the same tones [unison].)
8. Repeat the song.

Extended Procedures

1. As the class becomes more confident on echo, divide the class and have one group sing the first part, the other answer.
2. Select a soloist to sing the first part with the class responding.
3. Reverse the procedure, the class singing first and the soloist responding.

4. Place a recording of the song in the learning center so that students can listen and echo the recording.

Modifications for Exceptional Learners

1. Given the letter name of the first tone of each phrase, a talented student may be able to find the "echo" on a xylophone.
2. Drawings of a man, goat, railroad track, and so forth may help slower students recall the sequence of events, thus the text of the song.

Evaluation

1. Were students able to accurately echo you?
   a) Which students had difficulty?
   b) Were the difficulties rhythmic, melodic, or both?
2. Were students able to identify the difference between the sound of the teacher's part and that of their own singing as a contrast of solo and ensemble?
3. Were students able to associate this story with other folk tales?

Long John

With his shin-y blade,— *With his shin-y blade,—*

Got it in his hand,— *Got it in his hand,—*

Gon-na chop out the live oaks, *Gon-na chop out the live oaks*

That are in this land,— *That are in this land.—*

He's Long John,— *He's Long John,—* He's long gone,—

He's long gone,— He's gone, gone,—— *He's gone, gone,——*

Like a tur-key in the corn,— *Like a tur-key in the corn,—*

With his long clothes on,—— *With his long clothes on,——*

He's long gone,— *He's long gone,—* He's long gone,——

He's long gone.— He's gone, *He's long gone.—*

ANALYSIS OF MUSIC FOR PERFORMING

TITLE: "LONG JOHN"
SOURCE: *MAKING MUSIC YOUR OWN*, BOOK 6, P. 26

MUSICAL KNOWLEDGE THAT CAN BE DEVELOPED
 MELODY *Contrasts of major and minor*
 RHYTHM *Syncopation*
 TIMBRE
 HARMONY
 DYNAMICS
 FORM
MUSICAL SKILLS THAT CAN BE DEVELOPED
 SINGING *Repeating patterns as heard*
 PLAYING
 MOVING
 LISTENING *For differences in major and minor*
 CREATING
 READING *Last phrase of the song*
 DESCRIBING
GENERAL KNOWLEDGE THAT CAN BE DEVELOPED
 OF THE WORLD *"Blues" as a form of jazz, Post-Civil War America*
 OF RELATIONSHIPS *Subtle changes between patterns (major
     and minor)*
 OF FEELINGS *Hopeless feelings of the underprivileged*
GENERAL SKILLS THAT CAN BE DEVELOPED
 PERCEIVING
 COMMUNICATING
 SOCIAL SKILLS
 PHYSICAL SKILLS
 OTHER

Echo Phrase

"Long John"
Making Music Your Own, Book 6, p. 26

Upper Grades

Instructional Objectives

1. Students will read notation and sing the last phrase of the song.
2. Students will echo-sing other phrases of the song.
3. Students will demonstrate awareness of the difference between major and minor modes through performance and discussion.
4. Students will discuss the "blues" as a form of American music and part of the post-Civil War culture.

Environment

This activity is designed for an autocratic environment, and could be part of a social studies lesson dealing with social conditions following the Civil War. (It is assumed that students are aware of social conditions in post-Civil War America and of the significant contribution made to this culture by black citizens.) For this activity, students should be working from music books or from notation on a large chart or projection screen. A set of chromatic melody bells will also be needed. Five to ten minutes should be ample for this activity.

Initial Procedures

1. The following points should be made in a discussion of post-Civil War social conditions:
   a) Blacks had very limited opportunities.
   b) They were sometimes unjustly imprisoned.
   c) They frequently expressed their thoughts and feelings through song.
   d) A kind of music that expressed their feelings was known as "the blues."
2. Provide notation for students and direct attention to the last phrase of the song—"He's gone; He's long gone."
3. Discuss melodic direction and the flatted B.
4. Discuss the *fermata.* Agree that students should sing that tone as long as the conductor's (teacher's) hand is in the air.
5. Clap and speak the rhythm of the last phrase.
6. Provide the starting pitch and have students sing the last phrase. (You should not sing; this will help students develop vocal independence.)

7. Direct attention to the beginning of the song, pointing out that the teacher sings the first phrase, and the students echo that phrase as a response.

8. Lead the class in singing the song in the manner described in procedure 7. All sing together on the last phrase.

9. Discuss the difference between the sixth and seventh phrases ("He's long gone")—the sixth is in the major mode, and the seventh has a B flat, making it in the minor mode.

10. Play these two patterns on melody bells, noting the difference between the B-natural and the B-flat (major and minor).

11. Sing the song again, you singing the first part, the class singing the response.

Extended Procedures

1. Provide a recording of the song in a learning center so students can echo the recording.

2. After students are familiar with the song, divide the class having one part sing the first phrase, the other part singing the response.

3. Identify individuals to sing the first phrase as solos, the entire class singing the response.

Modifications for Exceptional Learners

1. Review the words from the text before beginning this activity with students of low reading ability.

2. Echo clapping or playing percussion instruments while echo singing will provide more physical involvement for children who need a high degree of activity.

Evaluation

1. Did the students' discussion of the notation in the last phrase indicate an understanding of musical notation?

2. Were students able to sing the last phrase independently?

3. Were students able to accurately echo the phrases sung by you?

4. Were students able to identify the sixth and seventh phrases as being different? Could they identify the difference as major and minor?

5. Did students enjoy this song?

PLAY ALONG

Play along is a teaching strategy that involves the students in performance the first time they hear the music. The basic assumption is that students will learn a song through active involvement in repeated performances by the teacher or by a recording.

When using this strategy, you should select rhythm patterns to be played on instruments or movement patterns that will provide appropriate accompaniments for the music. These patterns may be simply the beat of the song; they may be a metric pattern in which students play or move on the first beat of each measure; or they may be patterns formed by the first and third beats of each measure. More interesting patterns for playing or moving can frequently be found within the word rhythms of the song text.

We suggest you begin by playing or clapping the patterns, asking students to join. When they can play, or move, with confidence, ask them to continue while you sing the song. After hearing the song several times, students should be able to join you in the singing of the melody. Although it may be necessary to remind students to listen to the song while they are playing or moving, it is important that the patterns that they are performing are not so complicated that they are unable to divide their attention between their own performance and the song that you are singing. It is also important that sufficient time be provided for students to hear the song several times on a number of successive days before they are expected to sing independently.

Fun to Do (Clapping Is Fun)

Clap-ping your hands is fun to do, Fun to do, fun to do.

Clap-ping your hands is fun to do, To do, to do, to do.

2. Nodding your head is fun to do, fun to do, fun to do.
   Nodding your head is fun to do, to do, to do, to do.

3. Tapping your toe is fun to do, fun to do, fun to do.
   Tapping your toe is fun to do, to do, to do, to do.

4. Singing a song is fun to do, fun to do, fun to do.
   Singing a song is fun to do, to do, to do, to do.

5. Standing up is fun to do, fun to do, fun to do.
   Standing up is fun to do, to do, to do, to do.

6. Jumping high is fun to do, fun to do, fun to do.
   Jumping high is fun to do, to do, to do, to do.

7. Bending low is fun to do, fun to do, fun to do.
   Bending low is fun to do, to do, to do, to do.

8. Sitting down is fun to do, fun to do, fun to do.
   Sitting down is fun to do, to do, to do, to do.

9. Waving good-by is fun to do, fun to do, fun to do.
   Waving good-by is fun to do, to do, to do, to do.

SOURCE: Adapted from Richard Berg et al., *Music for Young Americans*, Book 1 (New York: American Book Co., 1963), p. 2. Used by permission.

ANALYSIS OF MUSIC FOR PERFORMING

TITLE: "FUN TO DO" ("CLAPPING IS FUN")
SOURCE: ADAPTED FROM *MUSIC FOR YOUNG AMERICANS*, BOOK 1, P. 2

MUSICAL KNOWLEDGE THAT CAN BE DEVELOPED
      MELODY   *Downward movement (last phrase)*
      RHYTHM   *Steady beat*
      TIMBRE
      HARMONY
      DYNAMICS
      FORM   *Phrases*
MUSICAL SKILLS THAT CAN BE DEVELOPED
      SINGING
      PLAYING
      MOVING   *Clapping, jumping, bending*
      LISTENING
      CREATING
      READING
      DESCRIBING
GENERAL KNOWLEDGE THAT CAN BE DEVELOPED
      OF THE WORLD   *Exploring body parts*
      OF RELATIONSHIPS
      OF FEELINGS   *Enjoyment in musical activity*
GENERAL SKILLS THAT CAN BE DEVELOPED
      PERCEIVING
      COMMUNICATING   *Following directions*
      SOCIAL SKILLS   *Suggesting ideas, working in a group*
      PHYSICAL SKILLS   *Large- and small-muscle coordination*
      OTHER

Play Along

"Fun to Do" ("Clapping Is Fun")
Adapted from *Music for Young Americans*, Book 1, p. 2

Lower Grades

Instructional Objectives

1. Students will participate in an enjoyable musical activity.
2. Students will perform a variety of body movements to the steady beat of the song.
3. Students will suggest additional activities and create new verses about these movements.

Environment

This activity provides an excellent beginning for a scheduled music class or a transition from one classroom activity to another. Initially, you will direct the activity, but as students become familiar with the song they can assume leadership. If large movements are planned, open space will be needed; much can be done, however, with students standing beside desks. Two to three minutes is sufficient for this activity.

Initial Procedures

1. Request students to "do what this song tells you to do," and proceed to sing several verses, leading students in the activity suggested by the text.
2. If students do not join in singing by the fourth verse, sing "Singing a Song Is Fun to Do" without any physical movement. This will invite students to join in the singing.
3. Ask students to suggest things they have fun doing. They can then create movements and song verses about those activities.

Extended Procedures

1. The number of activities that students find are "Fun to Do" is endless, so this song can be constantly renewed.
2. Have students play the last phrase on the melody bells. Discuss the downward direction. Look at the last phrase in notation.

Modification for Exceptional Learners

Most all children will enjoy singing this song. Physical handicaps may limit some movement responses, but students with handicaps could be encouraged to find ways to "make their hands jump" or to "swim with their feet." A project for gifted students might be creating a book with pictures showing children doing the things mentioned in each verse of this song.

Evaluation

1. Did children enjoy this activity?
2. Were students' movements with the beat of the music?
3. Did students suggest additional activities and verses for this song?

The Elephant

Source: From Eunice Boardman and Beth Landis, *Exploring Music*, Book 1 (New York: Holt, Rinehart and Winston, 1975), p. 27. Used with permission.

ANALYSIS OF MUSIC FOR PERFORMING

TITLE: "THE ELEPHANT"
SOURCE: *EXPLORING MUSIC*, BOOK 1 P. 27

MUSICAL KNOWLEDGE THAT CAN BE DEVELOPED
    MELODY   *Downward in steps, upward octave leap*
    RHYTHM   *Steady beat, slow tempo*
    TIMBRE
    HARMONY
    DYNAMICS
    FORM
MUSICAL SKILLS THAT CAN BE DEVELOPED
    SINGING   *Expanding range (C–C octave)*
    PLAYING
    MOVING   *To steady beat or slower (in half notes)*
    LISTENING
    CREATING
    READING
    DESCRIBING
GENERAL KNOWLEDGE THAT CAN BE DEVELOPED
    OF THE WORLD   *Elephants*
    OF RELATIONSHIPS   *Numerical sequences*
    OF FEELINGS   *Heaviness*
GENERAL SKILLS THAT CAN BE DEVELOPED
    PERCEIVING
    COMMUNICATING
    SOCIAL SKILLS
    PHYSICAL SKILLS   *Large-muscle coordination*
    OTHER   *Counting*

Play Along

"The Elephant"
Exploring Music, Book 1, p. 27

Lower Grades

Instructional Objectives

1. Students will move to a slow, steady beat while the teacher sings the song.
2. Students will count in numerical sequence.
3. Students will describe upward octave as a "big skip up."

Environment

You will direct this activity in an autocratic environment. Some space will be needed for movement; however, room for a single line of students moving around desks and chairs will be adequate. Five minutes should be ample for the initial experience.

Initial Procedures

1. With students standing, ask them to walk as though they were large, heavy animals.
2. Discuss some large animals.
3. Establish a beat by clapping, then suggest students walk to the beat as though they were elephants.
4. When students are moving to the beat, sing the first verse of the song.
5. Ask the question: "If one elephant asks another elephant to come and play, how many elephants would there be?"
6. Clap the beat and start students moving, then sing another verse of the song.
7. Continue with as many verses as desired.
8. There is one place in the song where the elephant raises his trunk high in the air. Say, "As I sing the song this time, listen and show me where the music goes up very high."
9. Begin singing, having students respond at the end of the first measure.
10. Discuss with students what in the music told them to raise "trunks" at a particular place. Develop the idea that the melody took a big jump up.
11. Sing the song again with students stepping on the steady beat and showing the octave leap.

Extended Procedures

1. On successive days, invite students to sing with you as they begin to feel comfortable with the song.
2. Establish a slower beat by clapping half notes. Have students move as bigger elephants to half-note rhythms while singing the song.
3. Form two circles, the outer circle moving to the steady beat of quarter notes and the inner circle moving to half notes (slow elephants) as students sing the song.

Modifications for Exceptional Learners

1. Students unable to walk because of physical handicaps could walk like elephants with their hands on a table top.
2. Pictures of one elephant, two elephants, three elephants, and so on for each verse of the song may help slower children learn to count.
3. Your playing a drum on the steady beat may help children hear the beat and move more accurately with the music.

Evaluation

1. Could students move to the steady beat of this song?
2. Could students count the elephants in proper sequence?
3. Did students identify the octave leap in the song?
4. How much of the song could the students sing at the conclusion of the initial experience?

Ifca's Castle

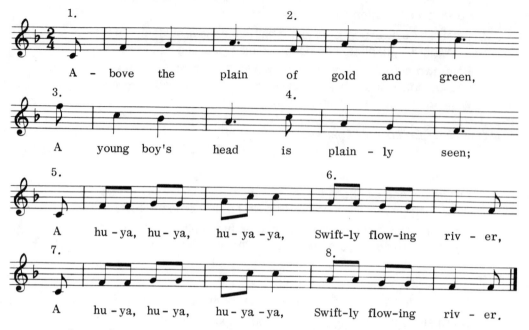

A - bove   the   plain   of   gold   and   green,

A   young   boy's   head   is   plain - ly   seen;

A   hu - ya,   hu - ya,   hu - ya - ya,   Swift-ly   flow-ing   riv - er,

A   hu - ya,   hu - ya,   hu - ya - ya,   Swift-ly   flow-ing   riv - er.

SOURCE: From Eunice Boardman and Beth Landis, *Exploring Music*, Book 5 (New York: Holt, Rinehart and Winston, 1975), p. 27. Used with permission.

ANALYSIS OF MUSIC FOR PERFORMING

TITLE: "IFCA'S CASTLE"
SOURCE: *EXPLORING MUSIC*, BOOK 5, P. 27

MUSICAL KNOWLEDGE THAT CAN BE DEVELOPED
    MELODY   *Up and down, steps and skips*
    RHYTHM   *Quarter-eighth note relationships*
    TIMBRE
    HARMONY   *Singing in a round and ostinato*
    DYNAMICS
    FORM
MUSICAL SKILLS THAT CAN BE DEVELOPED
    SINGING   *Extending range to high-F, singing in a round*
    PLAYING   *Playing simple ostinato on bells*
    MOVING
    LISTENING   *To one part while singing another*
    CREATING
    READING   *Rhythm of ostinato*
    DESCRIBING
GENERAL KNOWLEDGE THAT CAN BE DEVELOPED
    OF THE WORLD
    OF RELATIONSHIPS
    OF FEELINGS
GENERAL SKILLS THAT CAN BE DEVELOPED
    PERCEIVING   *What is the castle?*
    COMMUNICATING
    SOCIAL SKILLS   *Working as part of a group*
    PHYSICAL SKILLS
    OTHER

Play Along

"Ifca's Castle"
Exploring Music, Book 5, p. 27

Upper Grades

Instructional Objectives

1. Students will read eighth- and quarter-note rhythm pattern:

2. Students will distinguish melodic movement by step and skip.
3. Students will perform ostinato while singing a melody.

Environments

An autocratic environment should be used, with all students working together in one group. You will need charts with the rhythm pattern and an F and low-C bell. Approximately fifteen minutes will be needed for this activity.

Initial Procedures

1. Lead the class in echo clapping ending with this pattern:

2. Show the class this rhythm pattern on a chart:

"Is this what we clapped? Clap again and compare. Who can clap what is on the chart?"

3. Practice clapping this pattern on thighs:

4. Select a student to play the pattern on the bells:

5. Instruct a student to continue playing while others in the class continue clapping and you continue to sing the melody of the song.
6. Does the ostinato pattern played on the bells move in steps or skips?

7. Does the melody of the song move mostly in steps or skips? (Sing again to verify.)

8. Does the rhythm of the bell part appear in the song? What words are sung to that rhythm? (Sing again to verify.)

9. Assign a different student to play the bell part and invite the class to sing the melody of the song with you.

Extended Procedures

1. After students can sing the melody with confidence, have them sing the song as a round.

2. Another vocal part can be added by singing words from the refrain with the ostinato part.

3. Have one part of the class sing the first line while another part sings the third line. How many notes are there in the third line for each note in the first? Point out the quarter-eighth note relationships.

Modifications for Exceptional Learners

1. Students with exceptional ability could play this melody on the melody bells or xylophone as the class sings.

2. Simplify the ostinato part for students with coordination problems by changing the rhythms to quarter notes:

WHAT'S IT ABOUT?

What's it about is probably one of the most common approaches to teaching a song by rote. It is equally effective when you are using your own singing to provide the model of the song and when you are using a recording. In using this strategy, you ask a series of questions that can be answered only by careful listening to the song itself. Each time a question is asked, the song is repeated to help students find the answer. As the process is repeated several times, students learn both the text and the music from repeated hearings.

The kinds of questions asked are extremely important. The words are usually the most difficult part of a song to learn, so you will want to ask some questions about the story that is told through the song. If the only questions you ask refer to the text of the song, however, you may be teaching children that music itself is unimportant and that they only need to listen to the words when listening to music. We believe that, each time this strategy is used, it is important to ask some questions about the melody, rhythm, dynamics, or form of the song or about the timbres heard on a recording.

Brother Noah

SOURCE: From *American Sea Songs and Chanteys*, compiled by Frank Shay. Musical arrangements by Christopher Thomas. Copyright 1948 by Frank Shay and Edward A. Wilson. Copyright renewed 1976.

ANALYSIS OF MUSIC FOR PERFORMING

TITLE: "BROTHER NOAH"
SOURCE: *MUSIC*, BOOK 2, P. 163

MUSICAL KNOWLEDGE THAT CAN BE DEVELOPED
    MELODY   *Repeated tones, downward scale*
    RHYTHM   *Uneven rhythm patterns*
    TIMBRE
    HARMONY
    DYNAMICS
    FORM
MUSICAL SKILLS THAT CAN BE DEVELOPED
    SINGING   *Octave range*
    PLAYING   *Melody bells on last phrase*
    MOVING
    LISTENING
    CREATING
    READING
    DESCRIBING
GENERAL KNOWLEDGE THAT CAN BE DEVELOPED
    OF THE WORLD   *Weather, story of Noah*
    OF RELATIONSHIPS   *Darkening sky frequently means a storm.*
    OF FEELINGS
GENERAL SKILLS THAT CAN BE DEVELOPED
    PERCEIVING
    COMMUNICATING   *Telling a story*
    SOCIAL SKILLS
    PHYSICAL SKILLS
    OTHER

What's It About?

"Brother Noah"
Music, Book 2, p. 163

Lower Grades

Instructional Objectives

1. Students will discuss the story told in the text of this song.
2. Students will identify the repeated note patterns.
3. Students will identify the downward direction of the last phrase.
4. Students will identify the long tones in the refrain.

Environment

This activity is designed for an autocratic environment. You may model the song, or a recording may be used. Students should be informally seated near you or the record player. Five minutes should be ample for this activity.

Initial Procedures

1. Say, "I'm going to sing a song that is about a man. Listen and find out who the song is about."
2. Sing or play a recording of the first verse.
3. Give students an opportunity to answer.
4. Say, "I'm going to sing the song again, and I would like you to listen and find out what is happening in the song."
5. Sing or play the recording again. Solicit a "growing very dark and raining very hard" response from students.
6. Say, "As I sing the song, I'm asking Noah a question. Listen again and tell me what that question is."
7. Sing the song or play the recording again.
8. Ask, "When I sing 'I come into the ark of the Lord,' is my voice going up, going down, or staying on the same pitch?" (Sing the phrase again for students and discuss.)
9. Ask, "At the end of the song when we sing 'Loo-oo-oo-oo-ia' (singing last phrase for students), will we be going up, going down, or staying on the same pitch?"
10. Say, "I'm going to sing just the last part of the song. There are some very long sounds there. Show me the long sounds by moving your hand through the air when I sing a long sound."
11. Sing the last phrase. Discuss the students' response if necessary.
12. Invite the class to sing the entire song.

Extended Procedures

1. Repeat the procedures on another day to help children learn the second verse.
2. Discuss the fact that the third phrase is also a repeated tone but higher than the second phrase.
3. Select students to play the second and third phrases on melody bells.
4. Select students to play the last phrase on melody bells.

Modifications for Exceptional Learners

1. For students with short attention spans, begin with the refrain of the song, teaching it on one day. On future occasions, the students can sing the refrain as you sing the verse; eventually they will learn the entire song.
2. Select outstanding students to learn and play autoharp as accompaniment to this song.

Evaluation

1. Could students identify the story of this song? Did they learn the text of the song?
2. Did students identify the repeated note pattern?
3. Did students identify the downward direction of the last phrase?
4. Did students' hand movements reflect an awareness of the length of the dotted half note in the refrain?
5. Did students enjoy this experience?

Drill, Ye Tarriers, Drill!

3. Next time pay day came around,
   Jim Goff was short one buck he found.
   "What for?" says he; then his reply,
   "You're docked for the time you were in the sky."

SOURCE: From Robert Choate et al., *Experiencing Music*, New Dimensions in Music (New York: American Book Co., 1976), p. 76. Used with permission.

ANALYSIS OF MUSIC FOR PERFORMING

TITLE: "DRILL, YE TARRIERS, DRILL!"
SOURCE: *EXPERIENCING MUSIC*, NEW DIMENSIONS IN MUSIC, P. 76

MUSICAL KNOWLEDGE THAT CAN BE DEVELOPED
    MELODY   *Wide range, downward stepwise pattern at end of each section*
    RHYTHM   *Steady beat in duple meter*
    TIMBRE
    HARMONY
    DYNAMICS
    FORM   *Verse and refrain*
MUSICAL SKILLS THAT CAN BE DEVELOPED
    SINGING
    PLAYING   *Triangle on steady beat*
    MOVING
    LISTENING   *Identifying pattern at end of sections*
    CREATING
    READING
    DESCRIBING   *Melodic movement*
GENERAL KNOWLEDGE THAT CAN BE DEVELOPED
    OF THE WORLD   *Construction of transcontinental railroad*
    OF RELATIONSHIPS
    OF FEELINGS
GENERAL SKILLS THAT CAN BE DEVELOPED
    PERCEIVING   *Meaning in story*
    COMMUNICATING
    SOCIAL SKILLS   *Developing drama that also tells the story*
    PHYSICAL SKILLS   *Large-muscle coordination*
    OTHER

What's It About?

"Drill, Ye Tarriers, Drill!"
Experiencing Music, New Dimensions in Music, p. 76

Middle Grades

Instructional Objectives

1. Students will tell the story conveyed through this song.
2. Students will demonstrate awareness of the steady beat by clapping.
3. Students will identify the two sections of this song.
4. Students will describe the downward melodic pattern that ends each section.

Environment

An autocratic environment with students informally seated around you in a storytime manner. Tone bells F, E♭, D, and C will be needed. Five to ten minutes should be provided for this activity.

Initial Procedures

1. Introduce the song as one sung by railroad workers. Say, "Listen as I sing this song and find out if it was sung by the people who built the railroad or the people who ran the trains."
2. Sing the song (or play a recording of the first verse) and establish through discussion that tarriers were Irish who helped build the first transcontinental railroad.
3. Ask, "What were these workers doing?"
4. Sing the song again and then discuss with the class workers breaking rock to clear way for roadbed and for rock put under the railroad ties to level the track.
5. Say, "This is a work song sung by people as they built the railroad. Show me the speed you think they were working by clapping while I sing the song again."
6. Continue modeling the song and discuss the following questions:
   a) What time did the workers start to work?
   b) How many were working on this job?
   c) What kind of a boss did they have?
   d) How does the melody move when I sing "Drill, Ye Tarriers, Drill"?
   e) How much did the workers get paid? (They were paid just enough to buy sugar for their "tay," or tea.)

     f) Do you hear the same melody every time I sing "Drill, Ye Tarr-iers, Drill"?
     g) What kind of an accident occurred?
     h) What was the result of the accident?
     i) Why was Jim Goff unhappy?

7. When discussing the last phrase of the first section, select a student to play it on the melody bells. On subsequent repetitions, have the student again play the pattern and have the class sing this phrase.

8. Invite students to sing with you as they become familiar with the song.

Extended Procedures

1. Have students play the triangle on the steady beat to represent the sound of a sledge hammer.

2. Select students to dramatize the story of this song while the class sings it.

Modifications for Exceptional Learners

1. Invite students who play the piano to accompany the class while singing. (See piano accompaniment in teacher's edition of *Experiencing Music.*)

2. Use call and response strategies with slow learners, having them sing only the "drill, ye tarriers, drill" phrase that ends each section.

Evaluation

1. Could students tell the story of this song after hearing it several times?

2. Did students clap the steady beat?

3. Could students describe the downward melody that ends each section?

4. Did the students enjoy this experience?

LISTENING TO A RECORD

The recordings that accompany current elementary music textbooks provide excellent models of music for children. These recordings can be used effectively in guiding children's musical performance. We point out, however, that there is a distinct difference between using recordings as part of teaching strategies and becoming a "disc jockey," merely playing records and inviting children to sing along.

     You can use many of the strategies previously discussed when teaching a song from a recording. Children may sing a response or echo phrases to recorded music. They may be asked to play, clap, or move to records or to discuss specific aspects of the music that they hear. When teaching from a record, it is important to remember that *the record does not teach*; it merely provides a model of the song. As a teacher, you are responsible for finding ways to help children develop knowledge and skill through experiences with the recording.

We offer some specific principles that we believe are important to follow when using recorded music to guide children's musical performances:

1. Know the recording very well. How long is the introduction? How many verses are recorded? Is there an instrumental interlude between verses?

2. Focus students' attention on the part of the music that will enable them to meet the specific objectives of the lesson. (If the objective of the lesson is to develop knowledge about melody and/or to learn to sing the melody, ask questions about the melody or have children move to the melodic direction.)

3. Provide the opportunity for students to hear the recording several times before expecting them to perform.

4. Give students some specific purpose for each listening.

5. Play only that part of the recording essential for the particular activity. (No need to play all verses of a song if you only plan to work with the first verse.)

6. Do not permit students to become dependent on the recording. As students gain confidence in performing, decrease the volume of the record player. Do not use the recording every time the students sing a song. Help them grow to musical independence!

We also point out that most people prefer "live" performances to listening to recordings. Children will find listening to the teacher's "live" performance, even without the "fancy accompaniment," more exciting than listening to a recording.

Wake Me

Wake me,   Shake me,   Don't let me sleep too   late!

1. Got – ta   get   up   so ear – ly   in the   morn – in',
2. Got – ta   wash my face   so ear – ly   in the   morn – in',
3. Got – ta   brush my shoes so ear – ly   in the   morn – in',
4. Got – ta   get   up   so ear – ly   in the   morn – in',

Goin' to   swing on   the gold – en   gate.

SOURCE: Taken from *American Negro Songs and Spirituals* by John W. Work. © 1940, 1968 by Crown Publishers Inc. Used by permission of Crown Publishers Inc.

ANALYSIS OF MUSIC FOR PERFORMING

TITLE: "WAKE ME"
SOURCE: *MUSIC*, BOOK 2, P. 1

MUSICAL KNOWLEDGE THAT CAN BE DEVELOPED
    MELODY
    RHYTHM   *Steady beat*
    TIMBRE   *Tambourine (on recording)*
    HARMONY
    DYNAMICS
    FORM
MUSICAL SKILLS THAT CAN BE DEVELOPED
    SINGING
    PLAYING   *Tambourine*
    MOVING
    LISTENING
    CREATING
    READING
    DESCRIBING
GENERAL KNOWLEDGE THAT CAN BE DEVELOPED
    OF THE WORLD   *Morning routines*
    OF RELATIONSHIPS
    OF FEELINGS   *Excitement of seeing a new day*
GENERAL SKILLS THAT CAN BE DEVELOPED
    PERCEIVING
    COMMUNICATING
    SOCIAL SKILLS   *Grooming*
    PHYSICAL SKILLS
    OTHER

Listening to a Record

"Wake Me"
Music, Book 2, p. 1

Lower Grades

Instructional Objectives

1. Students will identify and discuss the message communicated through the text of the song.
2. Students will identify the tambourine part on the recording and clap that pattern.
3. Students will sing the melody of the song with the recording.

Environment

This activity is designed for an autocratic environment and is suggested for an early morning time. You and the record player should be in front of the students, and some space for minimal movement will be necessary. Less than five minutes is needed for this song. We suggest that it be repeated frequently to start the school day.

Initial Procedures

1. Ask, "Is this a song you would sing in the morning or in the evening?" Play the introduction and the first verse of the song.
2. Discuss student responses. Ask, "Why is it a morning song? What does the song say we are going to do in the morning?"
3. Show students a tambourine; play it for them.
4. Ask students to listen to the recording and count the number of times the tambourine plays. (Play only the very beginning of the introduction.)
5. Play the recording again—through the first verse—asking students to clap the part the tambourine plays.
6. Select a student to play the tambourine. Then play the recording through the first verse again, having the student play the tambourine and the rest of the class clap the tambourine part.
7. Select another student to play the tambourine. Play through the first verse again, inviting students to sing with the recording as well as clap the tambourine part.
8. Ask students to listen to the recording and find out what other things the song tells about doing in the morning.

9. Play the entire recording; then discuss the other activities mentioned.

10. Invite the class to sing along with the entire recording.

Extended Procedures

1. Lead the class in singing the song without the recording. As children gain more confidence in their own singing, you should sing less, helping them to develop vocal independence.

2. Let children suggest additional morning activities and create new verses for the song.

Modifications for Exceptional Learners

1. The tempo of the recording may be too fast for some students. The teacher can provide a model of the song at a slower tempo.

2. Pictures of a washcloth, shiny shoes, a toothbrush, a glass of juice, and so forth will help students remember the sequence of verses in this song.

Evaluation

1. Could students identify and discuss the morning activities described in the song?

2. Could students identify and clap the tambourine part from the recording?

3. Could students sing the melody of this song? Which individual students had difficulty?

4. Did the students enjoy this activity?

Old Brass Wagon

2. Swing oh, swing, Old Brass Wagon, *(3 times)*
   You're the one, my darling.

3. Skipping all around, Old Brass Wagon, *(3 times)*
   You're the one, my darling.

SOURCE: From Eunice Boardman and Beth Landis, *Exploring Music*, Book 2 (New York: Holt, Rinehart and Winston, 1975), p. 3. Used with permission.

ANALYSIS OF MUSIC FOR PERFORMING

TITLE: "OLD BRASS WAGON"
SOURCE: *EXPLORING MUSIC*, BOOK 2, P. 3

MUSICAL KNOWLEDGE THAT CAN BE DEVELOPED
    MELODY   *Repeated tones*
    RHYTHM   *Steady beat, duple meter*
    TIMBRE
    HARMONY
    DYNAMICS
    FORM   *Phrasing*
MUSICAL SKILLS THAT CAN BE DEVELOPED
    SINGING   *Within the range of a sixth*
    PLAYING
    MOVING   *To steady beat and phrases*
    LISTENING
    CREATING
    READING
    DESCRIBING
GENERAL KNOWLEDGE THAT CAN BE DEVELOPED
    OF THE WORLD   *Play-party games of early settlers*
    OF RELATIONSHIPS
    OF FEELINGS   *Celebration, enjoyment*
GENERAL SKILLS THAT CAN BE DEVELOPED
    PERCEIVING
    COMMUNICATING
    SOCIAL SKILLS   *Working together*
    PHYSICAL SKILLS   *Large-muscle coordination*
    OTHER

Listening to a Record

"Old Brass Wagon"
Exploring Music, Book 2, p. 3

Lower Grades

Instructional Objectives

1. Students will clap the steady beat to the song.
2. Students will step to the steady beat.
3. Students will sing the melody of the song.
4. Students will follow directions given in the song text for the play-party game.

Environment

This activity is designed for an autocratic environment and a large, open space. The first few procedures could be carried out with the students seated, or they could take place with students standing in the open space. Five minutes should be ample for this activity.

Initial Procedures

1. Invite students to lightly clap the steady beat while listening to the recording. (Play the introduction and first verse only.)
2. Ask, "What did the words of this song tell you to do? Were those words repeated in the song? Did the melody sound the same when you heard those words repeated? How was it different?" (Replay portions of the recording when necessary to verify students' answers.)
3. Listen to the recording again, this time walking to the steady beat. Form a circle and have the circle move to the left.
4. Play the recording again (first verse only), inviting students to sing as they walk the steady beat to the left.
5. Ask, "What are some other things we could do to this music?" Create new verses, singing and moving to the ideas suggested by students, such as:
   a) Circle to the right
   b) Jump up and down
   c) Bend down low
   d) Stretch up high

Extended Procedures

1. Use the following lyrics with this song as a vehicle to teach square-dance steps:

a) "Swing, oh, swing, Old Brass Wagon"
b) "Promenade around, Old Brass Wagon"
c) "Do-si-do, Old Brass Wagon"

2. Select students to play the rhythm pattern of the first measure of each of the first three phrases on melody bells G, A, and B as a way of discovering that each phrase starts one pitch higher than the previous phrase.

3. Develop in the class a feeling for duple meter by having students stamp on the first beat of each measure and clap on the second beat.

Modifications for Exceptional Learners

1. Select a group of gifted students to learn this song and the dance simply by listening to the recording. They can perform for the class and in this way teach the song to their peers.

2. Students with poor coordination may find the tempo of this recording too fast. Teach the song without the recording or make a new recording on tape at a slower tempo.

3. Use this song as a means for teaching concepts of right and left. Have students draw circles in the air with their left hand for the first verse, their right hand for the second verse. Then swing left leg, right leg, and so on.

Evaluation

1. Could the students identify and clap the steady beat to this song?

2. Which individuals had difficulty stepping to the steady beat?

3. Which individuals had difficulty singing this melody?

4. Did students enjoy playing the play-party game?

OSTINATO

An *ostinato* is a melodic or rhythmic pattern that is repeated throughout a composition as an accompaniment. Vocal ostinatos provide an excellent means for initial experiences in singing harmony. Instrumental ostinatos provide the opportunity to develop playing skills. Patterns that make appropriate ostinatos are sometimes given in the teacher's edition of music textbooks, or they can be derived from a song itself. Ostinato patterns will not fit with every song. Generally, the simpler the rhythmic and harmonic structure of the song, the more likely that ostinato patterns will provide effective accompaniment.

Because ostinato patterns are usually short and relatively simple, they can be taught by a note-reading strategy. It is sometimes effective to have the class learn the ostinato first and then perform it as accompaniment while the teacher provides a model of the song itself. The patterns frequently provide effective introductions and codas to the songs. Ostinatos may also be performed as accompaniments to recorded songs or instrumental compositions.

Down at the Station

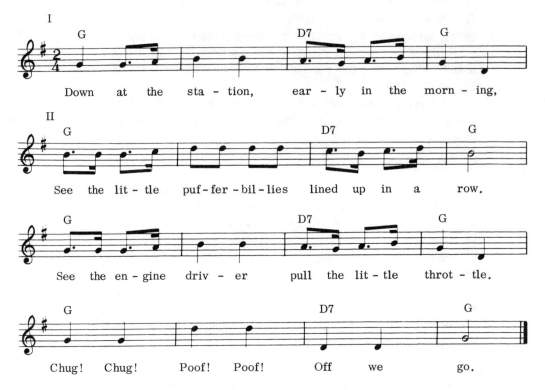

SOURCE: From Beatrice Landeck et al., *Making Music Your Own*, Book 3 (Morristown, N.J.: Silver Burdett Co., 1971), p. 133.

ANALYSIS OF MUSIC FOR PERFORMING

TITLE: "DOWN AT THE STATION"
SOURCE: *MAKING MUSIC YOUR OWN*, BOOK 3, P. 133

MUSICAL KNOWLEDGE THAT CAN BE DEVELOPED
    MELODY   *High and low, large skip and stepwise movement*
    RHYTHM   *Steady beat, duple meter, uneven rhythm patterns*
    TIMBRE
    HARMONY   *Round and ostinato*
    DYNAMICS
    FORM
MUSICAL SKILLS THAT CAN BE DEVELOPED
    SINGING   *In parts*
    PLAYING   *Sand blocks and tone bells*
    MOVING   *To steady beat (as a train)*
    LISTENING
    CREATING
    READING
    DESCRIBING
GENERAL KNOWLEDGE THAT CAN BE DEVELOPED
    OF THE WORLD   *Trains, transportation*
    OF RELATIONSHIPS   *Several ideas may occur at the same time.*
    OF FEELINGS
GENERAL SKILLS THAT CAN BE DEVELOPED
    PERCEIVING
    COMMUNICATING
    SOCIAL SKILLS   *Working together*
    PHYSICAL SKILLS   *Small-muscle coordination*
    OTHER

Ostinato

"Down at the Station"
Making Music Your Own, Book 3, p. 133

Middle Grades

Instructional Objectives

1. Given the notation of the last phrase of the song, students will identify high, middle, and low tones and the octave skip.
2. Students will identify high, middle, and low tones as played on the melody bells.
3. Students will sing and play the last phrase of the song as an ostinato as the teacher sings the melody.

Environment

This activity is designed for an autocratic environment with students seated at desks facing a projection screen. You will present the song on a projection transparency and will need these melody bells: high-D, low-D, and G. Five to ten minutes are ample for this activity.

Initial Procedures

1. Project the song on the screen, covering all but the last phrase. Ask the following questions:
   a) On what word will we sing the highest note in this phrase?
   b) On what word will we sing the lowest note in this phrase?
   c) Are there any notes that will sound more than once in this phrase?
   d) How many melody bells would we need to play this phrase?
2. Select a student to play the bells. With the student playing, lead the class in a discussion of the following:
   a) Play all three bells. Which is the highest? Which is the lowest? Which sounds in the middle?
   b) Which will you play first in this phrase? Which will you play second? (Physically arrange the bells with the G on the student's left, followed by high-D, then low-D.) Which will you play last?
   c) Pointing to the notation, have a student play the bells.
   d) Lead the class in singing the phrase, repeating it several times as students gain confidence.
3. Request that students sing phrases over and over while you sing something else. Start bell player, bring class in singing the second

time, and on the third repetition, begin singing the first phrase of the song. Have the class continue ostinatos for one additional phrase after song is completed.

4. Uncover the notation of the entire song, select a different student to play the bells, and repeat procedure 3.

Extended Procedures

1. Divide the class, having one part sing the ostinato while the other sings the melody of the song.
2. Divide the class in three parts, one singing the ostinato, the other two singing the melody as a round.
3. Add to the "train effect" by having selected students play the steady beat on sand blocks.
4. Provide further experience with the steady beat by having students form a "human train" and move to the steady beat as they sing the song.
5. Reinforce the harmonic concept by forming three trains, one singing the ostinato, the other two groups singing the melody as a two-part round. Students in each train move to the steady beat when they sing, stopping "at the station" when they are not singing.

Modifications for Exceptional Learners

1. Teach the ostinato bell part by rote, playing it for students yourself, then having them sing. Later a student may be selected to play the bell pattern while the class sings.
2. Play a recording of the melody so that you can continue singing the ostinato with the students, giving them necessary reinforcement but still providing them with a harmonic experience.

Evaluation

1. Could students visually identify pitch relationships from the notation of the last phrase of the song?
2. Could students aurally identify the pitch relationships of the melody bells?
3. Could students continue the ostinato part as you sang the melody of the song?

READING MUSICAL NOTATION

Although students are frequently given complete notation for songs as early as second grade, it is indeed an unusual elementary class that can perform a new composition simply by reading the notes. Note reading, however, can help students develop musical knowledge and skill and, ultimately, enable them to find increased enjoyment and satisfaction in their musical performances.

Some school districts have adopted one of several well-developed systems for teaching music reading. These are usually coordinated throughout the district by the music specialist. It is extremely important that the classroom teacher be aware of the system used in a particular school and reinforce music reading skills at every opportunity. We will not attempt to describe the various music reading systems, but instead we will discuss and demonstrate a few basic principles that are common to several systems.

1. Call attention to some aspect of the notation whenever students are using books or other materials containing notes. (Give students a reason to look at the notes, not just the words.)

2. Call attention to aspects of the notation that are essential to the the students' performance (melodic direction, rhythm pattern, dynamic markings).

3. Be certain students have had aural experiences with a particular musical pattern before expecting them to read it from notation. (Students who do not know what an elephant is will probably not learn to read the word. Students who have not experienced a major scale will have great difficulty reading a notated scale.)

4. Work from generalities to specifics. (Work with general upward or downward movement and steps and skips before naming precise intervals.)

5. Music reading activities should be used in a musical context. If drill is necessary, it should lead immediately to a performance of music and should not become an end in itself.

Since students are seldom expected to perform entirely by reading notation, these strategies will be combined with rote strategies in guiding musical performance.

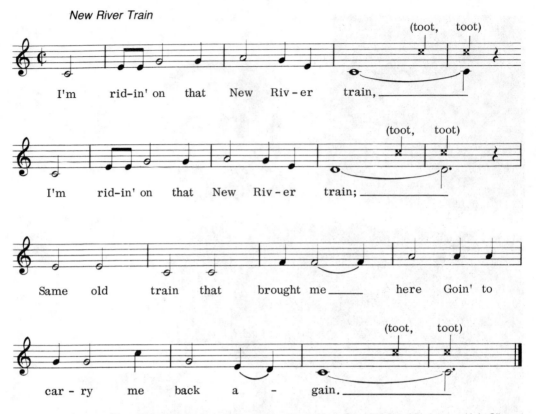

SOURCE: From Beatrice Landeck et al., *Making Music Your Own*, Book 1 (Morristown, N.J.: Silver Burdett Co., 1971), p. 80.

ANALYSIS OF MUSIC FOR PERFORMING

TITLE: "NEW RIVER TRAIN"
SOURCE: *MAKING MUSIC YOUR OWN*, BOOK 1, P. 80

MUSICAL KNOWLEDGE THAT CAN BE DEVELOPED
    MELODY   *Up and down*
    RHYTHM   *Steady beat; quarter-, eighth-note, and rest relationships*
    TIMBRE
    HARMONY
    DYNAMICS
    FORM
MUSICAL SKILLS THAT CAN BE DEVELOPED
    SINGING   *"Train whistle" response*
    PLAYING   *Percussion instruments as response*
    MOVING
    LISTENING
    CREATING
    READING   *Quarter and eighth notes and rests*
    DESCRIBING
GENERAL KNOWLEDGE THAT CAN BE DEVELOPED
    OF THE WORLD   *Trains*
    OF RELATIONSHIPS   *Two-one relationships, sound and silence*
    OF FEELINGS   *Anticipation, suspense*
GENERAL SKILLS THAT CAN BE DEVELOPED
    PERCEIVING
    COMMUNICATING   *Decoding symbols*
    SOCIAL SKILLS
    PHYSICAL SKILLS   *Small-muscle coordination*
    OTHER

Reading Musical Notation

"New River Train"
Making Music Your Own, Book 1, p. 80

Lower Grades

Instructional Objectives

1. Students will maintain the steady beat while singing the song.
2. Students will sing and/or play the "whistle response" at the ends of phrases.
3. Students will read response patterns using quarter and eighth notes.

Environment

This activity is designed for an autocratic environment. Any grouping of students will be satisfactory. It is assumed that students have had some previous experience reading quarter and eighth notes. You will need cards with the following notational patterns:

Initial Procedures

1. Establish the steady beat by having students slide palms of hands together, imitating the sound of a train.
2. As students continue the steady beat, sing the song. Repeat this process several times.
3. Suggest that students sing the "toot, toot" response at the end of the first, second, and last phrases. (Be certain students *sing* the response.)
4. Review rhythms on cards, having students clap each.
5. Suggest that students sing the "whistle response" on the rhythms printed on the cards. Sing the song again, holding up one of the cards as students sing the response.
6. Repeat, using another card each time.

Extended Procedures

1. By the second day, students should be singing the first part of the song as well as the response.

2. Have students select percussion instruments on which to play the responses.

3. Make additional rhythm cards containing quarter rests.

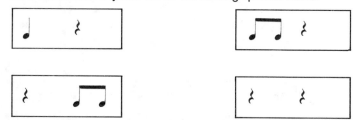

Modifications for Exceptional Learners

1. When working with a class of uncertain singers, begin with the percussion instrument response and work toward the singing response.

2. When working with slow learners, teach the song first. After children are quite familiar with the melody, work with the notational activity.

3. Use graphic notation for students unable to work with the abstract qualities of musical notes.

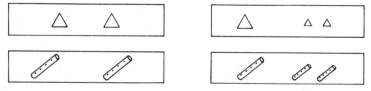

Evaluation

1. Could students maintain the steady beat while you sang the song?

2. Did students accurately sing and/or play the response at the end of the phrases? Which students did not?

3. Were students able to perform the response indicated on the rhythm cards?
   a) Which pattern was most difficult?
   b) Which students had difficulty reading the notation?

My Little Ducklings

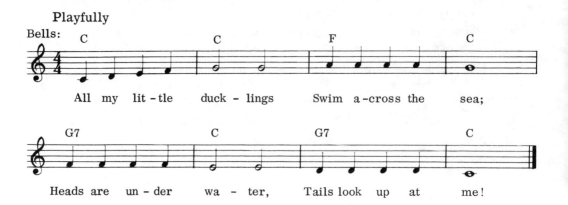

Playfully

Bells:

All my lit-tle duck-lings Swim a-cross the sea;

Heads are un-der wa - ter, Tails look up at me!

ANALYSIS OF MUSIC FOR PERFORMING

TITLE: "MY LITTLE DUCKLINGS"
SOURCE: TRADITIONAL

MUSICAL KNOWLEDGE THAT CAN BE DEVELOPED
     MELODY   *Up and down*
     RHYTHM
     TIMBRE
     HARMONY
     DYNAMICS
     FORM
MUSICAL SKILLS THAT CAN BE DEVELOPED
     SINGING   *Within a range of a sixth*
     PLAYING   *Melody bells*
     MOVING
     LISTENING
     CREATING
     READING   *Melodic direction*
     DESCRIBING   *Melodic direction*
GENERAL KNOWLEDGE THAT CAN BE DEVELOPED
     OF THE WORLD   *Animals*
     OF RELATIONSHIPS   *High and low*
     OF FEELINGS
GENERAL SKILLS THAT CAN BE DEVELOPED
     PERCEIVING
     COMMUNICATING   *Decoding symbols*
     SOCIAL SKILLS
     PHYSICAL SKILLS   *Playing melody bells (small-muscle coordination)*
     OTHER

Reading Musical Notation

"My Little Ducklings"
Traditional

Lower Grades

Instructional Objectives

1. Students will identify the upward direction of the notes of the first phrase.
2. Students will identify the repetition of the last note in the first phrase.
3. Students will arrange five melody bells in ascending order.
4. Students will sing the melody of the song.

Environment

This activity is designed for an autocratic environment and will be most effective with a small group of students; however, it may be carried out with the entire class. The notation should be available on a large chart or projection transparency. Melody bells C, D, E, F, and G will also be needed. Five to eight minutes will be required for this activity.

Initial Procedures

1. Show students the notation, directing their attention to the first phrase. Ask, "Do these notes tell us to sing up, down, or stay the same?"
2. In discussing the students' responses, develop the understanding that the general direction of the notes is upward but that the final note, G, is repeated.
3. Distribute the melody bells, one each, to five students in random order. Have these students stand in front of the group.
4. Say, "Let's find out who has the bell with the lowest sound." Have each student in turn play his or her bell. When the lowest has been identified, have the student who played it stand on the left, facing the other students.
5. Repeating the above procedures, find the next highest bell, and continue until all the bells are in scalewise order, the lowest on the class's left, the highest on the right.
6. Say, "These bells go up like the beginning of this song. Listen as I sing." (As you sing the first phrase, point to each student, cueing him to play as you sing his tone. The student with the highest bell will play twice.)

7. Repeat the above and continue singing the second phrase of the song.

8. Help students recall the text of the song by asking what's-it-about? questions:
   a) What animals are mentioned in this song?
   b) Whose ducklings are they?
   c) What are they doing?
   d) Where are their heads?

9. Lead the class in singing the song, students still playing the first phrase on the melody bells.

Extended Procedures

1. On another day, examine the notation of the second phrase of the song. It comes down, repeating each note several times.

2. Have students play the notes of the second phrase on the melody bells. (One additional bell, A, will be needed.)

3. Place a card with the notation and a set of melody bells in the learning center so that students can practice reading notes and playing.

Modifications for Exceptional Learners

1. For children with weak reading skills, the notation and bells can be color-coded (red—C, Green—D, Yellow—E, and so on).

2. If students have week aural perception, omit the procedure on arranging bells. You can provide the proper sequence before students begin reading and playing.

Evaluation

1. Did students identify the upward direction of the notes?

2. Did students identify the repetition of the last note in the first phrase?

3. Did students have difficulty hearing the pitch relationships of the bells and arranging them in the proper order?

4. Did students learn the melody of the song?

5. Did students eagerly participate in the experience?

Old Abram Brown

Old   A-bram Brown is   dead and gone, We'll nev - er   see him   more.

He   used to wear an   old gray coat, All   but-toned down be - fore.

SOURCE: Music by Benjamin Britten, text from *Tom Tiddler's Ground* by Walter de la Mare. Copyright 1936, Boosey & Co., Ltd. Reprinted from Beatrice Landeck et al., *Making Music Your Own*, Book 4 (Morristown, N.J.: Silver Burdett Co., 1971), p. 31. Used with permission.

ANALYSIS OF MUSIC FOR PERFORMING

TITLE: "OLD ABRAM BROWN"
SOURCE: *MAKING MUSIC YOUR OWN*, BOOK 4, P. 31

MUSICAL KNOWLEDGE THAT CAN BE DEVELOPED
    MELODY   *Repeated tones, octave leap*
    RHYTHM
    TIMBRE
    HARMONY   *Singing a round*
    DYNAMICS
    FORM
MUSICAL SKILLS THAT CAN BE DEVELOPED
    SINGING   *In a round*
    PLAYING
    MOVING
    LISTENING
    CREATING
    READING   *Melodic notation—repeated tones, descending scale line*
    DESCRIBING   *Melodic direction*
GENERAL KNOWLEDGE THAT CAN BE DEVELOPED
    OF THE WORLD
    OF RELATIONSHIPS
    OF FEELINGS   *Suspense, mystery—acceptance of people who are different*
GENERAL SKILLS THAT CAN BE DEVELOPED
    PERCEIVING
    COMMUNICATING   *Reading notation*
    SOCIAL SKILLS   *Working in a group*
    PHYSICAL SKILLS
    OTHER

Reading Musical Notation

"Old Abram Brown"
Making Music Your Own, Book 4, p. 31

Middle Grades

Instructional Objectives

1. Given notation of the song, students will identify the octave skip, the repeated tones of the first measure, and the downward direction of the last phrase.

2. Students will sing the melody of the song with limited assistance from the teacher.

Environment

This activity is designed for a democratic environment. The notation should be available on a projection transparency, and several marking pens will be needed. Students should feel free to participate in the discussion and independently sing the song from the notation. Five to ten minutes will be needed for this activity.

Initial Procedures

1. Show the notation of the song on a projection transparency. Ask students to identify the large skip and invite a student to circle the notation at the end of the second line.

2. Identify the letter names (D–D octave) and play this skip on the melody bells.

3. Ask students to describe the melody of the first line. (It stays on the same pitch.) Select a student to draw an arrow above the notation to show the repeated pitch level.

4. Ask students to describe the melody of the last two measures. (It goes downward in steps, or is going down the scale.) Draw an arrow to show this relationship.

5. Guide a discussion in which students describe the melody of this song. If possible include a description of the second and third lines.

6. Ask students to describe the rhythm of this song. Are most notes long or short? Where are the long tones?

7. Give the starting pitch and have students sing the first phrase by themselves. Join them when they lose confidence, but let them have the satisfaction of reading and singing as much as possible on their own.

8. Discuss places where students had difficulties singing the melody. Have them re-examine the notation and ask, "What do the notes tell us to do?" If necessary, practice these sections.

9. Give the starting pitch and have the class sing the entire song again.

Extended Procedures

1. Select a student to play octave Ds in eighth notes as an ostinato as the class sings this song.

2. When students sing with confidence, divide the class and have them sing the song as a two-, three-, or four-part round.

3. Try ending the song on a different pitch. (Play the last phrase on melody bells, going back up to E or F for the final pitch.) Discuss the feeling for tonal center, or "musical force of gravity," that pulls a melody to an ending tone that is often the same as the beginning tone of a composition.

Modifications for Exceptional Learners

1. While the rest of the class discusses the melodic direction, have slower students connect note heads in a "dot-to-dot" manner with a crayon in order to "draw a picture" of the melody.

2. Demonstrate to students how to draw a "picture" of this melody in the air by moving their hands to show upward and downward movement of the melody.

3. If you have a few nonreaders mainstreamed in a regular class, perhaps they could learn the song by listening to a tape recording several times while the rest of the class discusses the notation. All students could come together for a final performance.

Evaluation

1. Could students identify, from the notation, the octave skip, repeated tones, and the downward direction of the melody?
   a) Which patterns presented the greatest problems?
   b) Which individual students had difficulty identifying these patterns in notation?

2. Were students able to sing this melody without your support?
   a) Which sections presented the most difficulty?
   b) Which individual students had difficulties?

3. Did students remain on-task throughout this activity?

Praise and Thanksgiving

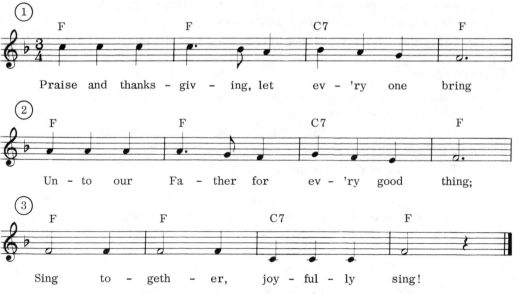

SOURCE: From Robert Choate et al., *Mastering Music*, New Dimensions in Music (New York: American Book Co., 1976), p. 217. Used with permission.

ANALYSIS OF MUSIC FOR PERFORMING

TITLE: "PRAISE AND THANKSGIVING"
SOURCE: *MASTERING MUSIC*, NEW DIMENSIONS IN MUSIC, P. 217

MUSICAL KNOWLEDGE THAT CAN BE DEVELOPED
    MELODY   *Downward, stepwise, sequence*
    RHYTHM   *Dotted-quarter rhythms*
    TIMBRE
    HARMONY   *Ostinato and round*
    DYNAMICS
    FORM
MUSICAL SKILLS THAT CAN BE DEVELOPED
    SINGING   *In a round*
    PLAYING   *Ostinato*
    MOVING
    LISTENING
    CREATING
    READING   *Melodic and rhythmic patterns*
    DESCRIBING
GENERAL KNOWLEDGE THAT CAN BE DEVELOPED
    OF THE WORLD
    OF RELATIONSHIPS   *Different ideas may be combined; one aspect may remain the same while another changes.*
    OF FEELINGS   *Worship*
GENERAL SKILLS THAT CAN BE DEVELOPED
    PERCEIVING
    COMMUNICATING   *Decoding*
    SOCIAL SKILLS   *Working together*
    PHYSICAL SKILLS   *Eye-hand coordination in reading notation and playing instruments*
    OTHER

Reading Musical Notation

"Praise and Thanksgiving"
Mastering Music, New Dimensions in Music, p. 217

Upper Grades

Instructional Objectives

1. Students will identify the letter names of the two notes in the last phrase.
2. Students will read and clap the rhythm of the last phrase.
3. Students will sing the last phrase.
4. Students will differentiate between the even rhythm of the first measure and the uneven rhythm of the second measure.
5. Students will discuss the melodic contour of the first two phrases.
6. Students will sing the melody of the song.

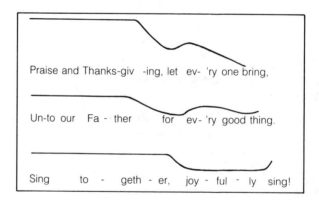

Praise and Thanks-giv -ing, let ev- 'ry one bring,

Un-to our Fa - ther for ev- 'ry good thing.

Sing to - geth - er, joy - ful - ly sing!

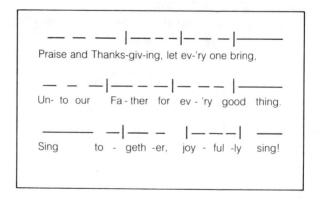

Praise and Thanks-giv-ing, let ev-'ry one bring,

Un- to our Fa - ther for ev - 'ry good thing.

Sing to - geth -er, joy - ful -ly sing!

Environment

This activity is designed for a democratic environment and will be most effect-tive with a small group of students. Each student should have the notation to the song, and melody bells C and F will be needed. Five to ten minutes will be needed for this activity.

Initial Procedures

1. Direct the students' attention to the last phrase of the song. Ask, "How many different pitches are used? What are the letter names of the notes?"

2. Discuss the rhythm of the last phrase. Ask, "Which measure has even rhythm? Which measure has one beat of silence? Which measure has a long sound followed by a short sound?"

3. Provide a countdown and have students clap the rhythm of the last line.

4. Repeat the chanting words of the last line.

5. Select a student to play the melody bells. Then lead the group in clapping and chanting while the student plays.

6. Lead the group in singing the last line.

7. Direct students' attention to the first phrase. Discuss the melodic contour (downward direction, beginning with three repeated tones).

8. Compare the melodic contour of the first phrase with that of the second. (They are very similar—the second begins lower and comes back up at the end.)

9. Discuss the rhythm of the first phrase. Ask, "Which measures have even rhythm? Which have uneven rhythm? Which has a long tone?"

10. Lead the class in clapping the rhythm of the first phrase.

11. Repeat the chanting words.

12. Compare with the second phrase. Clap and chant second phrase.

13. Give the starting pitch and let students sing the song without your support.

14. Lead the class in singing the entire song, adding melody bells on the last phrase.

Extended Procedures

1. After students become confident in singing the melody, have students use melody bells to play the last phrase throughout as an ostinato.

2. Divide the class and sing the song as a two-part round.

Modifications for Exceptional Learners

1. Some upper-grade students have considerable experience reading notation. Place notation for this song with melody bells in a learning center and have them play the entire song on the bells.
2. If two sets of bells are available, have an instrumental round.
3. Select an outstanding student to practice autoharp accompaniment and play while the class sings the song.
4. Color-code the notes and bells of the last phrase for students having reading difficulties.
5. For students unable to interpret notation, connect notes with a red line to emphasize melodic contour.

Evaluation

1. Could students name the notes of the last phrase?
2. Could students correctly clap the rhythm of the last phrase? What rhythms were most difficult?
3. Did students correctly sing the last phrase?
4. What did the students' discussion of the melody and rhythm of the first two phrases reveal about their musical knowledge?
5. Were students able to sing the second phrase independently?
6. Could students sing this song at the conclusion of the class?
7. Did students remain on-task during this activity?

He's Got the Whole World in His Hands

1. He's got the whole world— in his hands,— He's got the
2. He's got the wind and rain— in his hands,— He's got the
3. He's got both you and me— in his hands,— He's got both

whole world— in his hands, He's got the whole world—
wind and rain— in his hands, He's got the wind and rain—
you and me— in his hands, He's got both you and me—

in his hands,— He's got the whole world in his hands.——
in his hands,— He's got the whole world in his hands.——
in his hands,— He's got the whole world in his hands.——

Pattern I   Pattern II   Pattern III

Counter Melody

He's got the whole wide world— in his hands, —

Whole wide world in his hands, Whole wide world—

in his hands, — Whole world in his hands.——

ANALYSIS OF MUSIC FOR PERFORMING

TITLE: "HE'S GOT THE WHOLE WORLD IN HIS HANDS"
SOURCE: SPIRITUAL

MUSICAL KNOWLEDGE THAT CAN BE DEVELOPED
    MELODY   *Identifying melodic patterns*
    RHYTHM   *Quarter- and half-note rhythms*
    TIMBRE
    HARMONY   *Countermelody*
    DYNAMICS
    FORM
MUSICAL SKILLS THAT CAN BE DEVELOPED
    SINGING   *In parts*
    PLAYING   *Melody bells*
    MOVING
    LISTENING
    CREATING
    READING   *Stepwise melodies*
    DESCRIBING
GENERAL KNOWLEDGE THAT CAN BE DEVELOPED
    OF THE WORLD   *Spirituals and black culture*
    OF RELATIONSHIPS   *Two different ideas may be combined.*
    OF FEELINGS   *Reverence*
GENERAL SKILLS THAT CAN BE DEVELOPED
    PERCEIVING
    COMMUNICATING   *Reading*
    SOCIAL SKILLS   *Working together*
    PHYSICAL SKILLS   *Small-muscle coordination in playing bells*
    OTHER

Reading Musical Notation

"He's Got the Whole World in His Hands"
Spiritual

Upper Grades

Instructional Objectives

1. Students will identify by letter name the notes in the three patterns.
2. Students will discuss similarities and differences among the three patterns.
3. Students will play the three patterns on melody bells.
4. Students will identify the relationship between the patterns and the countermelody.
5. Students will play and sing the countermelody.

Environment

This activity is designed for a democratic environment and will be most effective with a small group of students. It is assumed that students know the melody of "He's Got the Whole World in His Hands" and that the coutermelody of this lesson will later be combined with the song. Cards displaying the three patterns and the entire countermelody will be needed, as well as a set of melody bells or xylophone. Ten to fifteen minutes will be needed for this activity.

Initial Procedures

1. Begin this activity by leading the class in singing the melody of "Whole World."
2. Direct students' attention to the patterns. Have students give the letter names of the notes. Discuss the similarities and the differences of the three patterns.
3. Select a student to clap the rhythm of each pattern. Then lead the class in clapping after the selected student has clapped.
4. Select students to play each pattern on the melody bells.
5. Direct students' attention to the countermelody. Discuss the relationship of the patterns to the countermelody (first line and third line, pattern I; second line, pattern II; fourth line, pattern III).
6. Discuss the beginning of the countermelody (pick-up notes).
7. Provide a countdown and have the class sing the countermelody while selected students play designated patterns on the bells.
8. Listen for problems, review patterns where they occur, and repeat the entire countermelody.

Extended Procedures

1. Have a small group perform the countermelody while the rest of the class sings the melody.
2. Invite students who play band or orchestral instruments to play the countermelody while the class sings. (Get the starting pitch from the instrument as some may be playing in a different key.)

Modifications for Exceptional Learners

1. Give a gifted student the challenge of playing the entire counter-melody (all three patterns) on melody bells as the class sings.
2. Have a gifted student play the countermelody on a recorder as the class sings.
3. Color-code notes and bells for students having reading difficulties.

Evaluation

1. Could students identify the letter names of the notes in the different patterns?
2. What did the students' discussion of the three patterns reveal about their musical knowledge and note-reading skill?
3. What difficulties did the students encounter in playing the patterns on the bells?
4. Were students able to recognize the relationships between the patterns and the countermelody?
5. Were students able to play and sing the countermelody?

SINGING IN PARTS

Much of the music that children hear every day, on their own records and on the radio, contains quite sophisticated harmony. There is little wonder that singing or playing in unison lacks excitement and appeal for older elementary school students. Singing in harmony begins in about the third grade with the singing of rounds, descants, and vocal ostinatos. In the middle grades, two-part harmony is introduced by singing and playing short segments of a song in parts. Children in the upper grades may sing entire songs in two and three parts.

As a general rule, the harmony part is not introduced until students can perform the melody independently and with confidence. Simple harmony parts can be learned by students reading the notation. In many cases, however, it will be necessary to utilize one of the rote teaching methods. The teacher can sing the harmony part while the class sings the melody. Another excellent way to introduce a harmony part is to have a student play the harmony on an instrument while the class sings the melody. The recorder or melody bells are good instruments for this, but remember also that many students in the upper grades are learning to play band or orchestral instruments and would welcome the opportunity to perform for their peers. If students are to play the harmony part on an instrument, they should be given the music a day or two in advance to provide time for practice. Also, starting pitches for the class singing the melody should be provided by the instrument so the class will be singing in the same key in which it is being played. Trumpets, clarinets, and saxophones are *transposing* instruments—that is, they do not sound in the key in which the music is written. If these instruments are used other accompaniments such as piano, autoharp, or recordings cannot be utilized unless parts are transposed.

ROUNDS

Rounds are an excellent way to provide beginning experience in performing in harmony. We point out, however, that not every song can be sung as a round. An exact repetition of a harmonic sequence is necessary for a song to be effectively performed as a round. The teacher's editions of music textbooks usually indicate those songs that can be performed as rounds.

Our experience has shown that students must be able to sing a melody with confidence before attempting to sing it as a round. It is very seldom that a song can be sung as a round on the same day that it is first introduced to students. We suggest using one of the rote or note-reading strategies to help children learn the melody. It may be necessary to review the song on several successive days before the students know the song well enough to sing it as a round. If a class can sing a song without your support, they can probably sing it as a round.

When first performing a round, it is quite effective to have the class sing the first part together while you sing the second part. When dividing the class into groups for singing rounds, be certain to include several strong singers in each part. It is sometimes helpful to select a student to serve as leader for one part while you lead the other.

We also point out that the goal for performing rounds is the harmonic experience that results from the combination of sounds. Students should be encouraged to listen to the other part as well as their own. Harmonic awareness can be further developed by selecting small groups of students to perform familiar rounds as their classmates listen.

Shalom, Chaverim

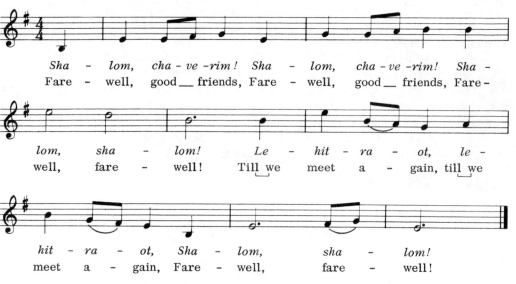

Sha - lom, cha - ve -rim! Sha - lom, cha - ve -rim! Sha -
Fare - well, good__ friends, Fare - well, good__ friends, Fare -

lom, sha - lom! Le - hit - ra - ot, le -
well, fare - well! Till we meet a - gain, till we

hit - ra - ot, Sha - lom, sha - lom!
meet a - gain, Fare - well, fare - well!

SOURCE: From Eunice Boardman and Beth Landis, *Exploring Music*, Book 4 (New York: Holt, Rinehart and Winston, 1975), p. 66. Used with permission.

ANALYSIS OF MUSIC FOR PERFORMING

TITLE: "SHALOM, CHAVERIM"
SOURCE: *EXPLORING MUSIC*, BOOK 4, P. 66

MUSICAL KNOWLEDGE THAT CAN BE DEVELOPED
    MELODY
    RHYTHM   *Pattern*
    TIMBRE
    HARMONY   *Minor*
    DYNAMICS
    FORM   *Round*
MUSICAL SKILLS THAT CAN BE DEVELOPED
    SINGING   *In a round*
    PLAYING
    MOVING
    LISTENING
    CREATING
    READING   *A rhythm pattern*
    DESCRIBING
GENERAL KNOWLEDGE THAT CAN BE DEVELOPED
    OF THE WORLD   *Jewish customs*
    OF RELATIONSHIPS   *Ideas may overlap one another.*
    OF FEELINGS   *Friendship*
GENERAL SKILLS THAT CAN BE DEVELOPED
    PERCEIVING
    COMMUNICATING   *Reading*
    SOCIAL SKILLS   *Working together*
    PHYSICAL SKILLS
    OTHER   *Researching customs of another culture*

Rounds

"Shalom, Chaverim"
Exploring Music, Book 4, p. 66

Middle Grades

Instructional Objectives

1. Students will discuss the customs of another culture.
2. Students will identify the rhythm pattern

    as it occurs in different melodic sequences throughout the song.
3. Students will sing the melody of the song.
4. Students will sing the song as a two-part round.

Environment

This activity is designed for an autocratic environment. The lesson described should be divided over at least two days, the first day being used to introduce the melody of the song. Singing in a round should come only after students can sing the melody with confidence. Each student should have a copy of the notation for the song, and you will also need a card showing the notation of the rhythm pattern. Five to ten minutes on each day will be needed for this activity.

Initial Procedures

First Day

1. Begin with a discussion of ways to greet one another—a hand-shake, a wave, saying hello, a smile, and so on.
2. Extend the discussion to greeting and parting customs in other cultures. Conclude with discussion of *Shalom* as Jewish greeting.
3. Show the rhythm pattern and have the class clap the pattern.
4. Direct students' attention to the notation of the song. Ask, "Where can you find this rhythm pattern in the song?"
5. Lead the class in chanting the words and clapping the rhythm of the song.
6. Have the class clap the rhythm and softly chant the words as you sing the melody.
7. Discuss the melody—in the first phrase, the first pattern is repeated a little higher; there are downward moving tones in the second phrase.

8. Lead the class in singing the melody.

Second Day

1. Lead the class in singing the melody.
2. Give the starting pitch and have the class sing without your support.
3. If the class can sing accurately and with confidence, continue; otherwise, review procedures from the first day in order to re-inforce learning.
4. Sing the song as a round with the class. Start the class singing at the beginning of the song, then you start at the beginning as the class begins to sing the second phrase.
5. If the class is able to maintain their part, divide them and have them sing as a round. Be certain to cue students singing the second part at their entrance.
6. Change parts, having students who were second begin the round.

Extended Procedures

1. Select a third group to sing the last two "Shaloms" as an ostinato throughout the composition.
2. Discuss the minor tonality of this composition. Play part of it using G ♯ so students can hear the difference between major and minor.

Modifications for Exceptional Learners

1. Invite students with instrumental experience to play this as a round for the class.
2. If students do not have experience reading notation, teach the rhythm of this song by echo clapping.

Evaluation

1. Could students discuss greeting and farewell customs of several cultures?
2. Could students clap the notated rhythm pattern?
3. Could students identify the rhythm pattern in the context of the song?
4. Could students sing this as a two-part round?

Merry Christmas   Harry R. Wilson

SOURCE: From *Rounds and Canons* copyright 1943 by Schmitt, Hall & McCreary (a division of Belwin-Mills Publishing Corp.). Copyright renewed 1971. Used by permission.

ANALYSIS OF MUSIC FOR PERFORMING

TITLE: "MERRY CHRISTMAS"
SOURCE: ADAPTED FROM *ROUNDS AND CANONS*, HARRY ROBERT WILSON

MUSICAL KNOWLEDGE THAT CAN BE DEVELOPED
    MELODY   *Repeated tones*
    RHYTHM   *Long and short*
    TIMBRE
    HARMONY
    DYNAMICS
    FORM
MUSICAL SKILLS THAT CAN BE DEVELOPED
    SINGING   *In a round*
    PLAYING
    MOVING
    LISTENING
    CREATING
    READING
    DESCRIBING
GENERAL KNOWLEDGE THAT CAN BE DEVELOPED
    OF THE WORLD   *Christmas holiday*
    OF RELATIONSHIPS
    OF FEELINGS   *Celebration*
GENERAL SKILLS THAT CAN BE DEVELOPED
    PERCEIVING
    COMMUNICATING
    SOCIAL SKILLS   *Working together*
    PHYSICAL SKILLS
    OTHER

Rounds (*What's It About?*)

"Merry Christmas"
Adapted from *Rounds and Canons* by Harry Robert Wilson

Middle Grades

Instructional Objectives

1. Students will celebrate the Christmas holiday through singing a song.
2. Students will identify the repeated tones of the third phrase.
3. Students will identify the long tones of the third phrase.
4. Students will sing the melody of the song.
5. Students will sing the song as a round.

Environment

This activity is designed for an autocratic environment. No special equipment is needed. Five minutes on each day should be ample for this activity.

Initial Procedures

First Day

1. Ask class to say "Merry Christmas."
2. Ask students to follow the tempo of your hand in saying "Merry Christmas." Use different tempos—some fast, some slow.
3. Give the pitch B$\flat$ and ask students to sing "Merry Christmas" on that pitch. (Direct them at a slow tempo.)
4. Sing the entire melody for students, asking them to raise their hands when they hear a section that sounds like what they just sang.
5. Discuss the following points about this song with students:
   a) The text is "Merry Christmas" repeated many times.
   b) The second phrase is higher than the first.
   c) The last phrase is the same as the first.
6. Lead the class in singing the song.

Second Day

1. Give the starting pitch and lead the class in singing the song. If they sing with confidence, proceed; otherwise, review procedures from the first day.
2. Start the class singing the song. As they begin the second phrase, start at the beginning, singing the song as a round.

3. Divide the class into two groups and have them sing the song as a round. Remind students to listen for both parts as they sing.

4. Reassign parts, starting with the other group, and sing again.

Extended Procedures

1. Select a small group of students to perform the round for the class so all can hear the harmony of the round.

2. Select students to play the repeated tones of the third phrase as an ostinato.

3. Divide the class in three or four parts for greater harmonic effect.

Modifications for Exceptional Learners

1. To help students learn the melody, as you model the song, show relative pitch levels in the air with your hand.

2. For students with limited singing ranges, transpose the song down to the key of C.

3. Challenge outstanding students by giving them melody bells of the tonic chord (E♭ , G, B♭) and have them improvise a descant using the rhythm of the words "Merry Christmas" as the class sings the song.

Evaluation

1. Could students follow your directions in chanting "Merry Christmas" with long and short sounds?

2. Could students sing "Merry Christmas" on repeated tones?

3. Could students sing the melody of the song at the end of the first day?

4. Could students sing the song as a two-part round at the end of the second day?

Keep Moving

1. One   fin - ger, one thumb, one hand   keep   mov - ing,   One

fin - ger, one thumb, one hand   keep   mov - ing,_____   One

fin - ger,   one thumb,   one hand   keep   mov - ing,   And   we'll

all   be   hap - py   and   gay. _____

2.   One finger, one thumb, one hand, two hands keep moving, etc.

3.   One finger, one thumb, one hand, two hands, one arm keep moving, etc.

4.   two arms

5.   one leg

6.   two legs

7.   stand up — sit down   8.   stand up — turn around — sit down

SOURCE: From Lilla Belle Pitts, Mabelle Glenn, Lorraine Waters and Louis G. Wersen, *Singing Teen-agers* of the series *Our Singing World* (Boston: Ginn and Company, 1961), p. 23.

ANALYSIS OF MUSIC FOR PERFORMING

TITLE: "KEEP MOVING"
SOURCE: *SINGING TEENAGERS*, P. 23

MUSICAL KNOWLEDGE THAT CAN BE DEVELOPED
    MELODY   *Repeated tones, melody built on chord tones*
    RHYTHM   *Uneven rhythms and steady beat*
    TIMBRE
    HARMONY
    DYNAMICS
    FORM
MUSICAL SKILLS THAT CAN BE DEVELOPED
    SINGING   *In a round*
    PLAYING
    MOVING
    LISTENING
    CREATING
    READING
    DESCRIBING
GENERAL KNOWLEDGE THAT CAN BE DEVELOPED
    OF THE WORLD   *Body parts*
    OF RELATIONSHIPS
    OF FEELINGS
GENERAL SKILLS THAT CAN BE DEVELOPED
    PERCEIVING
    COMMUNICATING
    SOCIAL SKILLS   *Working together*
    PHYSICAL SKILLS   *Large- and small-muscle movement*
    OTHER

Rounds (*Move Along*)

"Keep Moving"
Singing Teenagers, p. 23

Middle Grades

Instructional Objectives

1. Students will engage in an enjoyable activity combining movement and singing.
2. Students will follow directions sung by the teacher.
3. Students will identify the repeated note patterns in the song.
4. Students will sing the song as a round while moving to the steady beat.

Environment

This activity is planned for an autocratic environment. Students should be seated in chairs and have space to stand, turn, and sit down again. Five to ten minutes will be needed on the first day to introduce the melody to the class. On subsequent days, three to five minutes is ample time for singing the song as a round. Because of the physical activity involved, this is a good song for a mid-morning or midafternoon break from work with other subject materials.

Initial Procedures

First Day

1. Say, "I'm going to sing a song that tells you to do some things. Listen and watch as I do them and do them with me."
2. Sing verses 1 through 4 with students taking part in the movement.
3. Say, "Just listen as I sing the first phrase of this song. Is the melody going up, down, or staying on the same pitch?" (Sing the first phrase.) Through discussion develop the idea of a repeated melody tone.
4. Ask, "How is the second phrase different?" (Sing the first two phrases.) Through discussion establish that the second phrase also stays on one tone, but it is a higher note than the first phrase.
5. Ask, "Is the third phrase like the other two?" (Sing the first three phrases.) Through discussion establish that it also stays on a repeated tone, but it is still higher than the other two.
6. Ask, "How would you describe the melody of the last phrase?" (Sing the last phrase.) Through discussion establish that the last phrase descends in steps (comes down the scale).

7. Give the starting pitch and lead the class in singing verses 1 through 4.
8. Inform the class that there are more verses to the song. Ask them to sing the first part again and then to continue singing the other verses, doing what you do. (You must be seated to sing verses 5 through 8.)
9. Give the starting pitch and then lead the class in singing the song.

Second Day

1. Lead the class in singing the song. After starting the class, you should sing more softly in order to determine the degree of confidence students have in singing this song. If they can sing it "on their own," proceed with singing it as a round. If they cannot, review procedures from the first day.
2. Select two students to be leaders. Give the starting pitch and have them lead the class in singing the song.
3. Divide the class in two groups with one leader in front of each. Give the starting pitch and help each group get started as they sing the song as a round.

Extended Procedures

1. Review this song frequently when a "change of pace" is needed in the classroom.
2. Divide the class in three groups and sing the song as a three-part round.
3. Introduce an F-major chord (F–A–C) on the melody bells. Point out that each phrase begins on a new note of this chord.
4. Accompany this song with an F chord on the autoharp.

Modifications for Exceptional Learners

1. Introduce the song one or two verses at a time, extending the introduction over several days.
2. Use a slow tempo for this song so that students can sing and perform movements.

Evaluation

1. Did students enjoy the activity?
2. Did students follow the directions you sang?
3. Were students able to identify the repeated note patterns in the song?
4. Were students able to sing the melody of the song?
5. Were students able to perform the movements while singing the song as a two-part round?

Lame Tame Crane

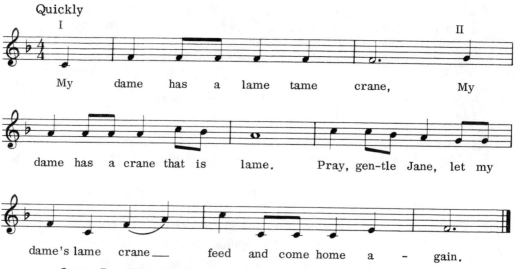

Quickly

My dame has a lame tame crane, My dame has a crane that is lame. Pray, gen-tle Jane, let my dame's lame crane feed and come home a - gain.

SOURCE: From William R. Sur, Mary R. Tolbert, Robert E. Nye, and William R. Fisher, *This is Music*, Book 6 (Boston: Allyn & Bacon, 1962), p. 9.

ANALYSIS OF MUSIC FOR PERFORMING

TITLE: "LAME TAME CRANE"
SOURCE: *THIS IS MUSIC*, BOOK 6, P. 9

MUSICAL KNOWLEDGE THAT CAN BE DEVELOPED
    MELODY   *Built on tones of F chord*
    RHYTHM
    TIMBRE
    HARMONY   *Major chord, singing in a round*
    DYNAMICS
    FORM
MUSICAL SKILLS THAT CAN BE DEVELOPED
    SINGING   *In a round*
    PLAYING
    MOVING
    LISTENING
    CREATING
    READING
    DESCRIBING
GENERAL KNOWLEDGE THAT CAN BE DEVELOPED
    OF THE WORLD   *Unusual pets*
    OF RELATIONSHIPS
    OF FEELINGS
GENERAL SKILLS THAT CAN BE DEVELOPED
    PERCEIVING
    COMMUNICATING   *Language—tongue twisters*
    SOCIAL SKILLS
    PHYSICAL SKILLS   *Speech development*
    OTHER

Rounds (*Play Along*)

"Lame Tame Crane"
This Is Music, Book 6, p. 9

Upper Grades

Instructional Objectives

1. Students will identify notes of the F-major chord.
2. Students will identify this melody as being based on the F-major chord.
3. Students will read and clap the melodic rhythm.
4. Students will sing the melody.
5. Students will sing the song as a two-part round.

Environment

This activity is designed to begin with an open environment and lead toward one that is more autocratic. Students will need copies of the notation of the song, several autoharps, and sets of melody bells or xylophones. Ten to fifteen minutes will be needed for the first day's activity and approximately five minutes for the second day's.

Initial Procedures

First Day

1. Divide the class into groups of four to eight students, giving each group an autoharp and a set of bells or a xylophone. The task is to play an F Chord on the autoharp and find three notes on the bells or xylophone that can be played together to make the same sound.
2. After approximately five minutes, have the groups report by playing F, A, and C combined to form the F chord.
3. Direct students' attention to the notation of the song. Ask, "How many notes of the song are notes of an F chord? How many are not? The first note in each measure is usually a very important note. What do you notice about the first note in each measure of this song?"
4. Clap and chant the rhythm of the words to this song.
5. Select three students to play these bells: F, A, and C.
6. Repeat the clapping and chanting. Have students with bells play the bell indicated at the beginning of each measure.
7. Lead the class in singing the melody of the song, students with bells again playing the first note in each measure.

Second Day

1. Lead the class in singing the song. If they sing with confidence, continue; if not, repeat procedures from the first day.
2. Give the starting pitch and start the class singing. Begin singing yourself at the beginning of the song when the class reaches the end of the second measure, singing the second part of the round.
3. Divide the class and have them sing in a two-part round. (Use a slow tempo the first time. As students' confidence in singing this song grows, increase the tempo.)

Extended Procedures

1. Select a small group of students (four to six) to perform the song as a round for the class so that all can hear the harmonic effect of two parts together.
2. Divide the class in three or four parts, starting each part one measure later than the previous part.
3. Select a student to accompany the song by using the F chord on the autoharp or by playing the three notes F, A, and C together on the melody bells.

Modifications for Exceptional Learners

1. Provide a tape recording of the song so non-readers can learn the song by rote while the class carries out procedures 1 through 6.
2. Use a very slow tempo for students with speech problems.
3. Provide color-coded notation and xylophone in a learning center so that individual students may play this song.

Evaluation

1. Were students in small groups able to identify the notes of the F-major chord?
2. Did students identify the melody as being based on the F-major chord?
3. Were students able to read and clap the melodic rhythm of this song?
4. Were students able to sing this melody at the end of the first day's activities?
5. Were students able to sing this song as a two-part round at the end of the second day's activities?
6. Did students enjoy this song?

PARTNER SONGS

Partner songs are two or more songs that can be performed simultaneously. Like rounds, they provide effective experiences in performing harmony. A rather limited number of songs can be combined as partner songs. The refrains of some songs, however, may be sung simultaneously with the verse, providing a partner-song effect.

The strategy for teaching partner songs is very much like that for teaching rounds. The two melodies should be taught by utilizing one of the rote teaching strategies or by reading from notation. Students must be able to perform both melodies independently and with confidence before singing them together.

Since both groups singing partner songs start performing at the same time, it is essential that starting pitches be given for both songs. (The two songs in the partnership do not always begin on the same pitch.) An additional problem for the leader is encountered if the two songs do not begin on the same beat of the measure. It can therefore be helpful to have student leaders for one or both groups when performing partner songs.

As in performing rounds, the goals of performing partner songs are to provide harmonic experiences and to develop awareness of group relationships. It is therefore essential that students in both groups listen as they perform.

Tzena, tzena

SOURCE: English words by Phyllis Resnick. From *Making Music Your Own*, Book 5. © 1971 Silver Burdett Company. Reprinted by permission.

ANALYSIS OF MUSIC FOR PERFORMING

TITLE: "TZENA, TZENA"
SOURCE: *MAKING MUSIC YOUR OWN*, BOOK 5, PP. 132–133

MUSICAL KNOWLEDGE THAT CAN BE DEVELOPED
    MELODY
    RHYTHM   *Steady beat, rhythm pattern* (♩ ♫ ♩ ♫)
    TIMBRE
    HARMONY   *Partner song (combined verse and refrain)*
    DYNAMICS
    FORM   *Repeat signs (verse and refrain)*
MUSICAL SKILLS THAT CAN BE DEVELOPED
    SINGING   *In two parts*
    PLAYING   *Tambourine (optional descant for clarinet)*
    MOVING
    LISTENING
    CREATING
    READING   *Rhythmic notation for tambourine part*
    DESCRIBING
GENERAL KNOWLEDGE THAT CAN BE DEVELOPED
    OF THE WORLD   *Folk music of Israel*
    OF RELATIONSHIPS
    OF FEELINGS   *Joyous celebration*
GENERAL SKILLS THAT CAN BE DEVELOPED
    PERCEIVING
    COMMUNICATING
    SOCIAL SKILLS   *Working together*
    PHYSICAL SKILLS   *Playing instruments (small-muscle coordination)*
    OTHER   *Researching folk customs*

Partner Song (*Reading Notation*)

"Tzena, tzena"
Making Music Your Own, Book 5, pp. 132–133

Upper Grades

Instructional Objectives

1. Students will clap the steady beat while the teacher sings the song.
2. Students will identify descending melodic patterns in the notation.
3. Students will identify and define repeat signs.
4. Students will sing the melody of the song.
5. Students will perform notated rhythm on the tambourine.
6. Students will sing the verse and refrain as partner songs.

Environment

This activity is designed for an autocratic environment. Students will need copies of the notation and sufficient space for clapping and playing instruments. Approximately ten minutes will be needed for the first day's activities; five minutes on each of several successive days should be devoted to this experience.

Initial Procedures

First Day

1. Sing the song, asking students to clap the steady beat.
2. Direct students' attention to the notation. Ask students to follow the notation as you sing again. Students are to identify phrases that begin with a descending melodic pattern (phrases three and four).
3. Through discussion compare these patterns with the up and down melodic patterns that begin phrases one and two.
4. Review the repeat sign found at the end of the first phrase and the function of the first and second ending.
5. Lead the class in singing the melody of the song.
6. Lead the class in clapping the rhythm of the tambourine part.
7. Lead the class in singing the melody while clapping the tambourine part.

Second Day

1. Review the melody of the song. If students can sing with confidence, continue partner song procedures, otherwise repeat some of the procedures from the first day.

2. Divide the class in half, instructing one part to sing the first part of the song (first two phrases) twice, while the rest of the class continues singing the entire song.

3. Add the tambourine part from the previous day and repeat two-part singing.

Extended Procedures

1. Select a student to play the accompaniment on the autoharp.

2. Select a small group of students to perform in two parts so the class can hear the harmonic effect of the partner songs.

3. Learn the dance steps to the *hora* and perform it while singing this song.

Modifications for Exceptional Learners

1. Select a student studying the clarinet to perform the clarinet ostinato given in *Making Music Your Own*.

2. Establish a slower tempo when working with students having weak reading skills.

3. Students without music reading skills and/or poor muscle coordination may play the steady beat on the tambourine rather than the part notated.

Evaluation

1. Could students clap the steady beat to this song?

2. Could students identify the descending melodic patterns in the notation?

3. Could students identify the repeat signs?

4. Could students sing the melody of the song?

5. Could students play the tambourine part while singing?

6. Could students sing this as a partner song?

7. Did students enjoy this activity?

There's Work to Be Done

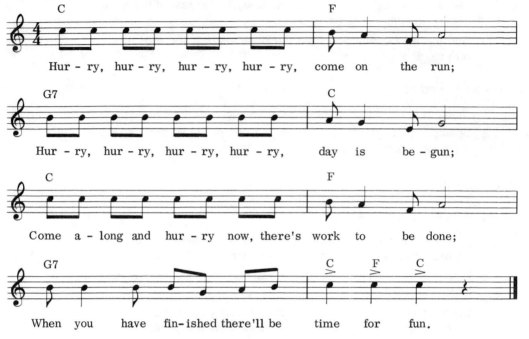

Hur - ry, hur - ry, hur - ry, hur - ry, come on the run;

Hur - ry, hur - ry, hur - ry, hur - ry, day is be - gun;

Come a - long and hur - ry now, there's work to be done;

When you have fin - ished there'll be time for fun.

SOURCE: From Robert Choate et al., *Experiencing Music*, New Dimensions in Music (New York: American Book Co., 1976), p. 138. Used with permission.

No Need to Hurry

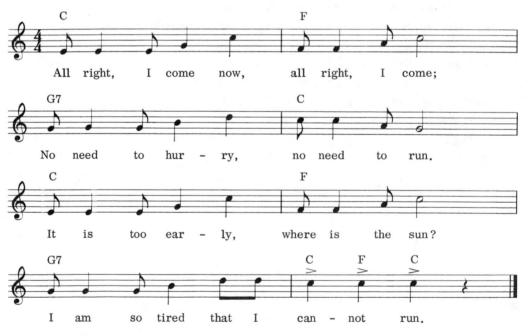

All right, I come now, all right, I come;

No need to hur - ry, no need to run.

It is too ear - ly, where is the sun?

I am so tired that I can - not run.

SOURCE: From Robert Choate et al., *Experiencing Music*, New Dimensions in Music (New York: American Book Co., 1976), p. 138. Used with permission.

ANALYSIS OF MUSIC FOR PERFORMING

TITLE: "THERE'S WORK TO BE DONE" AND "NO NEED TO HURRY"
SOURCE: *EXPERIENCING MUSIC*, NEW DIMENSIONS IN MUSIC, P. 138

MUSICAL KNOWLEDGE THAT CAN BE DEVELOPED
  MELODY   *Repeated tones*
  RHYTHM   *Syncopated patterns*
  TIMBRE
  HARMONY   *Partner songs*
  DYNAMICS
  FORM
MUSICAL SKILLS THAT CAN BE DEVELOPED
  SINGING   *Partner songs*
  PLAYING   *Calypso rhythms, Latin instruments*
  MOVING
  LISTENING
  CREATING
  READING   *Identifying syncopated patterns in notation*
  DESCRIBING
GENERAL KNOWLEDGE THAT CAN BE DEVELOPED
  OF THE WORLD   *Latin America, work ethic*
  OF RELATIONSHIPS   *Different ideas may be combined into one.*
  OF FEELINGS
GENERAL SKILLS THAT CAN BE DEVELOPED
  PERCEIVING
  COMMUNICATING
  SOCIAL SKILLS   *Working together*
  PHYSICAL SKILLS   *Small-muscle coordination for playing instruments*
  OTHER

Partner Songs (*Reading Notation*)

"There's Work to Be Done"
"No Need to Hurry"
Experiencing Music, New Dimensions in Music, p. 138

Upper Grades

Instructional Objectives

1. Students will clap and discuss the relative values of notes in this rhythm pattern:

2. Students will identify the rhythm pattern within the notational context of the song.

3. Students will identify the repeated tones that begin each phrase of "There's Work to Be Done."

4. Students will sing the melody of "There's Work to Be Done."

5. Students will play this rhythm pattern on Latin American instruments:

6. Students will identify the pattern in the notational context of "No Need to Hurry."

7. Students will play and clap the word rthythms of "No Need to Hurry."

8. Students will sing the melody of "No Need to Hurry."

9. Students will sing these two songs together as partner songs.

Environment

This activity is designed for an autocratic environment and should be spread over at least three days. Students will need copies of the notation for both songs, and an assortment of Latin American percussion instruments should also be available. Five to ten minutes each day should be devoted to work with these activities.

Initial Procedures

First Day

1. Direct students' attention to the rhythm pattern, which you have written on the board. Lead them in clapping and discussion of the relative length of quarter and eighth notes. (This activity should include at least as much clapping as discussing!)

2. Direct students' attention to the notation of "There's Work to Be Done." Ask, "Where do you find the pattern?"

3. What do students notice about the rhythm of the first measure in the first, second, and third phrases?

4. What do students notice about the melody of the first measure?

5. Direct students' attention to the notation of the first measure in each phrase:
   a) Will the rhythm be even or uneven?
   b) Will the melody go up, down, or stay the same?

6. Give the starting pitch and lead students in singing the melody.

Second Day

1. Review the song "There's Work to Be Done."

2. Review the rhythm pattern of the previous day.

3. Direct students' attention to notation for "No Need to Hurry":
   a) The second measure of each phrase has the same pattern.
   b) The first measure of each phrase has a pattern that is quite similar.

4. Distribute several Latin percussion instruments. Lead students in playing and clapping the word rhythm of the song.

5. Sing the melody while students softly play and clap word rhythms.

6. Give the starting pitch and lead the class in singing the melody.

7. Have students play instruments while singing the melody.

8. End the activity by again reviewing the song "There's Work to Be Done."

Third Day

1. Review the melody of both songs.

2. Divide the class, having the first half sing the melody of "There's Work to Be Done" while the second half listens.

3. Have the second half sing "No Need to Hurry" while the first half listens.

4. Give starting pitches to both groups and have them sing the songs together as partner songs.

Extended Procedures

1. Tape-record the performance of the class and replay the tape so students can hear the effect of the two songs combined.

2. Select a small group of students to perform combined songs for their classmates.

3. Have students create percussion accompaniment for Latin instruments.

    4. Select students to play accompaniment on autoharp or guitar.

Modification for Exceptional Learners

Provide a tape recording of the songs in a learning center. Encourage students to listen to the songs and sing along with the tape to develop confidence in their own singing. Later, encourage students to sing the partner song while listening to one song on tape.

CHORD ROOTS

Singing *chord roots* is another way to provide beginning experiences in part singing. *Chord roots* are the fundamental tones of chords that are used in accompaniment to songs. Since chord roots result in a part that is very similar to the part sung by basses in a choir, singing chord roots may be especially appealing to boys.

    We suggest that songs for use with chord roots be ones which can be accompanied with two or three chords and ones in which the chord changes do not occur frequently. It is also important that the tones of the chord roots be within the students' singing ranges. For this reason, songs in the keys of F and G are usually more appropriate than a song in the key of C.

    Students should have prior experience in hearing chord changes. This experience can be gained through playing the autoharp and through movement exercises such as sitting for the I chord or standing for the V^7 chord. It is not necessary for students to know the melody of a song before singing chord roots. In fact, in some instances, it may be desirable to have students sing the chord root part before learning the melody to avoid the tendency of some students to always sing the melody. We also suggest reinforcing singing experiences by having some students play chord roots on bells or xylophone and other students play chordal accompaniments on the autoharp while singing the chord root part.

Noah's Ark

1. Old   No - ah built him - self   an ark; There's one more riv-er to   cross.

He built it out of   hick-o-ry bark; There's one more riv-er to   cross._

REFRAIN

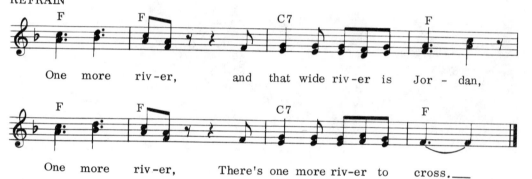

One   more   riv-er,   and   that wide riv-er is   Jor - dan,

One   more   riv-er,   There's one more riv-er to   cross.___

2. The animals went in one by one; There's one more river to cross.
   The elephant chewing a caraway bun; There's one more river to cross.

3. ... two by two; Rhinoceros and the kangaroo;

4. ... three by three; The bear, the bug and the bumblebee;

5. ... four by four; The hippopotamus stuck in the door;

6. ... five by five; "It's raining," said Noah, "so look alive;"

7. ... six by six; The monkeys did their silly tricks;

8. ... seven by seven; Said the ant to the elephant, "Who are you shovin'?"

9. ... eight by eight; "That's all!" said Noah and slammed the gate;

10. And as they talked of this and that
    The ark, it bumped on Ararat.

SOURCE: From Charles Leonhard et al., *Discovering Music Together*, Book 4 (Chicago: Follett Publishing Co., 1966), p. 17.

ANALYSIS OF MUSIC FOR PERFORMING

TITLE: "NOAH'S ARK"
SOURCE: *DISCOVERING MUSIC TOGETHER*, BOOK 4, P. 17

MUSICAL KNOWLEDGE THAT CAN BE DEVELOPED
    MELODY
    RHYTHM   *Uneven ($\frac{6}{8}$) rhythms*
    TIMBRE
    HARMONY   *Chord roots, two parts on refrain*
    DYNAMICS
    FORM   *Verse and refrain*
MUSICAL SKILLS THAT CAN BE DEVELOPED
    SINGING   *Chord roots*
    PLAYING   *An autoharp*
    MOVING
    LISTENING
    CREATING
    READING
    DESCRIBING
GENERAL KNOWLEDGE THAT CAN BE DEVELOPED
    OF THE WORLD   *Animals, story of Noah's Ark*
    OF RELATIONSHIPS   *Complex structures can be built on simple foundations.*
    OF FEELINGS
GENERAL SKILLS THAT CAN BE DEVELOPED
    PERCEIVING
    COMMUNICATING   *Story telling*
    SOCIAL SKILLS
    PHYSICAL SKILLS   *Small-muscle coordination for playing instruments*
    OTHER

Chord Roots (*Play Along*)

"Noah's Ark"
Discovering Music Together, Book 4, p. 17

Middle Grades

Instructional Objectives

1. Students will echo the teacher, chanting the rhythm of each phrase.
2. Students will identify chord changes within this song.
3. Students will play the melodic rhythm and correct chords on the autoharp.
4. Students will play chord roots on melody bells.
5. Students will sing chord roots.
6. Students will sing the melody of the song.
7. Students will sing the song in two parts.

Environment

This activity is designed for an autocratic environment. Students will essentially learn the song by rote; however, copies of notation will be needed for reading chord changes. An autoharp and melody bells F and C will be needed. Approximately ten minutes should be provided for this activity.

Initial Procedures

1. Clap and chant the words of the first phrase. Have students echo you.
2. Continue for each phrase of the song.
3. Chant word rhythms while playing the same rhythms on the autoharp. Ask students to raise their hands when they hear a chord change.
4. Select a student to play the autoharp. Have the class clap word rhythms and chant while the autoharp is played.
5. Select two students to play the melody bells. The F bell will play word rhythms in parts of the song where the F chord is indicated. The C bell will play word rhythms in parts of the song where a C^7 chord is indicated.
6. Have students practice bells on the first phrase.
7. Lead students in singing word rhythms on the pitches of the bells (chord roots). An autoharp may continue accompaniment.
8. When the class can sing chord roots with some confidence, have them continue their part while you sing the melody of the song.

9. Divide the class, having some students sing the melody while others continue on chord roots.

Extended Procedures

1. Sing through the entire song to tell the story of Noah's Ark.
2. Teach students the second part to the refrain, then divide the class in three groups—melody, chord roots, and second part.

Modifications for Exceptional Learners

1. Invite a student studying guitar to accompany the class, directing attention to the chord changes on the guitar.
2. Spend several days helping students develop confidence in singing chord roots before attempting the melody.

Evaluation

1. Did students correctly echo the rhythms of the teacher?
2. Could students aurally identify the chord changes when they were played on the autoharp?
3. Could students play the melodic rhythm on melody bells?
4. Could students sing the chord roots?
5. Could students sing the melody of the song?
6. Did students successfully sing the song in two parts?
7. Do students enjoy part singing?

DESCANTS

A *descant* is a vocal part that can be combined with a melody. Descants usually are at a higher pitch level than the melody and typically contain simpler rhythms and melodic patterns than the melody. Elementary music texts for upper grades usually contain several songs with descants.

The procedures for teaching descants are much like those that we suggest for teaching partner songs. Both the melody and the descant should be taught separately using either rote or note-reading strategies. After students can sing both with confidence, they can be combined to create the harmonic effect. We have found that students taking lessons on flute, violin, or clarinet can frequently play descants to the songs sung in the upper grades. Inviting these students to play as the class sings is another way to help students learn the descant and experience harmony.

Hush, Little Baby

3. If that billy goat won't pull,
   Mammy's goin' to buy you
   a cart and bull.
   If that cart and bull turn over,
   Mammy's goin' to buy you
   a dog named Rover.

4. If that Rover dog won't bark,
   Mammy's goin to buy you
   a horse and cart.
   If that horse and cart fall down,
   You'll still be the prettiest
   one in town.

SOURCE: From Charles Leonhard et al., *Discovering Music Together*, Book 4 (Chicago: Follett Publishing Co., 1966), p. 131.

ANALYSIS OF MUSIC FOR PERFORMING

TITLE: "HUSH, LITTLE BABY"
SOURCE: *DISCOVERING MUSIC TOGETHER*, BOOK 4, P. 131

MUSICAL KNOWLEDGE THAT CAN BE DEVELOPED
    MELODY
    RHYTHM   *Quarter- and eighth-note rhythms*
    TIMBRE
    HARMONY   *Descant*
    DYNAMICS
    FORM
MUSICAL SKILLS THAT CAN BE DEVELOPED
    SINGING   *Descant*
    PLAYING
    MOVING
    LISTENING
    CREATING
    READING   *Quarter- and eighth-note rhythms*
    DESCRIBING
GENERAL KNOWLEDGE THAT CAN BE DEVELOPED
    OF THE WORLD   *Lullabies, American folk music*
    OF RELATIONSHIPS   *Two ideas may be combined.*
    OF FEELINGS   *Gentleness*
GENERAL SKILLS THAT CAN BE DEVELOPED
    PERCEIVING
    COMMUNICATING   *Reading*
    SOCIAL SKILLS   *Working together*
    PHYSICAL SKILLS
    OTHER

Descant (*Reading Notation*)

"Hush, Little Baby"
Discovering Music Together, Book 4, p. 131

Middle Grades

Instructional Objectives

1. Students will read and clap quarter- and eighth-note rhythm patterns.
2. Students will sing the melody of the song.
3. Students will develop an understanding of the dotted quarter-note rhythm.
4. Students will sing the descant.
5. Students will sing the song in two parts.

Environment

This activity is designed for an autocratic environment. The teacher will need several cards with the following rhythms notated:

Five to ten minutes will be needed for this activity.

Initial Procedures

1. Direct students' attention to rhythm cards and lead them in clapping.
2. Show students cards 1, 2, 3, and 4. Ask them to listen as you sing a song. Ask, "Which card shows the rhythm of the beginning of the song?"
3. Sing one verse of the song and discuss students' responses. Clap the rhythms on the cards and resing the song if necessary.
4. Ask, "Does the second phrase begin with the same rhythm?" Sing the song again and establish through discussion that the second phrase begins with rhythm 4.
5. Lead the class in singing the first verse of the song. Give the words to the second verse and again lead the class in singing the first two verses.
6. Discuss and demonstrate rhythm card 5, taking one eighth note from the last beat and adding it to the third beat.
7. Lead the class in clapping cards 5 and 6.
8. Sing the descant for the class, pointing out the dotted eighth-note rhythm.
9. Lead the class in singing the descant part.
10. Divide the class, having one part sing the melody, and the other part sing the descant.

Extended Procedures

1. Introduce other verses to this song. Suggest that students make up some new verses.
2. Provide notation of the song and a set of melody bells in a learning center so students can play the descant on the bells.
3. Select a student to play autoharp accompaniment as the class sings the song in two parts.

Modifications for Exceptional Learners

1. Teach the melody of the song using a clap-along or what's-it-about strategy rather than the note-reading strategies suggested.
2. Spend several days helping students gain confidence in singing the melody before introducing the descant.
3. Introduce the descant by playing the bells while the class sings the melody.
4. Have students play the descant on the bells using color coding of the notation to guide their playing.

Evaluation

1. Could students read and clap quarter- and eighth-note rhythms?
2. Could students sing the melody of the song?
3. Did students correctly clap the dotted quarter-note patterns?
4. Did students accurately sing the descant?
5. Could students sing the song in two parts?

Battle Hymn of the Republic

REFRAIN

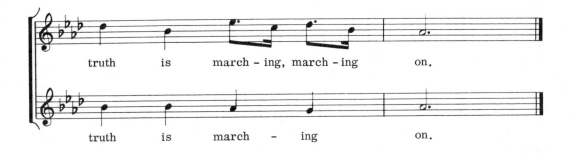

Battle Hymn of the Republic   continued

1. Mine____ eyes have seen the glo - ry of the
2. He has sound - ed forth the trum - pet that shall

com - ing of the Lord; He is tramp - ling out the
nev - er call re-treat; He is sift - ing out the

vin - tage where the grapes of wrath are stored; He hath
hearts of men be - fore the judg - ment seat. Oh, be

loosed the fate - ful light - ning of His ter - ri - ble swift
swift, my soul, to an - swer Him! Be ju - bi - lant, my

sword; His truth is march - ing on.
feet! Our God is march - ing on.

SOURCE: From Beatrice Landeck et al., *Making Music Your Own*, Book 5 (Morristown, N.J.: Silver Burdett Co., 1971), pp. 136–37.

ANALYSIS OF MUSIC FOR PERFORMING

TITLE: "BATTLE HYMN OF THE REPUBLIC"
SOURCE: *MAKING MUSIC YOUR OWN*, BOOK 5, PP. 136–37

MUSICAL KNOWLEDGE THAT CAN BE DEVELOPED
    MELODY
    RHYTHM   *Steady beat, march tempo; dotted eighth-sixteenth note patterns*
    TIMBRE
    HARMONY   *Descant*
    DYNAMICS
    FORM   *Verse and refrain*
MUSICAL SKILLS THAT CAN BE DEVELOPED
    SINGING   *A descant*
    PLAYING
    MOVING   *Marching*
    LISTENING   *To two parts.*
    CREATING
    READING
    DESCRIBING
GENERAL KNOWLEDGE THAT CAN BE DEVELOPED
    OF THE WORLD   *Civil War*
    OF RELATIONSHIPS   *Two different ideas may be combined.*
    OF FEELINGS   *Patriotism*
GENERAL SKILLS THAT CAN BE DEVELOPED
    PERCEIVING
    COMMUNICATING
    SOCIAL SKILLS   *Working together*
    PHYSICAL SKILLS   *Marching*
    OTHER   *Researching music of the Civil War*

Descants (*Reading Notation*)

"Battle Hymn of the Republic"
Making Music Your Own, Book 5, pp. 136–37

Upper Grades

Instructional Objectives

1. Students will discuss the music of the Civil War.
2. Students will sing the melody of a patriotic hymn.
3. Students will march to the steady beat while singing.
4. Students will read the notation and clap the rhythm of the descant.
5. Students will sing the descant.
6. Students will sing the song using two parts on the refrain.

Environment

This activity is designed for an autocratic environment. It is assumed that at least some students will be familiar with this well-known Civil War song. Open space will be needed for marching; however, a circle around the outer perimeter of the desks will be adequate. Students should have copies of the notation of the song. Ten to fifteen minutes should be provided for this activity.

Initial Procedures

First Day

1. Begin with a brief discussion of the Civil War and introduce this as the "battle hymn" of the North.
2. Direct students' attention to notation, provide the starting pitch and lead the class in singing the song.
3. Have students stand and lead a "march" with students stepping to the steady beat as they sing the melody.
4. Return students to their seats and direct their attention to the descant. Be certain all students know which lines of notation to read.
5. Lead students in clapping the rhythm and chanting the words of the descant.
6. Lead the class in singing the descant. (Students may continue to clap the rhythm as they continue singing.)

Second Day

1. Begin by reviewing the descant, all singing.

2. Have the class again sing the descant. After getting the class started, switch to singing the melody yourself.

3. Divide the class, half singing the melody and half singing the descant (refrain only).

4. Have the class sing the song from the beginning, dividing into two parts at the refrain.

5. Have students switch parts and sing from the beginning again.

Extended Procedures

1. Teach the class the second verse of this song.

2. Have students improvise a drum accompaniment to be played while the song is sung in two parts.

3. Make a tape recording of the students' performance and replay the tape for the class so they can hear the harmonic effect of the combined parts.

Modifications for Exceptional Learners

1. Select a student studying violin or flute to learn the descant and play it as the class sings the melody.

2. Provide a set of melody bells and notation of the song in a learning center so students can play the descant on the bells.

3. Find a recording of the melody to which a student can sing this descant.

Evaluation

1. Could the students sing the melody of this song?

2. Could students march to the steady beat while singing?

3. Could students read and clap the rhythms of the descant?
   a) Which students had difficulty?
   b) Which rhythmic patterns were too difficult?

4. Could students sing the descant?

5. Could students sing this song in two parts?

Streets of Laredo

3. "Get six jolly cowboys to carry my coffin,
   Get six purty maidens to sing me a song,
   Take me to the valley and lay the sod o'er me,
   For I'm a young cowboy and know I've done wrong.

4. "Oh, beat the drum slowly and play the fife lowly,
   Play the dead march as you carry me along;
   Put bunches of roses all over my coffin,
   Roses to deaden the clods as they fall."

SOURCE: From James Mursell et al., *Music Around the World*, Music for Living Series (Morristown, N.J.: Silver Burdett Co., 1956), p. 116.

ANALYSIS OF MUSIC FOR PERFORMING

TITLE: "STREETS OF LAREDO"
SOURCE: *MUSIC AROUND THE WORLD*, MUSIC FOR LIVING SERIES, P. 116

MUSICAL KNOWLEDGE THAT CAN BE DEVELOPED
    MELODY
    RHYTHM   *Triple meter*
    TIMBRE
    HARMONY   *Descant, chord changes in each measure*
    DYNAMICS
    FORM   *Phrasing*
MUSICAL SKILLS THAT CAN BE DEVELOPED
    SINGING   *Melody with a descant*
    PLAYING   *Chords on melody bells*
    MOVING
    LISTENING
    CREATING
    READING
    DESCRIBING
GENERAL KNOWLEDGE THAT CAN BE DEVELOPED
    OF THE WORLD   *Cowboys*
    OF RELATIONSHIPS   *Two different ideas may be combined.*
    OF FEELINGS   *Loneliness*
GENERAL SKILLS THAT CAN BE DEVELOPED
    PERCEIVING
    COMMUNICATING
    SOCIAL SKILLS   *Working together*
    PHYSICAL SKILLS   *Small-muscle coordination in playing bells*
    OTHER   *Researching the life of a cowboy*

Descant (*Play Along*)

"Streets of Laredo"
Music Around the World, Music for Living Series, p. 116

Middle Grades

Instructional Objectives

1. Students will demonstrate an awareness of triple meter by playing the melody bells.
2. Students will demonstrate an awareness of chord changes and musical phrases by playing the melody bells.
3. Students will sing the melody of the song.
4. Students will identify the stepwise melodic movement of the descant.
5. Students will sing the descant.
6. Students will sing the melody and descant together.

Environment

This activity is designed for an autocratic environment. The melody of the song will be taught by rote; however, notation will be needed for the second day when students will learn the descant. A set, preferably two sets, of melody bells will also be needed. Ten to fifteen minutes should be available for the first day's activities and approximately five minutes for the second day's.

Initial Procedures

First Day

1. Distribute bells to students and have them stand in front of the class in the following groupings:
   a) G B D
   b) D F♯ C
   c) A C E
2. Direct students to play as you point to each group, giving them distinct "beats" with hand motions. Each group should play three beats. Establish a steady beat and work until students can play together, keeping the beat as chords change.
3. Sing the song yourself, continuing to conduct the students playing the bells, pointing to each group when their chord should be played.
4. Ask questions to direct students' attention to the text of the song:
   a) What town is mentioned in this song?
   b) What happened in Laredo?

5. Repeat procedure 3 to verify students' responses.

6. Ask questions to direct students' attention to the melody:
   a) How many phrases are in this song?
   b) Are any of the phrases similar?

7. Repeat procedure 3 to verify students' responses.

8. Invite the class to join you in singing the melody of the song.

9. Choose different students to play the bell accompaniment and lead the class in singing again.

Second Day

1. Review the melody of the song (without bell accompaniment today).

2. Direct students' attention to the notation of the descant. Ask, "Are any phrases alike? Does the descant move mostly by step or skip?"

3. Sing the descant, inviting students to read the notation and sing along with you.

4. Discuss any problem spots, then sing them in isolation and again in the context of the entire descant.

5. Divide the class, having one part sing the descant while the other part sings the melody. (NOTE: The descant begins on a different pitch and a beat later than the melody.)

Extended Procedures

1. Select students to play the autoharp as an accompaniment.

2. Suggest that students improvise a rhythmic accompaniment on wood blocks to represent horses walking through the streets of Laredo.

3. Dramatize the story told in this song.

Modifications for Exceptional Learners

1. Invite students who play the guitar to accompany the class as they sing this song in two parts.

2. Ask students who read musical notation to play the descant on melody bells or xylophone.

3. Students with poor motor coordination may be unable to play the melody bells on the steady beat as suggested in first day initial procedures 1 through 3. Suggest that they play only on the first beat of each measure; be certain they have large mallets with which to play.

4. Draw a picture of the scene described to help slow learners grasp the text of this song.

Evaluation

1. Did the students playing of the bell accompaniment reveal an awareness of triple meter?
2. Were students able to change chords appropriately?
3. Were students able to sing the melody of the song?
4. Were students able to discuss the melodic movement after examining the notation of the descant?
5. Were students able to sing the descant?
6. Were students able to sing the two parts together?

SONGS IN TWO AND THREE PARTS

Students in the upper grades can sing songs written with two- and three-part harmony. We have found that it is best to avoid the terms *soprano* and *alto* since boys sometimes resent being classified with these labels traditionally given to women's vocal parts. Identifying parts as *high, middle,* and *low* is usually more satisfactory.

As a general rule, the harmony part should not be introduced until students can perform the melody independently and with confidence. Harmony parts can be introduced either through rote or note-reading strategies. Another excellent way to introduce a harmony part is to have a student play the harmony on an instrument while the class sings the melody. The recorder or melody bells are good instruments for this, but we also point out that many students in the upper grades are learning to play band or orchestral instruments and would welcome the opportunity to perform for their peers. If students are to play harmony parts on an instrument, they should be given the music several days in advance to provide time for practice. Starting pitches for singing the melody should also be taken from the instrument so that the class will be singing in the same key as the instrument is sounding. Trumpets, clarinets, and saxophones are "transposing" instruments—that is, they do not sound in the key in which the music is written. If these instruments are used, other accompaniments such as piano, autoharp, or recordings cannot be used unless parts are transposed.

Whether the harmony part is modeled by the teacher singing it or by a student playing it on an instrument, it should first be heard along with the melody. After hearing the harmony part several times, all students can be invited to sing along with the model until they reach some degree of confidence in singing it. (A good way to test this level of confidence is for the teacher to sing the melody. If the class can maintain the harmony part, they are probably ready to "put the two together.") When this level of confidence is reached, the class can be divided into groups with one group singing or playing each part.

In choosing songs for beginning experiences in two-and three-part harmony, we suggest songs in which small sections are harmonized while the rest is sung in unison. Dividing into parts for the last chord or last phrase is frequently quite effective. As students gain more knowledge and skill in harmony, entire songs can be performed in two or three parts.

When harmony is performed in the elementary school, parts should not be assigned on a permanent basis as they are in a choir or instrumental ensemble. Students need experience in singing and playing both melody and harmony and should, therefore, have the opportunity to perform both parts of a song. An important thing to remember about teaching a song and its harmony part is to progress slowly. Students may need to perform the melody of the song many times, over several days, before they are ready to hear the harmony. They may then need several more days to learn the harmony part before combining it with the melody.

Night Herding Song

1. Oh, slow up, do - gies, quit rov - ing a - round

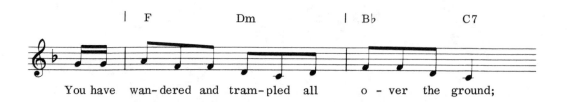

You have wan - dered and tram - pled all o - ver the ground;

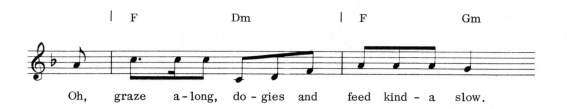

Oh, graze a - long, do - gies and feed kind - a slow.

And don't for - ev - er be on the go, Oh move slow,

do - gies, move slow, ___ Hi - o, hi - o, hi - o! ___

SOURCE: From Mary Val Marsh; Carroll Rinehart; Edith Savage; Ralph Beelke; and Ronald Silverman, *The Spectrum of Music, Book 4* (New York: Macmillan, 1974), p. 141.

ANALYSIS OF MUSIC FOR PERFORMING

TITLE: "NIGHT HERDING SONG"
SOURCE: *THE SPECTRUM OF MUSIC*, BOOK 4, P. 141

MUSICAL KNOWLEDGE THAT CAN BE DEVELOPED
    MELODY
    RHYTHM   *Uneven ($\frac{6}{8}$) rhythms*
    TIMBRE
    HARMONY   *Intervals of the third, harmonic variation*
    DYNAMICS
    FORM
MUSICAL SKILLS THAT CAN BE DEVELOPED
    SINGING   *In thirds*
    PLAYING   *The autoharp*
    MOVING
    LISTENING   *To different harmonizations of the same song*
    CREATING
    READING
    DESCRIBING
GENERAL KNOWLEDGE THAT CAN BE DEVELOPED
    OF THE WORLD   *Cowboys*
    OF RELATIONSHIPS   *One idea may be treated in several different ways.*
    OF FEELINGS   *Loneliness*
GENERAL SKILLS THAT CAN BE DEVELOPED
    PERCEIVING
    COMMUNICATING
    SOCIAL SKILLS   *Working together*
    PHYSICAL SKILLS
    OTHER

Songs in Two and Three Parts
(*Play Along; What's It About*)

"Night Herding Song"
The Spectrum of Music, Book 4, p. 141

Middle Grades

Instructional Objectives

1. Students will clap and play percussion instruments to typical $^6_8$ rhythm patterns:

2. Students will sing the melody of the song.
3. Students will draw a line showing the melodic contour of the last phrase.
4. Students will sing the harmony part of the last phrase.
5. Students will sing the song, dividing into two parts for the last phrase.

Environment

This activity is designed for a democratic environment. Several wood blocks, rhythm sticks, or similar instruments will be needed. A large sheet of paper and two colors of marking pens should also be available. Five to ten minutes will be needed for the first day's activities. Three to five minutes should be ample for the second day's.

Initial Procedures

First Day

1. Begin with echo clapping in $^6_8$ rhythms, being certain to include the following patterns:

2. Suggest the class clap

   as you sing the song.
3. Select several students to play the preceding pattern on the wood block. Have the rest of the students clap while you sing the song again.

4. Ask some questions to direct students' attention to the text:
   a) What is this song about?
   b) What is the cowboy trying to get the dogies to do?
   c) What have they been doing?

5. Divide the class; have half continue the clapping pattern from procedure 2 and the other half clap this rhythm:

   Sing the melody again yourself as students continue clapping.

6. Select several students to play the pattern from procedure 5 on rhythm sticks or claves. Combine this with the pattern played on the wood block, while you sing the song again.

7. Give the starting pitch and lead the class in singing the melody.

8. Repeat procedure 7 several times, selecting different students to play the instruments.

9. Direct students' attention to the last phrase of the song, singing it several times and having students draw the melodic contour in the air with their hands.

10. Select a student to draw the melodic contour for the last phrase on a large sheet of paper.

11. Sing the melody of the song again.

Second Day

1. Review the melody of the song. Can students sing with confidence, especially the last phrase?

2. Direct students' attention to the line showing the melodic contour of the last phrase and lead the class in resinging the last phrase.

3. Using a different color of marking pen, draw another line, paralleling the first at a higher level.

4. Using A as the starting pitch, lead the class in singing the last phrase at a higher pitch level. Repeat this several times until students are confident.

5. Divide the class, give one part the starting pitch of F and the other part the starting pitch of A, and lead the group in singing the last phrase.

6. Sing the song from the beginning, dividing into two parts on the last phrase.

Extended Procedures

1. Tape-record the performance of the class so students can hear the harmonic effect of the last phrase.

2. Accompany the song on the autoharp. Point out and compare the two parts given for the autoharp.

3. Select students to play on the melody bells the two parts of the last phrase.

Modifications for Exceptional Learners

1. Select an outstanding singer to sing this song as a solo, the entire class joining with the harmony part of the last phrase.
2. Some students may have difficulty clapping the rhythm patterns suggested in the initial procedures. They could instead play the steady beat on a drum.

Evaluation

1. Could students continue to clap patterns while you sang the song?
2. Could students sing the melody of the song?
3. Did students reveal an awareness of melodic contour by the shapes they drew in the air and on paper?
4. Did students sing the last phrase in two parts?
5. Did students enjoy this activity?

Tum Balalyka

REFRAIN

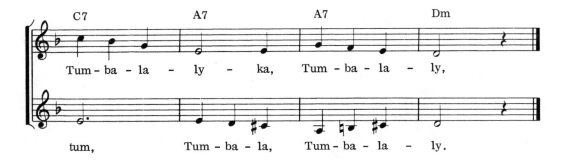

Tum Balalyka continued

(Boys) 1. Maid — en, maid — en, tell ___ me true,
(Girls) 2. Sil — ly lad, the an — swer true;

What can grow with — out ___ the dew?
A stone can grow with — out ___ the dew.

What ___ can burn for years ___ and years?
Love ___ can burn for years ___ and years;

What ___ can cry and shed ___ no tears?
A heart ___ can cry and shed ___ no tears.

ANALYSIS OF MUSIC FOR PERFORMING

TITLE: "TUM BALALYKA"
SOURCE: *EXPLORING MUSIC*, BOOK 6, PP. 136–37

MUSICAL KNOWLEDGE THAT CAN BE DEVELOPED
    MELODY
    RHYTHM   *Triple meter*
    TIMBRE   *Violin; balalyka*
    HARMONY   *Minor, intervals of the third*
    DYNAMICS
    FORM   *Verse and refrain*
MUSICAL SKILLS THAT CAN BE DEVELOPED
    SINGING   *In two parts (thirds)*
    PLAYING   *The tambourine*
    MOVING
    LISTENING   *Identifying a harmony part*
    CREATING
    READING
    DESCRIBING
GENERAL KNOWLEDGE THAT CAN BE DEVELOPED
    OF THE WORLD   *Russia*
    OF RELATIONSHIPS
    OF FEELINGS
GENERAL SKILLS THAT CAN BE DEVELOPED
    PERCEIVING
    COMMUNICATING
    SOCIAL SKILLS   *Working together*
    PHYSICAL SKILLS
    OTHER   *Researching Russian culture*

Singing in Two and Three Parts
(*Listening to a Record*)

"Tum Balalyka"
Exploring Music, Book 6, pp. 136–37

Upper Grades

Instructional Objectives

1. Students will identify two violins playing accompaniment on the recording.
2. Students will identify two vocal parts on the refrain of the song.
3. Students will clap and play

   on the tambourine.
4. Students will identify the phrase in which two vocal parts move separately.
5. Students will sing the melody of the song.
6. Students will sing the second part of the refrain.
7. Students will sing the refrain in two parts.

Environment

This activity is designed for an autocratic environment. It is expected that the initial procedures will be carried out over several days. Students will learn the song by listening to the recording, but copies of the notation should be available. Several tambourines will also be used in the lesson. Five to ten minutes each day should be devoted to this activity.

Initial Procedures

First Day

1. Introduce the term *Balalyka*—a Russian instrument similar to a guitar.
2. Play the instrumental introduction of the recording and then ask students to identify the instruments being used. Through discussion develop the idea that two violins are playing, one the melody and the other, a higher part.
3. Ask students to describe the voices they hear. Ask, "Are they the same for the verse and the refrain? Are all the voices singing the same part?"

4. Play the recording through the first verse. Through discussion develop the idea that the verse is sung by a man while children sing the refrain in two parts.

5. Review the concept of *triple meter*. Have students clap this pattern:

6. Select some students to play tambourines. Then play the recording through the first verse again, having students play and clap this pattern:

7. Direct students' attention to the notation, give the starting pitch, and lead them in singing the melody of the song (without the recording).

8. Lead students in singing the song again, adding the tambourine part.

9. Ask students to listen to the recording again. Ask, "Do the two parts in the refrain always sing together?"

10. Have students identify the third phrase of the refrain as a section in which two parts do not sing together. Also discuss the second part of the first two phrases of the refrain—it moves the same as the melody but at a lower pitch.

11. Give the starting pitch and lead the students in singing the second part of the refrain.

12. Review the melody of the entire song again.

Second Day

1. Review by singing the melody without the recording.

2. Lead the class in singing the second part of the refrain.

3. Play the recording, having the class sing the melody on the verse, the second part on the refrain.

4. Divide the class, having one part sing the melody on the refrain, the other part sing the harmony.

Extended Procedures

1. Have the class sing the combined parts with tambourine accompaniment.

2. Teach the class the second verse, having boys sing first, girls sing second, and all students sing the two-part refrain.

3. Tape-record the students' performance, replaying the tape so that students can hear the harmonic effect of the refrain.

Modifications for Exceptional Learners

1. Select students who study instruments to play the refrain in two parts.

2. A descant for flute is given in the teacher's edition of *Exploring Music*. A talented student could play this as the class sings the verse.

3. If students have difficulty playing the suggested pattern on the tambourine, have some play the first beat of each measure on a drum.

Evaluation

1. Did students hear the two violin parts in the introduction?

2. Did students hear the two vocal parts in the refrain?

3. Could students maintain the rhythm pattern as they listened? As they sang?

4. Did students accurately sing the melody of the song?

5. Did students accurately sing the harmony part?

6. Did students successfully sing the two parts together?

SELF-CHECK: PERFORMING

1. Performing music in the classroom is assumed to be
   a) Singing
   b) Playing instruments
   c) Singing, playing instruments, and moving to music
   d) Any musical activity

2. Which of the following was *not* considered to be an important reason for including performing activities in the classroom?
   a) Development of musical knowledge
   b) Development of knowledge of people and events in the world
   c) Development of general skills such as perceiving and communicating
   d) Development of the ability to use leisure time wisely

3. The general knowledge that is developed through musical experiences is
   a) Knowledge of the world, or relationships, and knowledge of feelings
   b) Knowledge of melody, rhythm, harmony, dynamics, timbre, and form
   c) Knowledge of composers and notation
   d) Knowledge of math, science, and geography

4. The skill of performing music
   a) Is unrelated to musical knowledge
   b) Is a way of developing musical knowledge
   c) Can be developed only after students learn to read music
   d) Can be developed only after students have acquired musical knowledge

5. Responsibility for guiding performing activities in the classroom
   a) Belongs to the classroom teacher
   b) Belongs to the music specialist
   c) Is shared by the classroom teacher and the music specialist
   d) Should be assigned to gifted students who can play the piano

6. Competencies for guiding performing activities
   a) Are a series of discrete behaviors that should occur in the prescribed order
   b) Are a series of discrete behaviors that may occur in random order
   c) Are a series of interrelated behaviors that may occur simultaneously
   d) Are the behaviors of planning, singing, playing, and moving

7. Competencies for guiding performance activities
   a) Are dependent on the ability of the teacher to read musical notation
   b) Are dependent on the performance skills of the teacher
   c) Are dependent on the degree to which the teacher appreciates good music
   d) Are a series of behaviors that can be developed by any teacher

8. Goals for performing activities
   a) Should be established by the teacher
   b) Should be based on an assessment of student needs
   c) Are the same for lower- and upper-grade classes
   d) Are the same for handicapped and normal learners

9. Which of the following was *not* considered an important goal for performing activities in the classroom?
   a) Experiencing the joy that comes from performing music
   b) Preparing students for performance in high school bands and choirs

Question	Key
1	c
2	d
3	a
4	b
5	c
6	c
7	d
8	b
9	b

c) Developing an increased understanding of melody, rhythm, harmony, dynamics, timbre, and form.

d) Developing skill in using musical notation

10. Assessment of musical needs
    a) Should occur at the beginning of every school year
    b) Is an ongoing process that is part of every musical activity
    c) Is necessary in special education classes but not in other classes
    d) Is necessary when individualized instruction is utilized but not for group instruction

    b

11. The assessment process is one of
    a) Giving tests to determine what students have learned
    b) Assigning grades on the basis of individual student progress
    c) Comparing students with national norms
    d) Collecting data about the degree to which students have met identified goals

    d

12. In assessing students' musical performances, the teacher should be concerned with
    a) The quality of music being performed
    b) The musical appreciation of the student
    c) The musical knowledge and skill developed through the performance
    d) The musical technique demonstrated by the performer

    c

13. A suggested procedure for assessing performing activities is
    a) Giving students a paper-and-pencil test on musical notation
    b) Observing student performances using a checklist to identify strengths and weaknesses
    c) Recording student performances and having them complete self-evaluations
    d) Administering the Test of Musical Performance or another standardized instrument twice each year

    b

14. An analysis of music for classroom performing activities should begin with
    a) An examination of the notation
    b) An examination of the text of the song
    c) Listening to either a recording or live performance of the song
    d) Identification of the key signature and starting pitch

    c

15. An analysis of music for performing activities is primarily concerned with
    a) Knowledge and skills that can be developed through the experience
    b) Anticipating performance problems so a more "polished" performance can be achieved
    c) Identifying music that is easy enough for the students to perform
    d) Learning to play accompaniments on the piano or autoharp

    a

16. Which of the following would not be a concern in analyzing a song for a classroom performing activity?
    a) Is this a song which I would enjoy singing?
    b) What musical knowledge can be developed through this song?
    c) What general knowledge can be developed through this song?
    d) Can I play the accompaniment of this song on the autoharp or piano?

    d

17. An autocratic environment is one which
    a) Is student-centered
    b) Is teacher-centered
    c) Involves much interchange between student and teacher
    d) Imposes no restrictions on either teacher or students

    b

Key

18. A democratic environment is one which   *Key*
    a) Is student-centered
    b) Is teacher-centered
    c) Involves much interchange between student and teacher   c
    d) Involves students and teachers voting on all class activities

19. An open environment is one which
    a) Is student-centered   a
    b) Is teacher-centered
    c) Involves much interchange between student and teacher
    d) Is material-centered

20. In planning learning environments, the teacher is concerned with
    a) Physical arrangement of things in the room
    b) Human interactions within the classroom
    c) Conservation of light and heat in the classroom
    d) Both human interactions and physical arrangements in the classroom   d

21. The time and space in which performing activities occur
    a) Are of little concern to the teacher in planning activities
    b) Must be considered as part of the total teaching/learning environment   b
    c) Comprise the total teaching/learning environment and must be carefully con-
       sidered by the teacher
    d) Present problems that the competent teacher can overcome

22. Which of the following was *not* considered as an effective management technique
    for performing activities?
    a) Establishing efficient classroom routines
    b) Providing clear and concise directions
    c) Using high-quality music   c
    d) Reinforcing good performance

23. Learning a song by rote implies
    a) A small group of children learning from a tape recorder
    b) Learning the song by reading notation
    c) Learning the song through repeated experiences with the song   c
    d) Echoing the teacher phrase by phrase

24. When giving children notation to a song
    a) Have students read through the entire song without singing yourself
    b) Give some problem or question that will require the use of notation   b
    c) Teach the song by rote first, then sing with notation
    d) Have students name the key signature, meter signature, and starting pitch

25. When teaching a song by rote, it is usually best to
    a) Find reasons to have students listen to the entire song on repeated occa-
       sions   a
    b) Have students hear only one phrase over and over until they learn it
    c) Have students learn the words first, then the song
    d) Have students read the song from notation

26. When teaching a song with a recording, the teacher should
    a) Have children sit quietly and listen
    b) Direct students' attention to some specific aspect of the recording   b
    c) Play the recording loudly in order to support the children's singing
    d) Play the recording only once

27. When teaching a round, descant, or other part song, the teacher should
    a) Direct students' attention to the harmonic effect by reminding them to listen to their part in relation to the other parts
    b) Help students stay on their own part by encouraging them to cover their ears in order to block out other parts
    c) Be certain to teach all parts of the song on the same day
    d) Have the boys sing the lower part

Key

a

ENABLING ACTIVITIES: PERFORMING

On your own (in the practice room or on your own)
1. Develop a repertoire of at least fifty songs that you can lead groups in singing. Memorize twenty-five of these songs.
2. Tape-record your singing of three songs. Listen to the recording and assess the performance as objectively as possible. The checklist on pages 9 and 10 will help. Make a list of things that will improve your performance and work toward achieving these. If you need help, ask your instructor.
3. Work out accompaniments for at least ten songs. You may use autoharp, ukulele, guitar, or piano.
4. Become familiar with at least ten instruments commonly found in the classroom. Be certain you know how to hold them, how to play them, and how they sound. (A good way to do this is to form a percussion ensemble to accompany class singing or to play along with records.)
5. Working with a group of your friends, create a dance to one of your favorite recordings. Do the movements reflect rhythm, phrasing, dynamics, pitch levels, and the form of the music? Perform your dance for the class.

In the schools
1. Observe a music performing lesson and list the teaching strategies and materials used.
2. Observe a music performing lesson and list several musical and general goals toward which the teacher may have been working. (You may need to discuss this with the teacher after the lesson.)
3. Examine the materials and resources that are available for musical performing activities in the classroom, in the music room, and in the media center. List categories of available materials and resources.
4. Assess the musical performance of several individual students and the general performance of the entire class using the checklist on pages 9 and 10. Suggest musical activities that will meet the identified needs of these students.
5. Lead a group of students in performing music that they already know.
6. Introduce a new musical composition to a group of students and work toward the attainment of at least one musical and one general learning goal.
7. Identify a student with special learning needs. Assess his or her present level of musical development and construct an IEP including a long-range goal, specific objectives, and some suggested musical activities that have been modified to meet the special learning needs.

In the library
1. Examine basic music textbooks commonly found in elementary schools. (See listing on page 182.)
2. Using the form found on page 17, complete an analysis of at least five songs found in elementary music textbooks.
3. Examine the scope and sequence charts and listing of goals and objectives found in the teachers' editions of elementary music textbooks.
4. Examine the goals and objectives listed in state and local district music curriculum guides.

5. Review the suggested teaching strategies for musical performance found in the teachers' guides of elementary music textbooks.

In the campus classroom

1. Begin each class period with a musical performance which includes singing, playing, or moving to music.
2. Assist one another in developing and refining performing skills.
3. Plan and lead a performing experience with a small group of your classmates. Evaluate the environment created, the teaching strategies used, and the musical performance of the "teacher."
4. Through a series of minilessons, gain experience in working in a variety of teaching/ learning environments and in using a number of teaching strategies.
5. Role-play a situation in which a teacher explains to a parent why performing is a necessary part of the classroom learning experience.

SOURCES OF MUSIC FOR PERFORMING ACTIVITIES

Discovering Music Together. Charles Leonhard, Beatrice Krone, Irving Wolfe, and Margaret Fullerton. Chicago, Ill.: Follett Publishing Co., 1966.

Exploring Music. Eunice Boardman and Beth Landis. New York: Holt, Rinehart and Winston, 1975.

Making Music Your Own. Beatrice Landeck, Elizabeth Crook, Harold C. Youngberg, and Otto Luening. Morristown, N.J.: Silver Burdett Co., 1971.

Music. Elizabeth Crook, Bennett Reimer, and David S. Walker. Morristown, N.J.: Silver Burdett Co., 1978.

Music Around the World, Music for Living Series. James Mursell, Gladys Tipton, Beatrice Landeck, Harold Nordholm, Roy E. Freeburg, and Jack M. Watson. Morristown, N.J.: Silver Burdett Co., 1956.

Music For Young Americans. Richard Berg, Daniel Hooley, Josephine Wolverton, and Claudean Burns. New York: American Book Co., 1963.

New Dimensions in Music. Robert Choate, Richard C. Berg, Lee Kjelson, and Eugene W. Troth. New York: American Book Co., 1976.

The Spectrum of Music. Mary Val Marsh, Carroll Rinehart, Edith Savage, Ralph Beelke, and Ronald Silverman. New York: Macmillan Publishing Co., 1974.

Learning Through Listening

OBJECTIVES

- State a rationale for listening to music in the elementary classroom
- Identify goals and objectives for listening activities
- Assess the musical needs of students through listening activities
- Analyze recorded compositions, identifying knowledge and skill that can be developed through listening experiences
- Plan effective classroom environments for listening activities
- Demonstrate a number of strategies for guiding listening activities

---

KINDS OF LISTENING

Because music is first of all *sound*, listening is basic to every musical activity. Children learn to sing by listening to songs sung by parents, teachers, other children, or on recordings. It is necessary to listen while performing alone or as part of a group to be certain that pitches, rhythms, dynamics, and tone are accurate and fit together in a pleasing and expressive way. Listening is essential if movement activities are to reflect reactions to the music. It is necessary to listen throughout the process of creating music in order to make musical decisions and value judgments. We also "listen" to our musical thoughts as we think sound patterns or recreate music in our memories. Listening is a vital part of every musical activity, and, in your role as a teacher, you will be responsible for helping children develop listening skills.

There is a special kind of musical listening. Although many people find enjoyment and satisfaction throughout their lifetime in musical performance, an even greater number find much meaning and pleasure in listening to the performances of others. We are told that the number of people attending musical concerts increases each year. The sale of records, tapes, and high-fidelity equipment is on an upward spiral. Listening to the musical performance of others is an important musical activity. This chapter will help you develop competencies in designing and guiding listening experiences for elementary school children.

WHY LISTEN IN THE CLASSROOM?

We are surrounded by sounds in our contemporary society—the sounds of machines, the sounds of people, and the sounds of nature, to say nothing of the sounds we have created for their own sake, such as the sounds of violins, trumpets, pianos, and electronic synthesizers. There are indeed few moments in the day that we are not experiencing sound. When we make a conscious effort to listen to a sound and to allow ourselves to respond to that sound with feeling, the sound becomes music.

Listening to music is a skill that, like other skills, becomes more refined as we practice and develop new techniques. Learning to listen is an important part of one's education as it is a means for acquiring both knowledge and skills.

Much knowledge about music can be gained by listening to musical performances, whether live or recorded. Live performances, of course, provide the opportunity to see the performers, and they often give us cues as to what we should hear. A soloist may stand so that we know what instrument is playing; the conductor's gestures may point out that the music is getting louder—or slower. By watching the fingers of the guitarist or pianist, we may become more aware of the scalelike passages we are hearing. Such visual cues are not available when listening to recorded music, and even at live performances many things frequently escape our attention because we do not know enough about the music that is being performed. Listening experiences in the classroom should help children become acquainted with music—with specific musical compositions and with broad concepts about music in general. For example, an effective way to learn about melodies is to listen to the patterns of pitch in a number of compositions. Likewise, an effective way to learn about rhythm is to listen to the rhythm of many compositions and an effective way to learn about musical form is to listen for the structure. One reason for listening in the elementary classroom is that *it is an effective way to develop knowledge about music.*

We have already pointed out that listening is a part of every musical experience and that listening is a skill that can be developed through practice. Learning to listen more critically will help children become better performers. Learning to listen more discriminately will help your students create more interesting musical compositions. Learning to listen more deeply will enable children to find more enjoyment and meaning as they go to concerts and listen to recorded music throughout their lives.

As was pointed out in our discussion of performing, knowledge and skill are interdependent. The same is true in listening. Greater listening skills will enable you to acquire greater musical knowledge, and greater musical knowledge will help you refine skills in listening to music. The second reason for including listening activities in the elementary classroom is that *such activities will enable students to develop sharper musical listening skills.*

Classroom listening activities can also provide the opportunity for children to acquire general knowledge. The text of songs and the "stories" of some compositions describe people, places, or events, thus providing children with a source of knowledge of the world. Much music, particularly instrumental compositions, is not intended to "describe" or "tell a story." Such *absolute* music, however, can provide an important source of knowledge about relationships. Learning to listen is learning to identify relationships—the ways things may be contrasted, varied, combined, and transformed in an unending number of ways.

Perhaps more importantly, listening to music provides a source of knowledge about human emotions and feelings. Because of its unique ability to capture and express feelings, music provides an excellent source of knowledge about human feeling. Learning to be aware of one's feelings and expanding the range of feelings are important parts of the development of *human* potential. Learning to listen is learning to hear the sound patterns in music and learning to *feel* our response to them. At times these feelings are familiar ones, brought back for reexamination, for a deeper understanding, or for savoring. At other times, the feelings that we experience in response to music may be entirely new, brought to us through the music and able to expand our knowledge of feelings. A third reason for including listening activities in the elementary classroom is that *listening to music provides the opportunity to develop general knowledge—knowledge about the world, knowledge about relationships, and knowledge of human feelings.*

Listening is also a means for developing some essential lifeskills. Our ears give us many cues about our world. As an aural art, music provides a means for developing aural perception. The difference in sound between a clarinet and an oboe, for example, might seem quite subtle, but so is the difference between the song of the robin and the bluebird. To be unaware of the differences in either instance is to miss important aspects of the world and living. We think that learning to listen for subtle differences in music will help one to become more aware of aural differences in environmental sounds, in language, indeed in all aural input.

Learning to listen to music also involves learning to decode and interpret meanings. For example, in program music the meanings are literate, in absolute music the meanings are more abstract, but present nevertheless. In the listening process, one must search for relationships among the sounds heard and identify implied meanings from the relationships. The process is not unlike the interpretation of meanings in verbal and in visual communication. It is assumed that learning to find meanings in music will help you become more proficient in finding meanings in other forms of communication. So, the fourth reason for listening to music in the classroom is that *listening experiences provide the opportunity to develop general skills which are part of general learning.*

COMPETENCIES FOR GUIDING LISTENING

If classroom listening experiences are to make a significant contribution to the development of musical knowledge and skills as well as general knowledge and skills, students must have frequent opportunities to listen to music. As with performing activities, the responsibility for guiding listening is shared between the music specialist and the classroom teacher. While the music specialist may have greater familiarity with the historical development of music, more highly refined skills in aurally analyzing music, and a more precise vocabulary for describing music, we have seen many classroom teachers guiding listening experiences with a high degree of effectiveness. The sincere sharing of delight and excitement found through listening is frequently more effective than a highly technical analysis of a musical composition. We urge all teachers to constantly seek to develop a greater musical understanding and familiarity with a wide variety of musical compositions. Our intent in this chapter, however, is to help you develop competencies in guiding the students in your classroom to greater enjoyment and satisfaction as they listen to music. These competencies are not directly dependent on your own understanding of music.

The process of guiding classroom listening activities is similar to that of guiding performing activities. That is, it consists of identifying goals, assessing student needs, identifying instructional objectives, analyzing musical materials, designing and managing learning environments, and selecting strategies and developing classroom procedures. (The specific competencies in each area, however, are significantly different from those needed for guiding performing activities.) We will discuss each discrete behavior, recognizing that in actual practice the behaviors are highly interrelated and often occur simultaneously during classroom listening activities.

The following are specific competencies for guiding listening activities that we believe are essential for all teachers. The competent teacher can

- Identify musical and general goals that can be achieved through listening to recorded music
- Assess students' musical knowledge and skill through listening experiences
- Identify instructional objectives for listening activities
- Analyze musical material identifying specific aspects to be brought to the attention of students
- Design and manage teaching/learning environments appropriate for listening activities
- Select and carry out specific strategies and procedures for guiding listening activities:

> Discussion
> Drawing to music
> Program music
> Call charts
> Test charts
> Visual guides
> Listening guides
> Following notation

IDENTIFYING GOALS FOR LISTENING ACTIVITIES

We have already indicated that the broad goal for listening, as well as for all other musical activities, is the development of knowledge and skill and that the identification of specific goals must be made in relation to an assessment of student needs. We can, however, identify some general goals for listening activities that can guide you in planning listening experiences for students of all ages. Our list is recognizable, minimal, and limited to goals for the development of musical knowledge and skill. As you make assessments of student needs in both music and in other developmental areas, we urge you to develop more specific goals for listening activities.

Classroom listening activities should provide students opportunities to

1. Experience the joy and satisfaction that comes from listening to music
2. Experience a wide variety of music representative of world history and culture
3. Develop an intimate familiarity with a few selected works of musical art

4. Develop an increasing understanding of melody, rhythm, harmony, dynamics, timbre, and form
5. Develop an increasing awareness of the ideas and feelings expressed through music
6. Develop skill in listening to music
7. Develop skill in describing music

We believe these goals can serve as general guides for listening experiences at all grade levels. The developmental level of students will, of course, influence such elements of any listening experience as the length of the musical selection or excerpt, the depth of students' understanding and awareness, and the degree of students' skill, but the general goals remain the same in kindergarten or sixth grade.

ASSESSING MUSICAL NEEDS THROUGH LISTENING

As you learned in Chapter 1, the main purpose of assessment is collecting information for making decisions about the abilities, interests, and attitudes of individual students and groups of students. It is also the process of comparing student achievement with established criteria to determine the degree to which instructional goals have been reached. You will be able to use assessment to determine how well children can aurally discriminate between musical events. It can also help you decide what they know or don't know about the music they hear. Assessment can be used to find out how well students like a particular listening activity.

Because listening is an internalized process, it presents special assessment problems. It is impossible to observe what a student is hearing, and it is frequently impossible to accurately observe how a student is responding to music. It is, nevertheless, important for you to determine what students hear and how they respond to music if you are to plan a sequence of listening activities that will assure the achievement of goals.

Like the assessment of performing activities, the assessment of listening experiences is an ongoing process. It is essentially a matter of asking these three questions:

1. Were students aware of a particular aspect of the composition before the lesson?
2. Did they become aware of a particular aspect of the music as a result of my teaching?
3. Did they enjoy this listening experience?

Data about what students hear and how they respond to music can be collected in a variety of ways. The verbal comments and the questions students ask about music reveal their knowledge, listening skill, and attitudes.

Specific listening strategies may also provide opportunities for assessment. Moving to music and drawing to music are techniques that may be used to focus students' attention on particular aspects of a composition. The way in which students move or the figures that they draw may also reveal what they are hearing and how they are responding to the composition. Test charts and listening guides calling for written responses are additional strategies that will be discussed later in this chapter. They also provide a means for assessing listening activities. The competent teacher is constantly collecting data about what students hear and how they respond to music and using the data as a means for planning future listening activities.

The checklist that we have provided on page 190 can serve as a basis for collecting and recording data regarding individual or group listening activities.

ASSESSMENT OF LISTENING ACTIVITIES

Student (Class) _____ School _____ Date _____
Observer _____

Did student's description (verbal and nonverbal) of the music reveal awareness of the following?

Melody
_____ direction of melody
_____ stepwise or skipwise movement
_____ smooth or jagged
_____ melodic sequences
_____ other melodic patterns
_____ repetition of melodies

Rhythm
_____ steady beat
_____ metric organization
_____ accents
_____ tempo and tempo changes
_____ specific rhythm patterns

Timbre
_____ names of instruments heard
specify instruments named _____
_____

Harmony
_____ one part or several parts
_____ major, minor, or other
_____ chords or counterpoint
_____ consonance or dissonance

Dynamics
_____ overall loudness level
_____ sudden changes in volume
_____ gradual changes in volume

Form
_____ phrases
_____ cadences
_____ sections
_____ structural patterns AB, ABA, rondo

Did student's reaction (verbal and nonverbal) indicate an awareness of the expressiveness of the composition?
_____ an overall mood
_____ changes in mood
_____ awareness of specific feelings expressed in the music

Did the student enjoy the listening experience?
_____ facial expressions
_____ nonverbal responses
_____ verbal comments
_____ requested to hear composition again

IDENTIFYING OBJECTIVES FOR LISTENING ACTIVITIES

After identifying long-range goals and assessing the needs of the students, you will want to identify specific objectives for listening activities. As was the case with performing activities, objectives for listening should be stated in terms of student behavior and should contain an action verb, a statement of content, and the conditions under which the behavior is to be carried out. The Instructional Objectives Guide on pages 12 and 13 may also help you in writing objectives for listening activities.

Objectives for listening activities are, in some ways, more difficult to state in terms of student behavior than are objectives for performing activities. "Listening" is a behavior, but it is frequently impossible to tell from observation if a student is really listening. For this reason, it is often desirable to specify a performance behavior that will indicate what the student is hearing in the listening process. The following are some examples of objectives stated in this way:

1. Students will demonstrate an awareness of upward melodic movement by drawing lines on the chalkboard.

2. Students will compare the rhythms of the two sections by clapping each while listening to the recording.

3. Students will demonstrate an awareness of the form by arranging colored geometric shapes in the proper sequence after listening to the recording.

4. Students will demonstrate an awareness of the changing tempo by walking to the pulse while listening to the recording.

Objectives of this type may be considered "skill" objectives because the behaviors that they identify require both listening skill and performing skill. At times you may be more concerned with helping students develop knowledge through the listening activity. Knowledge itself cannot be directly observed, so we suggest specifying some overt behavior through which students can demonstrate knowledge. The following are examples of some objectives for the development of knowledge through listening experiences:

1. Students will demonstrate their knowledge of syncopated rhythm by raising their hands when they hear syncopated patterns in the recording.

2. Students will demonstrate knowledge of form by correctly labeling the sections of music after listening to the recording.

3. Students will demonstrate knowledge of jazz by discussing the jazz characteristics of this composition.

4. Students will demonstrate knowledge of melody and texture by discussing the ways in which the two composers used these elements in the two compositions.

5. Selected students will demonstrate knowledge of Aaron Copland by reporting the results of their research on this composer to the class.

6. Students will demonstrate knowledge of composers' styles by correctly identifying the composers of the five compositions analyzed in this unit.

On several occasions in this book, we have discussed the importance of children's finding the joy and satisfaction that comes from positive musical experiences. We strongly believe that positive affective responses should result from most classroom musical experiences. At the same time, we recognize that many teachers become so involved in developing knowledge and skill that this essential part of the musical experience is overlooked and that it is difficult to state objectives for affective responses in terms of student behavior. Nevertheless, we believe that teachers need to constantly remind themselves that it is essential for children to experience the joy of music. We therefore suggest that you develop competence in stating affective objectives and that you frequently make such objectives part of your lesson planning. The following are examples of some affective behaviors for listening experiences:

1. Students will reveal enjoyment of this experience by requesting to hear the recording again.

2. Students will demonstrate satisfaction in drawings made to music by electing to display them on the bulletin board.

3. Students will show excitement for this activity by discussing it with other students during free time.

4. Students will demonstrate enjoyment in listening to this recording by electing to listen to it again in the listening center.

5. Students' facial expressions and physical movements during this activity will demonstrate enjoyment and satisfaction.

While objectives of this kind may not be as easily assessed as those objectives dealing with the development of knowledge or skill, we believe that competent teachers consider them of at least equal importance.

ANALYSIS OF MUSICAL MATERIALS FOR LISTENING

The first step in planning a listening experience for children is to choose the selection to which students will listen. Although there are frequently opportunities for listening to "live" performances of musicians from the community, we will be concerned with listening only to recorded music in this chapter. The procedure for choosing and analyzing music for the listening experience is the same for live performances as for recorded listening selections.

Although there are several excellent collections of records for classroom listening experiences, you need not feel limited to these. Most any musical selection can be appropriate for some classroom listening activity. It is important to remember that children's attention spans are relatively short so musical selections should not be excessively long. It is usually better to play a short excerpt of a composition several times than to play a long selection only once. As in choosing music for performance, the first criterion for choosing listening selections should be whether or not you enjoy listening to the piece. If you can share your enjoyment and excitement about a musical composition with your students, they also will very likely find the experience enjoyable and exciting. The second criterion for choosing a musical selection for listening is what you can help the children gain from the music that they would not get by listening on their own. This means that at times you may assume children will hear the obvious parts of a recording, so you will need to deal with the more subtle aspects. The following are some of the specific questions you should consider in analyzing a musical composition for a listening experience:

1. What musical knowledge can be developed through this composition?
   a) What aspects of melody are illustrated?
   b) What aspects of rhythm are illustrated?
   c) What aspects of timbre are illustrated?
   d) What aspects of harmony are illustrated?
   e) What aspects of dynamics, tempo, or tone color are illustrated?
   f) What aspects of form are illustrated?

2. What musical skills can be developed through this composition?
   a) What singing skills might be developed?
   b) What playing skills might be developed?
   c) What moving skills might be developed?
   d) How might this composition help children develop specific listening skills?
   e) How might an experience with this composition help children develop music reading skills?
   f) How might an experience with this composition help children develop skills of describing music?

3. What general knowledge can be gained through listening to this composition?
   a) What facts about people, places, or events in the world can be gained?
   b) What facts about relationships can be gained?
   c) What facts about feelings can be gained?

4. What general skills can be developed through a listening experience with this composition?
   a) What skills of perceiving can be developed?
   b) What skills of communicating can be developed?
   c) What social skills can be developed?
   d) What physical skills can be developed?
   e) What other skills (specific skills that are important to your students at this particular time) can be developed?

We suggest that you complete a form like the following one to help you identify a particular composition's most important aspects which you can point out to your students through a listening experience. We would not expect you to fill in all of the spaces on the form, but rather you should select those things that appear most important to you as you listen and analyze the music. You may choose only one or two aspects for a particular lesson.

We would hope that you would find many occasions to return to the same composition for future listening lessons so that your students may come to know the music more completely. Although, hopefully, every listening experience will be enjoyable, even the first listening experience can be one through which students gain knowledge and skills. The competent teacher can ensure that this will occur by analyzing the music to determine what knowledge and skills are to be emphasized in each listening experience. The following analyses are an example of some made by a competent teacher.

ANALYSIS OF MUSIC FOR LISTENING

TITLE: "UNSQUARE DANCE," BRUBECK
SOURCE: *LEARNING TO LISTEN TO MUSIC*, RECORD II

MUSICAL KNOWLEDGE THAT CAN BE DEVELOPED
    MELODY
    RHYTHM   *Repeated patterns, $\frac{7}{4}$ meter*
    TIMBRE   *String bass, hand clapping, piano, drums*
    HARMONY   *Layers of sound*
    DYNAMICS
    FORM
MUSICAL SKILLS THAT CAN BE DEVELOPED
    SINGING
    PLAYING   *Hand clapping, playing percussion in $\frac{7}{4}$*
    MOVING
    LISTENING   *To several layers of sound at once*
    CREATING
    READING
    DESCRIBING
GENERAL KNOWLEDGE THAT CAN BE DEVELOPED
    OF THE WORLD
    OF RELATIONSHIPS   *Several events may occur simultaneously.*
    OF FEELINGS
GENERAL SKILLS THAT CAN BE DEVELOPED
    PERCEIVING
    COMMUNICATING
    SOCIAL SKILLS
    PHYSICAL SKILLS   *Clapping, playing instruments for coordination*
    OTHER

ANALYSIS OF MUSIC FOR LISTENING

TITLE: "GREETING PRELUDE," STRAVINSKY
SOURCE: *MASTERING MUSIC, NEW DIMENSIONS IN MUSIC*, P. 102

MUSICAL KNOWLEDGE THAT CAN BE DEVELOPED
    MELODY   *Familiar melody with some tones misplaced*
    RHYTHM
    TIMBRE   *Orchestra*
    HARMONY   *Consonance and dissonance*
    DYNAMICS
    FORM
MUSICAL SKILLS THAT CAN BE DEVELOPED
    SINGING
    PLAYING
    MOVING
    LISTENING   *For changes in a familiar melody*
    CREATING   *A new composition using displacement technique*
    READING
    DESCRIBING
GENERAL KNOWLEDGE THAT CAN BE DEVELOPED
    OF THE WORLD   *Stravinsky, a Russian composer who lived
                         in the United States*
    OF RELATIONSHIPS   *Old ideas can form the basis for new.*
    OF FEELINGS   *Celebration*
GENERAL SKILLS THAT CAN BE DEVELOPED
    PERCEIVING   *Subtle relationships*
    COMMUNICATING
    SOCIAL SKILLS
    PHYSICAL SKILLS
    OTHER

ANALYSIS OF MUSIC FOR LISTENING

TITLE: "DESERT WATER HOLE" FROM *DEATH VALLEY SUITE*, GROFE
SOURCE: *ADVENTURES IN MUSIC*, GRADE 4, VOL. 1

MUSICAL KNOWLEDGE THAT CAN BE DEVELOPED
    MELODY   *Familiar melodies, "Oh Susanna" and "Old Joe"*
    RHYTHM   *Contrasts of slow and fast in duple meter*
    TIMBRE   *Orchestra*
    HARMONY   *Contrasts of major and minor, chords of*
                 chorale, countermelodies of the dance
    DYNAMICS
    FORM
MUSICAL SKILLS THAT CAN BE DEVELOPED
    SINGING   *Familiar melodies*
    PLAYING
    MOVING   *Creating a celebration dance*
    LISTENING
    CREATING
    READING
    DESCRIBING   *Musical events and the story they describe*
GENERAL KNOWLEDGE THAT CAN BE DEVELOPED
    OF THE WORLD   *Gold rush of 1849*
    OF RELATIONSHIPS
    OF FEELINGS   *Changing from despair to excitement*
GENERAL SKILLS THAT CAN BE DEVELOPED
    PERCEIVING
    COMMUNICATING
    SOCIAL SKILLS
    PHYSICAL SKILLS
    OTHER   *Historical research, collecting information about*
             the gold rush

ENVIRONMENTS FOR LISTENING

Creating a suitable environment for listening experiences will be an important part of your task as a teacher. As with environments for performing, there are a number of aspects of listening environments to be considered and a number of different kinds of listening environments that may be appropriate in given situations. You will need competence in working within a number of different environments and in choosing the most suitable environment for a particular listening experience.

The Human Environment

The Autocratic Environment

Listening experiences are frequently more highly structured than experiences in either performing or creating music. Therefore an autocratic environment in which the teacher, through the use of various strategies, points out specific aspects of the music to the students is probably the most common for listening experiences. The following would be some typical teacher behaviors found in an autocratic listening environment:

1. Telling students a "story" about the composer or the particular musical composition
2. Listing the instruments in the order in which they will be heard
3. Instructing students to clap a particular rhythm pattern as they listen
4. Asking questions such as
   a) Does the melody played by the flute move up or down?
   b) Does this composition have duple or triple meter?
   c) What instrument is playing the melody?
   d) Is the form of this composition ABA or AB?
5. Providing work sheets or call charts to guide students' listening

Within an autocratic listening environment, the teacher directs students' attention to specific aspects of the music. The individual student's role is to follow the direction of the teacher. Student response is a means through which the teacher can assess the degree to which the student is hearing the particular part of the music pointed out by the teacher. An autocratic environment can be an effective way to deal with knowledge of some facts and skills. Because it does not provide the opportunity for individual responses from students, however, an autocratic environment is not very effective in developing knowledge about feelings.

The Democratic Environment

There are more opportunities for student response in the democratic environment, where the teacher and students share responsibility for learning. While helping children find things in the music that they would not have found on their own remains the ultimate goal, the democratic teacher does not assume that he or she has already found all of the important aspects of the music. The approach is more one of "Let's listen to this piece together and share what we hear in it." The following would be some typical teacher behaviors found in a democratic listening environment:

1. Asking individual students to research the life of the composer or the circumstances under which a particular composition was written and report their findings to the class

2. Asking questions such as
   a) Is the primary interest of this piece in the melody, rhythm, or harmony? What makes you think so?
   b) What in this music describes (an elephant)?
   c) What does this music tell you about (Japan)? How does the music do that?

3. Asking students to compare two compositions—how are they similar, how are they different?

4. Asking students to compare their personal responses to two compositions—how are they similar, how are they different?

5. Asking students to use movement or visual design to illustrate some aspect of the music

While specific aspects of the music are very important in a democratic listening environment, the aspects considered important are not all predetermined by the teacher. Students will frequently hear and point out a particular aspect that the teacher might have overlooked or considered unimportant. The democratic environment also offers an opportunity for students to consider their own personal reactions to music. A very important aspect of a democratic environment is that all students feel free to offer their ideas and reactions. Great care must therefore be taken so that students do not feel that what they have heard is wrong or that their personal responses to music are inappropriate. A democracy is a place where individuals may disagree with one another but still respect one another's individual worth and right to different opinions.

The Open Environment

Knowledge and skills can also be gained through listening experiences in an open classroom environment. Open environments are usually designed for individuals or small groups of students rather than for an entire class. In such student-centered environments, the teacher provides time, space, and materials for listening and offers guidance to children as they seek answers to their own questions through listening. Listening activities may take place in designated listening centers and at particular times, but in an open environment they will more frequently grow out of more informal experiences in which students happen to hear music and begin talking about it. In contrast to the autocratic environment in which the content of the music is the primary concern, the responses of the students are the most important consideration in an open environment.

The following would be some typical teacher behaviors found in an open listening environment:

1. Placing in a music center several different recordings from which students may choose a listening selection
2. Listening as students engage in the choice process and asking questions to help them develop reasons for their choices:
   a) Why do you want to hear _____ instead of _____?
   b) What about that piece makes it better for you?
   c) How are the _____ (instruments, rhythm, words, melody, etc.) different in _____ compared to _____?
   d) No one mentioned this record. Have any of you heard it?
3. Watching students' physical responses as they listen and asking them to talk about what they heard:
   a) Mary, what part of the music were you showing as you _____ (tapped your toe, moved your hand, drew the line, etc.)?
   b) Gary, something in the music made you smile. Can you tell us what it was?
4. Listening as students discuss what they heard and asking questions to help them analyze the experience more deeply:
   a) What did the composer do to make the music sound _____ (happy, sad, lonely, excited, etc.)?
   b) What about the music did you like?
   c) What in the music made you think of _____ (Japan, elephants, rain, race cars, etc.)?
5. Playing recorded music for informal, nondirective listening during study time, lunch time, and free time

In an open environment, the students generally initiate the listening activity and set the general direction of discussion. The teacher's role is primarily that of helping them focus on specific aspects of the music and their responses to the music.

The Physical Environment

Time

Providing time for listening activities will be an important part of establishing the learning environment. In the preface, we pointed out our belief that life in schools should be as much as possible like life out of schools. In "real life," people set aside special times for listening to music—for going to concerts or listening to recorded music. We believe that special time should also be set aside in the classroom for listening. This time may be part of a "music class" with the listening activity's being related to performing or creating activities, or the listening experience may grow out of other classroom activities. In either case, we believe that some time should be set aside each week when students can listen to music.

Listening experiences are part of many other experiences in "real life." We also believe that listening to music can be a part of many other classroom experiences. The next time you watch your favorite television program, notice the many roles that music fulfills—it introduces the program, sets the mood for many scenes, reinforces the drama, provides a transition between scenes, announces the ending, and may even help to sell products during the commercials. Music can serve similar roles in your classroom. The following is a list of some of the times you could play recorded music:

1. As children enter the room in the morning, after recess, or lunch
2. Between classes—as a signal for children to change groups
3. At the end of a work period—as a signal for children to put materials away and get ready for the next class
4. During rest or snack time
5. At the end of the day as children prepare to go home

The time devoted to listening in either the formal "listening time" or in the more informal, nondirected listening experiences just described should be relatively short. For younger children, the musical selection should not exceed two to three minutes in length. The length of listening selections for upper-grade students should not be over five or six minutes. We can probably all agree that our favorite music is that with which we are familiar. It is quite important that children hear musical selections frequently so that they can become "old friends." (We will discuss this point more fully under the section on materials.) Our point here is that children need *time* to listen to each musical selection. This time may be given in a formal listening "class" or in a more informal way in the classroom. We suggest the following time schedule for weekly listening in the elementary classroom:

Monday   Informal listening (selection A) as children enter the room in the morning
Informal listening (selection B—from last week) at the end of afternoon work time

Tuesday   Informal listening (selection B) as children enter the room in the morning
Directed listening—fifteen-minute follow-up lesson on selection B focusing attention on rhythm and form
Informal listening (selection A) as children prepare to go home

Wednesday Informal listening (selection B) as children enter the room in the morning
Directed listening (selection A)—ten-minute lesson focusing attention on melody and timbre
Informal listening (selection A) during "inside recess" while children play seat games

Thursday Informal listening (selection A) during morning work time
Informal listening (introducing selection C) between reading and math

Friday Informal listening (student's choice) during morning work time
Informal listening (selection A) as children prepare to go home

So far we have discussed time when the entire class can listen to music. You may also provide time for individual listening. You should be aware, however, of the need to plan time for individuals to use the listening centers. This may be "free time," after students have completed other assigned work, or a part of "center time," a designated time period each day when students are to work at one of several classroom centers.

Space

Most any classroom space can be easily adapted for listening. It is important that students be comfortable while listening and that potential distractions be avoided. If movement activities are to be used as a means of guiding listening, ample space must be provided for moving. If guide sheets or drawing-to-music strategies are to be used, students should probably be seated at desks for the listening experience. Listening may take place in large groups, but space should also be provided for listening by individuals and small groups. (A music center within the classroom is ideal for this purpose.) Since listening activities are intended to focus children's attention on fine details of music, it is especially important that other sounds be kept to a minimum. For example, it may be difficult for children to hear a delicate oboe solo if another class is having recess outside the window of the classroom. In planning listening experiences, the competent teacher will plan space that is most appropriate for the particular learning experience.

Materials

Listening experiences probably require more careful planning for materials than any other musical activity. We have been discussing listening to recorded music, so it is essential that a good-quality record player be available. Since sophisticated high-fidelity equipment is found in many homes, it is unreasonable to expect children to find listening to music through inferior equipment to be enjoyable or exciting. Electronic technology has made high-quality equipment available at a reasonable cost. It is your responsibility as a teacher to insist on the availability of such equipment in your classroom.

We have indicated that several excellent record collections are available for classroom listening experiences. In addition to at least one of these, you should have a small collection of your own favorite recordings and recordings that your students find enjoyable. We also point out that phonograph records should be considered expendable items. While they may provide several years of good-quality listening, they do wear out and should be replaced when their sound quality becomes at all questionable.

Many teachers prefer to work with a tape recorder during listening experiences. If your tape recorder has a "counter," you can easily locate specific places in the music which you want to point out to your students. Good-quality cassette tape players are now available; however, inexpensive "portable" players are seldom of sufficient quality for listening to music.

A record player or tape recorder in a classroom listening center can be equipped with headsets so that three to six children can listen at the same time. Tape players are easier for young children to operate, but be certain that both the tape and the player are of high quality.

Establishing an appropriate learning environment in which you have considered human interactions, time, space, and materials is one of your important roles as a teacher. In planning listening activities, we urge you to consider each carefully.

Managing The Environments

The way in which the human and physical elements of the listening environment are managed will be an important factor in the success of the listening experience. The more familiar you are with both the students and the musical materials, the better you will be able to manage listening activities. As with performing activities, careful planning is essential. You must predetermine the behaviors you will expect of your students and clearly communicate those expectations to them. We urge you as a beginning teacher to think through each detail of the listening activity: How will students be seated? How will they get in that grouping? What materials will you have on the chalkboard? Where will the record player be located? How much of the recording will you play? How many times will you play it? We also suggest that you determine precise wording for your listening directions and questions so that they clearly focus the students' attention on precise aspects of the music. As you gain more experience in guiding listening activities, concern for such detail will become "second nature" and this degree of precision in planning may not be necessary.

It is also essential that you model good listening behaviors yourself. Your students will not listen attentively if you are talking, reading, or writing material on the chalkboard while a recording is playing. If you want listening to music to be an enjoyable and exciting experience for your students, you must show them that it is such an experience for you.

MANAGEMENT TECHNIQUES FOR LISTENING ACTIVITIES

1. *Know the music well.*
   a) Be able to make one or two statements about each of the important musical aspects of the composition as well as about the composer, performer, or circumstances under which the music was written.
   b) Identify aspects of the music you want to point out to students.
   c) Know where to locate specific sections of music on the record or tape.
   d) Be familiar enough with the selection that you would recognize it if it were played on the radio.

2. *Establish effective classroom routines.*
   a) Plan procedures for grouping and seating students during listening.
   b) Plan procedures for passing out listening guides, call charts, and other materials.
   c) Keep talking to a minimum; let the music do the communicating. Discussions should take place before and after listening. There should be no talking while the record is playing.
   d) Adjust the volume of the record player to simulate a live performance. If music is too soft, it will become background music; if it is too loud, listening becomes uncomfortable.
   e) Turn the volume down when starting and stopping a record to avoid the "thud" or scratch of the needle being placed on the record.

3. *Provide clear and concise directions.*
   a) Plan a way to introduce music to students. Give only the information that will help them meet the specific objectives of a particular lesson.
   b) In a few carefully worded statements, give students specific aspects for which they are to listen.
   c) Plan wording for questions using both "open" and "closed" questions.
   d) Make frequent use of traditional and graphic notation. Music is frequently difficult to describe with words.

4. *Involve students as active listeners.*
   a) Ask questions that can only be answered through listening.
   b) Frequently focus attention on short excerpts, playing only enough of the recording to illustrate a point or to provide answers to questions.
   c) Provide visual guides or paper-and-pencil work sheets to focus students' attention while listening.
   d) Use physical movement as a means to focus attention on specific aspects of the music.

e) Help students develop an adequate vocabulary for discussing music.

5. *Model good listening behavior.*
   a) Approach listening as a pleasurable experience.
   b) Listen with the students.
   c) Do not talk or ask additional questions while a record is playing.
   d) Do not prepare materials for the next activity while the record is playing.

STRATEGIES FOR GUIDING LISTENING

After determining the needs of the students, establishing specific objectives, and selecting a musical composition for the listening experience, you must then select teaching strategies that will most effectively guide students in hearing and responding to particular aspects of the music that will enable them to meet the objectives. On the following pages, we have described a number of strategies for guiding listening and have provided model lessons demonstrating each strategy. We realize that the distinctions among the strategies are sometimes blurred and that in our model lessons we frequently combine elements from different strategies. Our classification and labeling of the various strategies, however, are intended to point out that there are a number of viable ways for guiding listening experiences in the elementary classroom. As a competent teacher, you must be aware of them and able to use those that are most appropriate for a given listening experience.

Drawing to Music

Drawing to music is a popular teaching strategy but one that must be used with exteme caution if objectives for musical growth are to be met. While music and the visual arts have some common characteristics, they also have some basic differences. For example, music exists in time, while a painting is a moment of time that has forever been frozen. Both do, however, express human feelings. One instance in which the drawing-to-music strategy might be effective would be a lesson in which the objective was concerned with the emotional response evoked by a particular composition. A teacher might, for example, have an upper-grade class listen to *American Salute* by Gould, which consists of a theme and variations on the familiar melody "When Johnny Comes Marching Home." The class could discuss the similarities and differences among the various sections (using discussion strategies), pointing out that each section not only sounds different but also conveys a different *feeling*. It is also important that students discuss the means through which the composer conveyed these different feelings—tempo, rhythmic patterns, instrumentation, melodic variation, and so on. After a second or third listening, students could each select *one* variation and draw or paint a picture that conveys feelings similar to those expressed by the musical variation they selected. The students' art should then also be compared, pointing out the differences and similarities and the means through which differences were obtained—use of different colors, shapes, textures, and forms.

Another instance in which drawing to music may be an effective teaching strategy involves drawing a kind of notation to the music. Using a short (less than one minute) composition or excerpt, students can draw lines that represent melodic and/or rhythmic movement. Such an exercise will help them focus on the up-and-down melodic movement or the long and short durations of the tones. (The visual result will be a rather abstract work of art.) Or, various colors may be used to represent different timbres. Finger painting works well for this kind of exercise if it is pointed out to students that the final visual product is probably not a composite of the entire musical composition since, in fingerpainting, early sections are painted over later.

While drawing to music is an interesting activity for both teacher and students, it is extremely important that the teacher keep the musical objectives of the lesson clearly in mind and be certain that they are met through the experience. This is not to say that general learning objectives cannot also be met through drawing-to-music strategies, but we urge you to include objectives for the development of *musical* knowledge and skill as well.

ANALYSIS OF MUSIC FOR LISTENING

TITLE: "LEAP FROG" FROM *CHILDREN'S GAMES* OP. 22, BIZET
SOURCE: *ADVENTURES IN MUSIC*, GRADE 1, VOL. 1

MUSICAL KNOWLEDGE THAT CAN BE DEVELOPED
    MELODY   *High and low, jagged and smooth*
    RHYTHM   *Fast tempo*
    TIMBRE
    HARMONY
    DYNAMICS   *Contrasts of loud and soft*
    FORM
MUSICAL SKILLS THAT CAN BE DEVELOPED
    SINGING
    PLAYING
    MOVING
    LISTENING   *For melodic direction*
    CREATING
    READING   *Using lines to represent the direction of the melody*
    DESCRIBING   *Verbalizing about timbres, dynamics, and melodic direction*
GENERAL KNOWLEDGE THAT CAN BE DEVELOPED
    OF THE WORLD   *Children in many parts of the world play the same games.*
    OF RELATIONSHIPS   *Opposites—up and down, loud and soft; contrasts and repetition*
    OF FEELINGS   *Happy, carefree, playful feelings may change rapidly.*
GENERAL SKILLS THAT CAN BE DEVELOPED
    PERCEIVING
    COMMUNICATING   *Using symbols to represent events*
    SOCIAL SKILLS
    PHYSICAL SKILLS   *Playing leap frog*
    OTHER

Drawing to Music

"Leap Frog," from *Children's Games* op. 22, Bizet
Adventures in Music, Grade 1, Vol. 1

Middle Grades

Instructional Objectives

1. Students will demonstrate an awareness of the melodic direction through the direction of lines in their drawings.
2. Students will demonstrate an awareness of melodic contour (smooth and jagged) through the shapes in their drawings.
3. Students will demonstrate an awareness of the loudness of the music by the intensity of their drawings.

Environment

Working in a formal environment, students will need large sheets of paper, crayons or colored chalk, and a large, flat surface (a large table or the floor will do). Ten to fifteen minutes will be ample for this activity.

Initial Procedures

1. Begin class by playing leap frog in the gym or out of doors. Have a few students stand aside and watch. Ask them what kinds of movements they see (up and down and forward).
2. Introduce the composition as a musical impression of the game. Listen to the way the music moves up and down just as the players moved up and down.
3. Ask, "Do all frogs look exactly the same when they jump? What might make a difference?" (Size, age, or skill might affect jumping.)
4. Ask, "How did the composer describe the different movements of different frogs?" Have students listen again and find out.
5. Discuss differences in timbre, dynamics, and melodic contour.
6. Have students take crayons and find places at a large sheet of paper. Play the recording again and have students draw lines to show how the music moves up and down. Have students think of ways to show different kinds of movement. (NOTE: Students are to draw lines, not frogs.)
7. Play the recording again as students draw lines representing musical movement.
8. Small groups may share drawings with the class. Be certain to play the recording again as students look at these drawings.

Some discussion might be appropriate regarding why certain lines, colors, and shapes were used.

Extended Procedures

1. On another day, play the recording again having students draw imaginary lines in the air with the music.
2. Using their drawings as notation, students could play their own versions of leap frog on classroom instruments.

Modifications for Exceptional Learners

1. Encourage outstanding students to illustrate rhythmic contrasts of long and short as well as the melodic contour in their drawings.
2. Finger painting may be easier than drawing with crayons for students with delayed motor development.

Evaluation

1. While drawing lines, were students moving with the music?
2. Did the drawings reflect the contrasts in melodic contour, dynamics, and texture heard in the music?
3. How effectively were students able to verbalize about the music and the relationship between what they heard and what they drew?
4. Which students seemed to be aware of many fine details in the music?
5. Which students seemed to have difficulty hearing the melodic contour, dynamics, and texture of the music?

DISCUSSION

Talking about music is probably the most widely used strategy for guiding listening. (It should be noted that almost all of the other strategies suggested in this chapter include some element of discussion.) As a teacher, however, you should be aware that there are many aspects of music that are difficult, if not impossible, to describe with words. This is particularly true when working with children who have limited vocabularies. Also it is impossible to carry on a discussion while listening to music, if you are to hear and respond to the subtleties of sound that make music expressive. Therefore, discussions about music should take place before or after the actual listening experience. Well-conducted discussion can be an effective means for guiding listening experiences if the limitations of this strategy are kept in mind.

Prior to listening, you can make some statements about the music. These should be designed to direct the students' attention to *specific aspects of the music* as they listen. Statements such as the following are often appropriate.

1. I'd like you to notice how the melody in this composition begins very low and moves upward in small steps.
2. The bassoon has an important solo at the beginning of this composition.
3. The rhythm that we just clapped is very important in this piece. See if you can find it and tell me after we listen what instrument was playing it.
4. This composition begins very calmly but builds a feeling of excitement. As you listen, try to find out what the composer did in the music to build this excitement.

Sometimes questions are more appropriate than statements since they will provide the basis for discussion after listening. It is important that you ask only one or two questions so that students can remember them and find the answers. It is also important that the questions be quite specific in nature. As a teacher, you may ask some questions or, particularly in the case of more experienced listeners, the students themselves may formulate questions to be answered through the listening experience. The following are examples of the kind of questions that are appropriate:

1. Is the melody of this composition jagged or smooth?
2. Do you recognize any familiar melodies in this composition?
3. What is the meter of this composition?
4. Does this piece begin in major or minor? Does it end the same way?
5. Do the feelings in this composition get stronger or weaker? What did the composer do in the music to make this happen?

If you are asking several questions about the music, we suggest writing the questions on the chalkboard since students sometimes forget what they are to be finding in a particular listening experience. If the answer to the question is to be found in a particular part of the composition, or if students' attention begins to wander from the listening experience, you can remind them of the question by pointing to the words written on the chalkboard without interrupting the sounds of music with your own voice.

The most important phase of the discussion strategy occurs after listening. Questions asked before listening can be used to initiate discussion. If students are unable to answer or seem unsure of their answers, the portion of the music that will provide the answer should be played again. It is important for you to remember that music cannot always be described. It may be easier for a student to clap a rhythm than to describe it, to sing a melody or show its contour in the air than to verbalize about it. Some students may not know the names of instruments, but they may be able to point to pictures of those they heard. One of your goals should be to help children expand their vocabularies so that they can more adequately discuss music. We suggest that each classroom develop a vocabulary list of words that describe music and of musical terminology. Also, it is important that you use correct terminology in describing music. In most instances, it is no more difficult for children to learn correct names of notes, instruments, and other aspects of music than it is for them to learn "simplified names" that inadequately describe what they hear.

We point out again that we are suggesting *discussion as a means for guiding listening.* At least as much time should be spent listening to music as talking about it. Within a given lesson, students should have the opportunity to listen to a composition or excerpt several times, with short discussion periods between each listening.

ANALYSIS OF MUSIC FOR LISTENING

TITLE: *CHILDREN'S SYMPHONY*, THIRD MOVEMENT, McDONALD
SOURCE: *ADVENTURES IN MUSIC*, GRADE 2, VOL. 1

MUSICAL KNOWLEDGE THAT CAN BE DEVELOPED
    MELODY   *Use of familiar melodies, melodic fragmentation*
    RHYTHM   *Even $\frac{2}{4}$, uneven $\frac{6}{8}$*
    TIMBRE   *Trumpet*
    HARMONY
    DYNAMICS
    FORM   *ABA, introduction, transitions, and coda*
MUSICAL SKILLS THAT CAN BE DEVELOPED
    SINGING   *Familiar melodies*
    PLAYING   *Even and uneven rhythms on classroom percussion*
    MOVING
    LISTENING   *Identifying familiar melodies and trumpet*
    CREATING
    READING
    DESCRIBING   *Discussing how the composer used familiar melodies*
GENERAL KNOWLEDGE THAT CAN BE DEVELOPED
    OF THE WORLD
    OF RELATIONSHIPS   *Making something new out of old materials*
    OF FEELINGS   *Feelings may suddenly grow in intensity.*
GENERAL SKILLS THAT CAN BE DEVELOPED
    PERCEIVING
    COMMUNICATING
    SOCIAL SKILLS
    PHYSICAL SKILLS
    OTHER

Discussion

Children's Symphony, Third Movement, McDonald
Adventures in Music, Grade 2, Vol. 1

Lower Grades

Instructional Objectives

1. After listening to the composition, students will name two melodies they heard.
2. Students will identify the point just before the entrance of "Jingle Bells" as one of building excitement and will name several musical devices used to achieve this effect.
3. Students will compare by clapping the even rhythm of "Jingle Bells" and the uneven rhythm of "Farmer in the Dell."
4. Students will discuss the structure of the composition, emphasizing the return of the original idea following a contrasting section (ABA).

Environment

This activity is designed for use with an entire class. You will lead the discussion in an autocratic atmosphere; the students, however, must feel free to enter into the discussion. Students should hear the recording several times during the lesson, so ten to fifteen minutes should be provided.

Initial Procedures

1. Ask students to listen to the entire recording and try to find melodies they have heard before. When the recording has finished, ask them to tell the class what they heard.
2. Play the recording.
3. Listen to the children's responses. (NOTE: Some may identify the melody "A Hunting We Will Go," which is the same as "The Farmer in the Dell.")
4. Say, "Composers often try to find ways to make music more exciting. Listen again and raise your hands when you feel the music become very exciting."
5. Play the recording through the beginning of "Jingle Bells."
6. Ask, "What did the composer do to help us feel excitement there?" (The music got louder, higher, faster. Replay this section of the recording as necessary to aid the discussion.)
7. Sing the melodies of each song ("The Farmer in the Dell" and "Jingle Bells") and clap the rhythms.

Compare the feeling of a horse trotting through snow and the smooth movements of the sleigh with a horse galloping over the hot, dry ground in the summer.

8. Using the wood block and rhythm sticks, play even rhythms

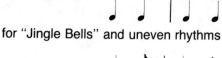

for "Jingle Bells" and uneven rhythms

for "The Farmer in the Dell."

9. Listen to the recording again having students play rhythm patterns on instruments when they hear each melody. (Students without instruments can clap patterns.)

10. Ask, "What melody did we hear first? What came next? Was that the end?"

11. Listen to the composition again.

Extended Procedures

1. Discuss the "hunting call" that introduces the farmer. Ask, "What instrument plays it? Is it the same every time?"

2. Discuss the second version of "Jingle Bells." Ask, "How did the composer make this version more interesting?" Different instruments play parts of the melody.

3. Have students move to the music, showing the even and uneven rhythm of the two sections.

Modifications for Exceptional Learners

1. When working with slow learners, sing both songs and play rhythm patterns on instruments *before* listening.

2. If students have short attention spans, it may be necessary to spread these activities over several lessons.

Evaluation

1. Did the majority of students recognize the two melodies?

2. Did students recognize the building excitement before the entrance of "Jingle Bells"?

3. What difficulties did students have in describing the musical means employed for building excitement?

4. Which students were able to clap the even and uneven rhythm patterns?

5. What difficulties were experienced in discussing the structure of the composition?

ANALYSIS OF MUSIC FOR LISTENING

TITLE: *VARIATIONS ON AMERICA*, IVES (SCHUMANN ORCHESTRATION)
SOURCE: LONDON RECORD # CSA 224S (LOS ANGELES PHILHARMONIC)

MUSICAL KNOWLEDGE THAT CAN BE DEVELOPED
    MELODY   *Variations on a familiar melody*
    RHYTHM   *A melody may have many different rhythmic accompaniments.*
    TIMBRE   *Contrasting timbres of an orchestra*
    HARMONY   *Major-minor, consonance-dissonance*
    DYNAMICS   *Many contrasts*
    FORM   *Theme and variations*
MUSICAL SKILLS THAT CAN BE DEVELOPED
    SINGING
    PLAYING
    MOVING
    LISTENING   *Identifying similarities and differences, the means through which the composer varied the melody*
    CREATING
    READING
    DESCRIBING   *Discussing the changes that were found in the familiar melody*
GENERAL KNOWLEDGE THAT CAN BE DEVELOPED
    OF THE WORLD   *Charles Ives was an American composer. America is a "melting pot" of world cultures.*
    OF RELATIONSHIPS   *One part may remain constant while other parts change.*
    OF FEELINGS   *Several feelings may be experienced at once.*
GENERAL SKILLS THAT CAN BE DEVELOPED
    PERCEIVING   *Relationships and changes made throughout this composition*
    COMMUNICATING   *Verbalizing a description of the music*
    SOCIAL SKILLS
    PHYSICAL SKILLS
    OTHER

TABLE 2   *Variations on America*—Description of the Music

Variation I	Full Orchestra; fanfarelike
Theme	Smooth; brass playing melody; pizzicato string accompaniment; triangle at end of phrase
Variation II	Melody played slowly by strings; woodwinds with fast-moving, scalewise accompaniment
Variation III	Minor; some melodic and rhythmic changes
Variation IV	Dissonant chords; loud; unfinished
Variation V	Lively, jogging rhythm ($\frac{6}{8}$)
Variation VI	Spanish rhythms; trombone melody; fast tempo
Variation VII	Slow; minor
Variation VIII	Fast tempo; countermelody by trumpet; tempo slows for last time, some melodic changes
Coda	Fanfares, like the beginning; excitement in the strings; low brass countermelody

Discussion

Variations on America, Ives (Schumann Orchestration)
London Record # CSA 224S (Los Angeles Philharmonic)

Middle Grades

Instructional Objectives

The students will discuss ways in which melodies, rhythms, harmonies, and timbres have been changed in the variations of this composition.

Environment

Students should be comfortably seated with paper and pencil for note taking. You will lead the discussion; however, most discussing should be done by students rather than by you.

Procedures

1. Show students two photographs of a similar scene (the seashore, a city street, workers in factories, etc.)
2. Ask the class to identify things in the two photographs that are similar. (The discussion should include both *things* in the photograph—water, sky, cars, birds—and the *visual elements* that comprise the photograph—circular shapes, the color blue, straight lines, curved lines.)
3. Ask students to identify things that are different.
4. Point out that music may also have similarities and differences. Have the class listen and identify them in this composition.
5. Play the recording—Variation I and Theme.
6. Discuss the similarities—same melody, both played by the orchestra.
7. Discuss the differences—Variation I is excited, interrupted; theme is smooth, continuous with phrases well marked by the triangle, and so on.
8. Mention the fact that Charles Ives was an American composer who liked to work with American ideas. In this composition, he used theme and variations to express important ideas about America.
9. Ask students to listen to the entire composition and list similarities and differences in each variation.
10. Play the entire recording.
11. Using notes taken during listening as a guide, discuss similarities and differences between variations. Return to the recording to verify anything mentioned that is in question.

12. Ask, "What important things does this say about America?" (Develop the concept of the melting pot.)

Extended Activity

1. Place a recording of this composition in the learning center with a set of cards labeled "Variations I, II, III, IV, V, VI, VII, Theme," and "Coda." As small groups of students listen to the recording again, have them sort the cards into a pile of those sections with the greatest variation in melody, another pile with greatest variation in rhythm, another in harmony, and a fourth in timbre.

Modifications for Exceptional Learners

1. Students with experience in playing band, orchestral, or keyboard instruments may be able to create their own variations on a familiar melody using some of the techniques demonstrated in this composition.

2. This recording may be too long for students with short attention spans. Select one or two variations and compare them in the first lesson. Longer attention spans can be developed by extending the length of listening during several successive lessons.

Evaluation

1. Which musical component (melody, rhythm, harmony, timbre) was most difficult for students to identify?

2. Which musical component was the most difficult for them to verbalize?

3. Which variation did they seem to enjoy most?

MOVING TO MUSIC

Moving to music is a particularly useful strategy for guiding listening because it provides opportunities for students' physical involvement in the listening process. As students move to music, they are translating what they hear and what they feel into observable behaviors making moving to music an excellent means for assessment. Short musical selections (one or two minutes in length) with distinct rhythmic and melodic patterns are generally best for movement activities. It is usually necessary for students to listen to the selection at least once before attempting movement. Statements and questions such as the following may be used to guide initial listening:

1. I'd like you to listen to this recording, noticing especially the way the melody moves up and down.

2. Listen to this recording, noticing the steady beat. Does it continue throughout the composition?

3. There is a rhythm pattern that is repeated over and over in this composition. As you listen this time, try to find it and think of ways you might move to show that pattern.

4. As you listen to this composition, notice that there are some high instruments and some low instruments. Do they play at the same time?

These statements and questions are not intended to initiate discussion but rather to direct listening. After the initial listening, you should provide adequate space for students to move; then rephrase the statements:

1. Now show me the way the melody moves up and down by moving your hands as it moves.

2. Show me the steady beat by walking to it. If the steady beat stops, show me by stopping.

3. Show me the rhythm pattern you heard by moving your head and shoulders.

4. This half of the room will show me where high instruments play by moving to the rhythms of their part. The other half will show me where low instruments play by moving to the low part. If both high and low instruments play together, I will see everybody moving.

Students may need to be reminded to listen carefully as they move and to let the music "tell them how to move." Experiences in moving to music may need to be repeated several times until students learn to adjust body movements to movement in the music. Moving to music in itself is a skill that must be learned. Students lacking previous experience in movement may have many inhibitions about moving that must be overcome. Moving to music, however, can be an effective way to guide students to a new awareness of specific aspects of a musical composition.

ANALYSIS OF MUSIC FOR LISTENING

TITLE: "BIG BLACK TRAIN," NIEHAUS
SOURCE: *THE SMALL DANCER*, BOWMAR RECORD # 391

MUSICAL KNOWLEDGE THAT CAN BE DEVELOPED
    MELODY
    RHYTHM   *Getting faster*
    TIMBRE
    HARMONY
    DYNAMICS
    FORM
MUSICAL SKILLS THAT CAN BE DEVELOPED
    SINGING
    PLAYING   *Sand blocks to steady beat*
    MOVING   *To increasing tempo*
    LISTENING
    CREATING
    READING
    DESCRIBING   *Changing tempo*
GENERAL KNOWLEDGE THAT CAN BE DEVELOPED
    OF THE WORLD   *Travel by steam locomotor*
    OF RELATIONSHIPS   *Things can change gradually.*
    OF FEELINGS
GENERAL SKILLS THAT CAN BE DEVELOPED
    PERCEIVING
    COMMUNICATING
    SOCIAL SKILLS   *Working in a group*
    PHYSICAL SKILLS   *Large-muscle development*
    OTHER

Moving to Music

"Big Black Train"
The Small Dancer, Bowmar Record # 391

Lower Grades

Instructional Objectives

1. Students will demonstrate an awareness of the increasing tempo of the music by clapping and playing sand blocks.
2. Students will demonstrate an awareness of the increasing tempo of the music by moving to the music.

Environment

This activity is designed for an autocratic environment. At the beginning, students should be informally seated near the record player with several pair of sand blocks available. For the second part of the activity, large, open space will be needed; however, students could move in wide aisles between chairs and desks. Five to ten minutes will be needed for this activity.

Initial Procedures

1. Introduce the music with a short discussion about trains. Ask, "How do they move when they are leaving a station? How do they move when they are traveling through the country?"
2. Play the recording having students play sand blocks and/or slide the palms of their hands together on the steady beat.
3. Say, "Show me how the train moves by moving the way it does." Have students form a single line, hands on the waist of the person in front, and then move by sliding their feet on the floor to the steady beat of the music.

Extended Procedures

1. Repeat the experience on another day with several smaller "trains" formed by six to eight students.
2. Have students create their own train music using classroom percussion instruments. Choose a conductor to lead the group in a composition which describes a train starting out, traveling through the country, and coming to a station.

Modifications for Exceptional Learners

Physically handicapped students may be able to move their hands on a desk or table rather than physically move around the room.

ANALYSIS OF MUSIC FOR LISTENING

TITLE: "BERCUSE," FROM *THE FIREBIRD SUITE*, STRAVINSKY
SOURCE: *ADVENTURES IN MUSIC*, GRADE 1, VOL. 1

MUSICAL KNOWLEDGE THAT CAN BE DEVELOPED
  MELODY   *Mostly stepwise, small range*
  RHYTHM   *Duple meter (in four)*
  TIMBRE   *Bassoon and harp within full orchestra*
  HARMONY   *Melody with ostinato accompaniment*
  DYNAMICS
  FORM   *ABA*
MUSICAL SKILLS THAT CAN BE DEVELOPED
  SINGING
  PLAYING
  MOVING   *To rhythm of the melody and the steady beat*
  LISTENING   *For melody and form*
  CREATING
  READING
  DESCRIBING   *Several musical events happening at the same time*
GENERAL KNOWLEDGE THAT CAN BE DEVELOPED
  OF THE WORLD   *Rituals of ancient tribes*
  OF RELATIONSHIPS   *Contrast and repetition, simultaneous events*
  OF FEELINGS   *Suspense, anticipation, building of tension*
GENERAL SKILLS THAT CAN BE DEVELOPED
  PERCEIVING   *Relationships and feelings*
  COMMUNICATING   *Nonverbal communication*
  SOCIAL SKILLS   *Working in a group*
  PHYSICAL SKILLS   *Large-muscle development*
  OTHER

Moving to Music

"Bercuse," from *The Firebird Suite*, Stravinsky
Adventures in Music, Grade 1, Vol. 1

Middle Grades

Instructional Objectives

1. Students will demonstrate an awareness of melodic contours through movement.
2. Students will demonstrate an awareness of the ABA form by designing movements that reflect this pattern of contrast and repetition.
3. Students will demonstrate an awareness of the feeling level contained in the music through their movements and through discussion.

Environment

A student-centered environment will be most effective for this activity. A large screen, preferably an entire light-colored wall and six to eight flashlights with colored cellophane over the lens will be needed. The room should be partially darkened.

Initial Procedures

1. Talk briefly of ritual dances, mentioning that dancers listen to music and move the way the music moves.
2. Ask the class what parts of the music may tell a dancer how to move. Point out the following:
   a) Rhythm establishes tempo and movement patterns.
   b) Melody suggests movement levels—high, low.
   c) Harmony (texture) suggests how many dancers move at once.
   d) Dynamics suggest the force of the movement.
   e) Form suggests an overall pattern—the end is like the beginning.
3. Ask students to listen to the recording for clues as to how dancers might move.
4. Give students flashlights with colored cellophane, and ask them to create a "dance of lights" as the music is played again.
5. Play the recording as students move lights on screen or wall.
6. Discuss the relationships between the light dance and the music. Ask, "Did the lights show melodic movement? How might the movement be changed? Did the lights show rhythmic patterns? Could rhythmic movement be improved? Did the lights show the texture and form?"

7. Repeat the light dance with the recording, making the refinements suggested in the discussion.

8. Repeat the discussion and light dance if time permits, perhaps with different students moving the lights.

9. Ask students to identify the places in the music where they felt the greatest tension. Ask, "How did the music create this feeling?" (Replay these sections in the discussion.)

10. Ask students to listen to the music again, without the dance of lights, becoming more aware of the feelings of tension and relaxation they experience in the music.

Extended Procedures

1. Provide the opportunity for students to listen and practice their dance of lights with this composition, perhaps performing it for parents or another class.

2. When students become comfortable with moving the flashlights, they may be ready to move their entire bodies to the music. Using overhead projectors with colored cellophane as light sources, dancers can move between the projectors and screen, making a dance of shadows.

Modifications for Exceptional Learners

1. Gifted students could conduct research on tribal rituals and create one of their own. Have them begin by writing a story about an event; then have them design masks and/or costumes and create music and a dance for the ritual.

2. Mentally handicapped students may have difficulty focusing attention on several aspects of the music at once. Deal only with rhythm in the first lesson, repeating the experience on other days in order to deal with melodic and dynamic contrasts.

Evaluation

1. To what degree did students' movements reflect an awareness of melodic and rhythmic movement of the music? What difficulties did individual students seem to have?

2. To what degree did the movement patterns reflect the ABA structure of the music?

3. To what degree did the final discussion reveal an awareness of feelings communicated through the music?

PROGRAM MUSIC

Program music is that which tells a story. In program music, the composer uses particular sounds or patterns to represent characters or events in the story. The most widely known programmatic composition for children is probably *Peter and the Wolf* by Prokofiev. This, like some other programmatic works, usually employs a narrator who tells the story as the music unfolds. Other programmatic music, such as *The Carnival of the Animals* or *The Grand Canyon Suite*, does not have a narrator, but instead the story is suggested by the titles of the composition and by program notes written by the composer.

A program, or story, can be used as a means to guide students' attention to specific aspects in the music as they listen, for example, for the sound of the horns to signal the arrival of the hunters or for the roll of tympani representing the sound of thunder. In such instances, we suggest that you summarize the story before the children listen and follow the listening experience with a discussion of specific events, relistening to excerpts to find details in both the story and the music.

Another approach to program music is to withhold the title and story, asking students what they think the music might be describing. In this instance, you must be prepared to accept whatever story a child might invent, even if it is quite different from that suggested by the composer, so long as the child can provide musical reasons for his or her version of the story. You must be certain that a child does not feel that his or her story is "wrong" simply because it differs from that of the composer.

The most important phase of listening to program music comes in the discussion which follows each listening. Your role as a teacher is to guide students to discuss the *musical events* as well as the events in the story. Some questions of the following type are generally useful:

1. How did the composer set the scene for this story?
2. What in the music told you that it was night?
3. What sounds told you that the animal was (big, little, fast, slow, etc.)?
4. What in the music told you that _____ had happened?
5. Was there anything in the music that told you how Peter felt when _____?
6. What musical devices did the composer use to build the feeling of tension?

Songs with texts may also be considered as program music since a message is usually contained in the words. Procedures similar to those described above can be used to guide the listening to vocal music, particularly those of current folk groups. It is again stressed that *at least equal emphasis should be placed on the music itself* as on the "story" contained in the words.

A final caution must be given. Not all music is intended to tell a story. A majority of our music is meant to be abstract, conveying sounds and feelings rather than ideas that can be verbalized. It is generally *inappropriate* for teachers or students to attempt to make up stories for such music.

ANALYSIS OF MUSIC FOR LISTENING

TITLE: "THE ELEPHANT," FROM *CARNIVAL OF THE ANIMALS*, SAINT-SAENS
SOURCE: *ADVENTURES IN MUSIC*, GRADE 1, VOL. 2

MUSICAL KNOWLEDGE THAT CAN BE DEVELOPED
    MELODY
    RHYTHM   *Triple meter*
    TIMBRE   *String bass*
    HARMONY
    DYNAMICS
    FORM   *AB*
MUSICAL SKILLS THAT CAN BE DEVELOPED
    SINGING
    PLAYING
    MOVING   *To the steady beat, showing the heaviness of the music*
    LISTENING   *For characteristics of the music that describe an elephant*
    CREATING
    READING
    DESCRIBING   *The two sections verbally and through movement*
GENERAL KNOWLEDGE THAT CAN BE DEVELOPED
    OF THE WORLD   *Elephants*
    OF RELATIONSHIPS   *Large is often equated with heavy and slow.*
    OF FEELINGS
GENERAL SKILLS THAT CAN BE DEVELOPED
    PERCEIVING
    COMMUNICATING
    SOCIAL SKILLS
    PHYSICAL SKILLS   *Large-muscle movement*
    OTHER

Program Music

"The Elephant," from *Carnival of the Animals*, Saint-Saens
Adventures in Music, Grade 1, Vol. 2.

Lower Grades

Instructional Objectives

1. Students will identify characteristics of the animal described by this music as being large, heavy, and somewhat clumsy.
2. Students will identify the low sounds and slow tempo as musical means used in this composition to describe the animal.

Environment

An informal, teacher-centered environment should be used. Space for moving would be desirable. A photograph of a string bass would also be helpful.

Initial Procedures

1. Ask students to name some large animals, some small animals, and some in-between animals. Ask, "What animals would be very heavy? What animals would be very light? What animals would be clumsy (have a hard time dancing)? What animals might be able to dance very well?"
2. The composer Saint-Saens used music to describe an animal. Say, "Listen to this music. What kind of animal do you think it is?"
3. Play the recording.
4. Ask, "Do you think it was a big or a little animal? What in the music told you so? (NOTE: Discourage attempts at this point to name an animal. The point of the discussion is to focus attention on the low-ness and slowness of the music.) When necessary, return to the recording to verify what students thought they heard.
5. Ask, "Do you think the animal was heavy or light? What in the music told you?"
6. Ask, "Do you think the animal was graceful or clumsy? (Do you think the animal could dance?) What in the music told you?"
7. Ask, "What animal did the music describe for you?" (NOTE: It is extremely important that both the teacher and students recognize that there is not one "right" answer. Music does not have exact meaning. Saint-Saens was thinking of an elephant, but the music could also be describing a hippopotamus, grizzly bear, or water buffalo.)

8. Say, "Let's listen again. Perhaps you can think of another animal the music may be describing."

Extended Procedures

1. On another day, students may move to the music as a large, heavy animal. Point out that movements in the second section should be more graceful than those in the first section.
2. Using photographs and recordings, compare a violin and a string bass. Ask, "Why did Saint-Saens use the bass in this composition?"
3. Listen to another selection from *Carnival of the Animals* and discuss it in a similar way.

Modifications for Exceptional Learners

1. For children with poorly developed verbal skills, begin by having them move to the music and then discuss the characteristics of the music that suggested particular ways of moving.

Evaluation

1. Which children had difficulty identifying the lowness and slowness of the music?
2. Which children had difficulty verbalizing about the music?
3. Which children had difficulty making associations between the music and animals?
4. Which children had difficulty attending to a musical selection of this length?

ANALYSIS OF MUSIC FOR LISTENING

TITLE: *DANCE MACABRE*, SAINT-SAENS
SOURCE: BOWMAR ORCHESTRAL LIBRARY #59

MUSICAL KNOWLEDGE THAT CAN BE DEVELOPED
    MELODY
    RHYTHM
    TIMBRE   *String instruments, particularly violin and cello; pizzicato; oboe*
    HARMONY   *Minor mode*
    DYNAMICS
    FORM   *Introduction, coda, fugue; program music—music that tells a story*
MUSICAL SKILLS THAT CAN BE DEVELOPED
    SINGING
    PLAYING
    MOVING
    LISTENING   *Identifying events and feelings expressed through music*
    CREATING
    READING
    DESCRIBING   *Musical devices used to depict events and feelings*
GENERAL KNOWLEDGE THAT CAN BE DEVELOPED
    OF THE WORLD   *Halloween and ghost stories*
    OF RELATIONSHIPS   *Events occur in a logical order and usually involve repetition and contrast.*
    OF FEELINGS   *Expectation, suspense, loneliness, excitement, celebration*
GENERAL SKILLS THAT CAN BE DEVELOPED
    PERCEIVING   *Subtle distinctions in sound*
    COMMUNICATING   *Recognizing symbols for events, story telling*
    SOCIAL SKILLS
    PHYSICAL SKILLS
    OTHER

Program Music

Dance Macabre, Saint-Saens
Bowmar Orchestral Library #59

Upper Grades

Instructional Objectives

1. Given the story and the opportunity to listen to the recording, the students will identify the musical aspects which represent
   a) Spirits coming out of graves
   b) The call to dance
   c) The dance
   d) The wind
   e) The approach of morning
2. Students will reflect on feelings aroused through the music and will discuss the musical means utilized to symbolize those feelings.
3. Students will identify the sounds of
   a) Violin
   b) Cello
   c) Xylophone
   d) Oboe
4. Students will identify the fugue, which is utilized in this composition.

Environment

The length of this composition requires that students be comfortably seated in an area relatively free from distractions. Lowering the lighting level may enhance the overall mood of the listening experience. A teacher-centered environment will be utilized; however, students should feel free to contribute during the discussion period. The following should be listed on the board:

   a) Spirits coming out of graves
   b) The call to dance
   c) The approach of morning

Procedures

1. Tell the story to the class.
2. Briefly discuss how different people may view an event in a slightly different way and may tell a different version of a story. A story told in music will not be exactly the same as a story told with words.
3. Referring to the list on the chalkboard, request that students find the way in which the composer told of these events.

4. Play the recording in its entirety.

5. Through discussion identify the way in which the music depicted the events listed on the board.
   a) Spirits coming out—soft, short, low sounds (pizzicato strings).
   b) Call to dance—violin playing open strings as in tuning.
   c) The approach of morning—oboe depicting rooster. (NOTE: Upper-grade students should be well acquainted with the string instruments, but a picture of an oboe may be helpful.)

6. Say, "In a drama the stage, set, and costumes establish the location and set the mood for the story. How did Saint-Saens establish location and set the mood for this story?
   a) Play the recording again through the "fiddle-tuning" call to dance.
   b) Discuss the "clock striking midnight," the suspense-building pizzicato patterns of spirits coming out of graves. Some students may also recall the minor tonality of the dance theme.

7. Ask students how the composer depicted many ghosts dancing. Return to the recording (about one-half inch from the beginning of the band, just after the rattling of the skeleton bones) and listen to the fugue. Through discussion point out that the cello entered first with the dance theme, followed by the violas, the high woodwinds, then the trumpets. More instruments were added to show that more ghosts were dancing.

8. Play the entire recording again, asking students to focus on their own feelings as they respond to the music. Notice how their feelings change throughout the recording.

Extended Procedures

1. Although this composition is rather long, students should have many opportunities to listen to it in its entirety.

2. Find notated themes and have students play them on piano, band instruments, or melody bells.

3. Have students create their own story and compose music to describe characters and events.

Modifications for Exceptional Learners

1. Gifted students with experience in dancing and drama may enjoy creating a dance for this composition that will further express the ideas and feelings of the story.

2. A series of pictures to illustrate events in the story may help hold students' attention and enable them to recall the events during the discussions.

Evaluation

1. Were students able to identify differences in the sounds of violin and cello?
2. Were students able to describe the musical means employed to depict events in the story? What vocabulary difficulties were encountered?
3. Were students able to identify changes in feelings communicated through the music? Were they able to identify the musical devices used to bring about the changes?

CALL CHARTS

Call charts are an especially effective means for guiding listening as they enable you to point out specific events as they occur in a composition. A *call chart* is a list of statements about specific musical events, arranged in the exact sequence of the music. Each statement is numbered, and as the event occurs you "call" out the number, directing students to read the statement and become aware of that particular aspect of the music they are hearing. Because of their verbal characteristics, call charts are most effective with students having well-developed language skills. Call charts using visual designs and notation can also be constructed. Although call charts are beginning to appear in elementary music textbooks, it will frequently be necessary for you to construct your own. This requires careful listening and analysis of the music. We have found that some students in upper grades enjoy constructing call charts for their own favorite records and sharing them with their classmates.

Prior to listening with a call chart, it is generally desirable to review terminology that has been used to describe the music. We remind you that it is important to demonstrate music as well as talk about it. For example, rather than merely describing *triple meter* as three beats to a measure, have students clap triple meter so that they directly experience the feel of 1 2 3 1 2 3 1 2 3. If you have included the notation of rhythmic patterns or melodic fragments as part of the call chart, students should clap those rhythms or hear the melodies before listening.

After listening to a composition and following a call chart, discussion strategies can be used to review important aspects of the composition. We also suggest replaying excerpts of the composition as they are discussed. Following a brief discussion, we suggest replaying the entire composition so that students can reexperience the music and their reactions at the deeper level that comes from increased understanding.

CALL CHART

"Pizzicato Polka"
Ballet Suite No. 1
Shostakovich

Adventures in Music, Grade 1, Volume 1

Time (seconds)	**Call Number**
0:00	1. Introduction, pizzicato strings, up and down
0:09	2. Pizzicato strings playing melody Medium loud
0:24	3. Tempo getting faster Strings and woodwinds imitating one another Getting louder
0:40	4. Very fast tempo Woodwinds playing melody with very short sounds Softer
0:50	5. Brass playing melody with very short sounds Louder sounds, thicker Getting slow at the end
1:05	6. Pizzicato strings playing melody Same as heard at Call 2 Slower at the end.

ANALYSIS OF MUSIC FOR LISTENING

TITLE: "PIZZICATO POLKA," FROM *BALLET SUITE #1,* SHOSTAKOVICH
SOURCE: *ADVENTURES IN MUSIC*, GRADE 1, VOL. 1

MUSICAL KNOWLEDGE THAT CAN BE DEVELOPED
    MELODY   *Melodic imitation*
    RHYTHM   *Gradual changes of tempo, use of short sounds (pizzicato)*
    TIMBRE   *String instruments playing pizzicato*
    HARMONY
    DYNAMICS
    FORM   *Imitation and repeated sections*
MUSICAL SKILLS THAT CAN BE DEVELOPED
    SINGING
    PLAYING
    MOVING
    LISTENING   *With a call chart to identify specific musical events*
    CREATING
    READING
    DESCRIBING   *Timbres and tempo changes*
GENERAL KNOWLEDGE THAT CAN BE DEVELOPED
    OF THE WORLD   *The polka is a popular dance in many parts of the world.*
        Shostakovich—a twentieth century Russian composer
    OF RELATIONSHIPS   *Gradual changes*
        Imitation
    OF FEELINGS   *Happy, carefree*
GENERAL SKILLS THAT CAN BE DEVELOPED
    PERCEIVING
    COMMUNICATING   *Reading from a call chart*
    SOCIAL SKILLS
    PHYSICAL SKILLS
    OTHER

Call Chart

"Pizzicato Polka," from *Ballet Suite No. 1*, Shostakovich
Adventures in Music, Grade 1, Vol. 1

Middle Grades

Instructional Objectives

1. Students and teacher will discuss the meaning of *pizzicato*.
2. Students will name instruments of the string family.
3. While listening to the recording, students will follow a call chart which points out contrasts of timbre and tempo.

Environment

A teacher-centered environment, preferably with students at desks, should be used. Each student may have a copy of the call chart, or it may be projected from a transparency. Photographs of string instruments would be desirable. Five to ten minutes should be adequate for this activity.

Initial Procedures

1. Introduce the term *pizzicato* and have students look up the dictionary definition—"playing a string instrument by plucking."
2. Have students identify string instruments, and ask how they are usually played.
3. Ask, "Would plucking make longer or shorter sounds than playing with a bow?"
4. Ask, "Could other instruments—woodwinds or brass—play pizzicato?"
5. Ask, "How could flute or trumpet performers imitate pizzicato sounds on their instruments?" (Students may need to listen to find this answer.)
6. Distribute copies of the call chart and then invite students to listen, while you call numbers at appropriate times.
7. Discuss the following questions:
   a) How did woodwind and brass imitate the pizzicato sound?
   b) Did the instruments imitate one another in any other way?
   c) Would this music be easy to dance to? (No, the tempo changes frequently.)
   Return to the recording as often as necessary to find the answers to these questions.

Extended Procedures

1. Listen on other days with the call chart. Can students add other things to the description of the various sections?
2. Have students clap or move their entire bodies to the pulse of the music, being certain to move faster and slower as the music does.
3. Make a string instrument from rubber bands and create your own "Pizzicato Polka."

Modifications for Exceptional Learners

1. Some students in the class may play string instruments. Invite them to demonstrate pizzicato playing.
2. Construct a call chart with drawings of the various instruments for students who have not developed reading skills.
3. Contrasts in tempo could be directly experienced through movement. Realize, however, that tempos may be extremely fast for students with poor motor development.

Evaluation

1. To what degree were students able to use the vocabulary from the call chart in their own verbal description of the music?
2. Which students were unable to recall instruments in the string family?
3. Which students were not following the call chart as the recording played? Was it a problem of attention, or might they have been unable to read the words on the chart?

CALL CHART

"Saturday in the Park," Chicago, *Chicago Album #10*
Columbia # PC 3110

Time	Call Number
0:00	1. Piano chords repeated:

Time	Call Number
0:15	2. Trumpet going down in half steps
0:24	3. Trumpet continues, voices enter, section repeats
0:40	4. New melody, softer
0:53	5. Voices continue, trumpets enter on long tones as accompaniment
1:00	6. Smoother melody, trumpets enter at end playing skipwise pattern
1:10	7. Instrumental interlude, mostly brass Trumpet and cymbal playing off the beat
1:20	8. Second verse—melody like 3 except there is vocal background on second phrase
1:35	9. Like section 4—solo voice with vocal group in harmony at end of phrase
1:45	10. Voices continue, trumpet accompaniment in long tones like 3
1:55	11. Smoother melody again—like 6
2:00	12. New idea—new melody, more driving rhythm, uneven rhythm
2:30	13. Material from the introduction returns
2:40	14. Descending half tone in trumpet, like 2
2:50	15. Third verse, musically like 3—sax on descending half tones
3:00	16. Solo voice, ensemble on end of phrases
3:10	17. Vocal with trumpet accompaniment, long tones
3:20	18. Smoother melody like that heard at 6
3:35	19. Instrumental coda with voices humming

ANALYSIS OF MUSIC FOR LISTENING

TITLE: "SATURDAY IN THE PARK," CHICAGO
SOURCE: *CHICAGO ALBUM #10*, COLUMBIA # PC 3110

MUSICAL KNOWLEDGE THAT CAN BE DEVELOPED
    MELODY   *Descending in half steps*
    RHYTHM   *Strong, steady beat; repeated pattern—*

    TIMBRE   *Voices, trumpet*
    HARMONY
    DYNAMICS
    FORM   *Repetition and contrast of sections*
MUSICAL SKILLS THAT CAN BE DEVELOPED
    SINGING
    PLAYING   *Rhythm pattern on classroom percussion*
    MOVING
    LISTENING   *For musical content of a "popular" composition*
    CREATING
    READING
    DESCRIBING   *Musical events that express feelings*
GENERAL KNOWLEDGE THAT CAN BE DEVELOPED
    OF THE WORLD   *Life in a city*
    OF RELATIONSHIPS   *Repetition as part of contemporary life*
    OF FEELINGS   *Loneliness, insignificance*
GENERAL SKILLS THAT CAN BE DEVELOPED
    PERCEIVING
    COMMUNICATING   *Reading from a call chart*
    SOCIAL SKILLS
    PHYSICAL SKILLS
    OTHER

Call Chart

"Saturday in the Park," Chicago
Chicago Album #10, Columbia # PC 3110

Upper Grades

Instructional Objectives

1. Students will clap the rhythm pattern.
2. Students will distinguish between whole and half steps.
3. Students will follow the call chart while listening to "Saturday in the Park."
4. Students will discuss the effectiveness with which this composition describes an event in contemporary life and the musical devices it employs.

Environment

A teacher-centered environment with students seated, preferably at desks, would be most effective. Call charts may be on individual sheets or on a projection transparency. The rhythm pattern should be written on a chalkboard and melody bells E, F, F♯, G, G♯ and A should be available. This rhythm pattern should be written on the chalkboard:

Initial Procedures

1. Play or have students play A, G♯, F♯, E and G, F♯, F, and E on the melody bells. Ask, "What is the difference between the two patterns?" (The tones of the second are closer together—it moves in half steps.)
2. Play both patterns again, having students sing the second pattern— the one that descends in half steps (G, F♯, F, E).
3. Play the beginning section of the recording (through the first two phrases of the vocal), having students sing the descending half-step pattern as trumpets play.
4. Refer to the rhythm pattern on the chalkboard. Have students clap.
5. Play the introduction from the recording again. What instrument plays this pattern?
6. Play through the first verse of the recording, having students clap the notated rhythm pattern.
7. Refer to the call chart and have students follow along as the entire recording is played.

8. Ask, "What does this composition tell us about life in the city? What facts are told by the words? What feelings are communicated by the music?

9. Ask, "What aspects of the music enable the composition to communicate facts and feelings about contemporary city life?"

Extended Procedures

1. On another day, listen again with the call chart. Can students add any words to describe more details of the music?

2. Play the notated rhythm pattern on several classroom percussion instruments. Select one timbre that would be most appropriate for each section of the recording and play along.

Modifications for Exceptional Learners

1. Advanced students may be able to construct call charts for their own recordings. Invite them to do so and lead the class in a listening activity in which they point out things they find interesting in their favorite recordings.

2. A call chart with photographs or drawings of instruments and people singing can be substituted for the verbal call chart for students unable to read at this level.

3. Mentally handicapped students can respond to the strong rhythmic drive of this composition. Rather than having them follow the call chart, have them clap the steady beat or the notated rhythm pattern throughout.

Evaluation

1. To what extent could students read the notated rhythm? Identify individuals having difficulty.

2. To what extent were the students able to identify and describe the difference between whole and half steps?

3. To what degree were students able to follow the call chart? Which students had difficulty? Was the problem one of attention, or were they unable to read the terminology on the chart?

TEST CHARTS

Test charts are quite similar to call charts in that they provide a means for you to direct students' attention to specific aspects of the music as it occurs. The primary difference is that the test chart presents the student with a number of choices as to what is occurring in the music. The student indicates what he or she hears by underlining or circling the best response. Some teachers prefer the test chart to the call chart since it provides for the students' direct physical involvement in listening. Also, the test chart is an effective way to assess students' listening. While most test charts are verbal statements, they may contain drawings and/or musical notation.

TEST CHART

"March Past of the Kitchen Utensils," from *The Wasps*, Williams
Adventures in Music, Grade 3, Vol. 1

As you listen to this recording, your teacher will call numbers. When you hear a number, read the descriptions of the music that follow that number on your paper, listening carefully to the recording. Circle the words that best describe what you hear at that time.

Time (seconds)	Call Number	
0:00	1. Dancelike	Marchlike
0:23	2. Short, detached tones	Longer, connected tones
0:40	3. Mostly strings	Mostly brass
0:58	4. Duple meter	Triple meter
1:16	5. Getting faster	No change in tempo
1:35	6. Dancelike	Marchlike
1:48	7. Mostly woodwinds	Mostly strings
1:58	8. Short, detached tones	Longer, connected tones
2:04	9. Duple meter	Triple meter
2:12	10. String section	Full orchestra
2:20	11. Trumpet	Clarinet
	New idea	Like the beginning
2:44	12. Accompaniment moving up the scale	Accompaniment using only a few tones
	Getting louder	Suddenly louder
3:02	13. Getting slower	No change in tempo

ANALYSIS OF MUSIC FOR LISTENING

Title: "March Past of the Kitchen Utensils," from *The Wasps*,
     Williams
Source: *Adventures in Music*, Grade 3, Vol. 1

Musical Knowledge That Can Be Developed
     Melody
     Rhythm   *March tempo, strong accent, duple meter*
     Timbre   *String orchestra and winds*
     Harmony
     Dynamics
     Form   *ABA, distinct phrases*
Musical Skills That Can Be Developed
     Singing
     Playing
     Moving   *Slow march*
     Listening
     Creating
     Reading
     Describing   *Rhythm and form*
General Knowledge That Can Be Developed
     Of the World   *Greek plays, court system, trial by jury*
     Of Relationships   *Contrast and repetition*
     Of Feelings   *Regimentation and ceremony*
General Skills That Can Be Developed
     Perceiving
     Communicating
     Social Skills
     Physical Skills   *Marching to music*
     Other

Test Chart

"March Past of the Kitchen Utensils," from *The Wasps*, Williams
Adventures in Music, Grade 3, Vol. 1

Upper Grades

Instructional Objectives

While listening to "March Past of the Kitchen Utensils," students will select words that best describe components of the music.

Environment

Within a teacher-centered environment, students should be seated at desks with test charts and pencils. In most instances, the test chart will not be a means of evaluating students for a grade but merely a means to help them hear more of what is in the music. Students should be made aware of this. We suggest playing the recording several times so students can "check" their responses before discussing them.

Initial Procedures

1. Pass out the test charts and review terminology. Whenever possible the review should be musical rather than verbal. Review the following information, for example:
    a) Short, detached tones—Sing a familiar song in a detached manner (*staccato*) and in a connected manner (*legato*).
    b) Duple meter, triple meter—Clap a duple pattern (1–2, 1–2, 1–2); Clap a triple pattern (1–2–3, 1–2–3, 1–2–3).
    c) Changing tempo—Sing a familiar song speeding up and slowing down.
    d) Woodwinds, strings—Find a recording of instrument families and listen to the difference in timbres.
2. Play the recording having students circle the best description on their sheets.
3. Review the "answers."
4. Play the recording and call numbers again so that students can verify the descriptions.

Extended Procedures

1. Using the descriptive words selected in the initial listening, have students construct a call chart, adding more descriptive words and phrases for other details in the music.

2. On another day, have students write in words that describe other details they hear in each section of this composition.

3. Construct shadow puppets of instruments and kitchen utensils and present a shadow play that illustrates each section of the music.

Modifications for Exceptional Learners

1. Invite outstanding students to make call charts pointing out musical content of their favorite recordings and to share them with the class.

2. Provide mentally handicapped students with several small geometric shapes cut from colored paper (four circles, four squares, four triangles). As they listen, have them arrange the shapes to represent what they hear. Use a circle to represent the first section. If the second is the same, place another circle beside it. If the second section is different, place a square beside the circle and so on.

Evaluation

1. How many of the words needed to be reviewed with the students before the initial listening? Which students had difficulty with musical terminology?

2. Which sections of the music seemed hardest for students to describe?

3. How adequate was the pacing of the chart? Did students daydream between numbers, or did they not have sufficient time to read, listen to music, and mark papers?

VISUAL GUIDES

Visual forms provide an excellent way to guide the listening of students with limited language skills. Realistic or abstract designs are used to point out specific aspects of the music at the time they are heard. An upward moving melody, for example, may be represented by a drawing of a set of steps, an upward moving line, a bird flying upward, or a series of geometric shapes placed in an ascending pattern. If this particular melody is repeated in the composition, the visual design can also be presented again. If the pattern is repeated in the music but played by a different instrument or at a different dynamic level, the visual pattern can be repeated in a different color or perhaps a different size.

In preparing a visual guide, you must first carefully analyze the musical composition, identifying major sections and the more important musical elements within each section. Some means for visualization must then be devised. The title or text of the music may suggest some visual designs.

It is important, however, that the visuals contain some reference to the musical content of the composition as well as the programmatic content. You must also constantly keep the teaching objectives in mind. Drawings of instruments playing, for example, are quite appropriate in a lesson designed to increase students' awareness of tone color, but they will do very little to point out melodic direction or rhythm patterns.

After the visuals have been designed, they may be placed on a large bulletin board where you can point to each one at the appropriate time in the music. This will help students know exactly what they are to hear in the music. Another way of using the visual guide is to provide each student with a sheet of paper containing the various designs, each having a letter or number. You can then call a number at the appropriate time in the music, directing the students to look at a particular design. In this way, the visual guide functions in the same manner as a call chart.

Visual Call Chart for *Prince of Denmark March*

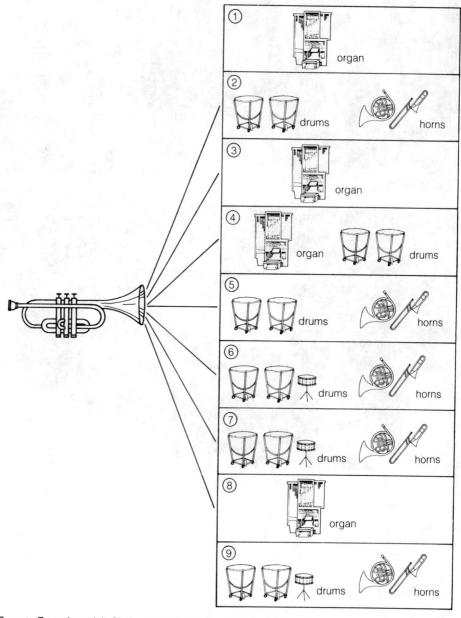

SOURCE: From Jeremiah Clark, *Holt Individualized Music Program* (New York: Holt, Rinehart and Winston), guide sheet T-2-3.

ANALYSIS OF MUSIC FOR LISTENING

TITLE: *PRINCE OF DENMARK MARCH*, CLARK
SOURCE: *HOLT INDIVIDUALIZED MUSIC PROGRAM*, LEVEL 2, CASSETTE #10

MUSICAL KNOWLEDGE THAT CAN BE DEVELOPED
    MELODY
    RHYTHM   *Slow, marchlike rhythm, strong accents*
    TIMBRE   *Trumpet, pipe organ, tympani*
    HARMONY   *Solo instrument and several instruments together*
    DYNAMICS
    FORM   *Contrast and repetition of sections*
MUSICAL SKILLS THAT CAN BE DEVELOPED
    SINGING
    PLAYING
    MOVING
    LISTENING   *For multiple timbres and repeated sections*
    CREATING
    READING
    DESCRIBING   *Elements that give this music a "majestic" sound*
GENERAL KNOWLEDGE THAT CAN BE DEVELOPED
    OF THE WORLD   *Royal ceremonies, country of Denmark*
    OF RELATIONSHIPS   *Part of an idea may remain the same while other parts change.*
    OF FEELINGS   *Majesty*
    Feelings may grow in intensity.
GENERAL SKILLS THAT CAN BE DEVELOPED
    PERCEIVING   *Simultaneous events*
    COMMUNICATING   *Reading instrument names from the chart*
    SOCIAL SKILLS
    PHYSICAL SKILLS
    OTHER

Visual Call Chart

Prince of Denmark March, Clark
Holt Individualized Music Program, Level 2, Cassette #10

Lower Grades

Instructional Objectives

1. Students will identify pictures of trumpet, pipe organ, and tympani.
2. Students will listen to an excerpt of the recording and identify the sounds of trumpet, pipe organ, and tympani.
3. Students will follow the call chart while listening to the recording.
4. Students will discuss the formal structure of the composition, identifying those sections that are the same, those that are similar, and those that are different.
5. Students will identify melody and texture as the elements that differ in the contrasting sections.

Environment

Students can best work with visual call charts while seated at desks. A formally structured environment will give you the control to guide listening; however, students should feel free to express ideas in an accepting atmosphere during discussions.

Initial Procedures

1. Refer students to the visual call chart. Have students identify instrument pictures. Also review word names for instruments.
2. Have students turn their papers over. Play the first two sections of music (about twenty seconds). Ask, "What instrument did you hear first? What did you hear second? What did you hear next? Did the instruments play one at a time, or did they play together?" Replay the excerpt as necessary to implement the discussion.
3. Refer students to the call chart again. Notice that the trumpet is indicated for all sections while the other instruments change.
4. Play the recording, having students follow the chart.
5. Discuss the structure of the composition. Ask, "Which sections were the same? Which sections were different? What made them different?"
6. Point out the title and discuss the location of Denmark and the role of the royal family. Ask, "What in this music expresses feelings of royalty?"

7. Replay the composition as students again follow the chart.

Extended Procedures

1. Place a tape recording of the music and copies of the call chart in a learning center for students to use during independent study time.

2. Divide the class into four groups: trumpets, pipe organ, tympani, and horns. Each group will move to the music when they hear their instrument being played.

Modifications for Exceptional Learners

Students with some kinds of learning disabilities may have difficulty following this chart. Finding pictures of the instruments and holding them in front of the children at the appropriate times may be more effective for these students.

Evaluation

1. Were students able to identify instruments by both sight and sound? Which individuals had difficulty?

2. Did students attend to the call chart while listening?

3. What musical perceptions were revealed in the students' discussion of form? Which students had difficulty verbalizing what they heard?

Visual Guide for *Walk to the Bunkhouse*

Illustration from *Learning to Listen to Music*
© 1969 General Learning Corporation.
Reprinted by permission of Silver Burdett Company

ANALYSIS OF MUSIC FOR LISTENING

TITLE: "WALK TO THE BUNKHOUSE," FROM *THE RED PONY*, COPLAND
SOURCE: *LEARNING TO LISTEN TO MUSIC*, RECORD II, P. 30

MUSICAL KNOWLEDGE THAT CAN BE DEVELOPED
    MELODY   *Smooth and jagged*
    RHYTHM   *Uneven, syncopated, changing meter*
    TIMBRE   *Trumpet and violin*
    HARMONY   *Melody with rhythmic accompaniment, two melodies combined in the last section*
    DYNAMICS
    FORM   *Rhythm provides unifying force, melodies provide contrast. Transition sections*
MUSICAL SKILLS THAT CAN BE DEVELOPED
    SINGING
    PLAYING
    MOVING
    LISTENING   *For several aspects occurring at the same time*
    CREATING
    READING
    DESCRIBING   *Differences between two melodies*
GENERAL KNOWLEDGE THAT CAN BE DEVELOPED
    OF THE WORLD   *Aaron Copland, an American composer of the twentieth century; cowboy legends*
    OF RELATIONSHIPS   *Several ideas may occur at once. Ideas or events may be connected by unrelated ideas or events.*
    OF FEELINGS   *Light, carefree, happy*
GENERAL SKILLS THAT CAN BE DEVELOPED
    PERCEIVING   *Several ideas and feelings at once*
    COMMUNICATING
    SOCIAL SKILLS
    PHYSICAL SKILLS
    OTHER

Visual Guide

"Walk to the Bunkhouse," from *The Red Pony*, Copland
Learning to Listen to Music, Record II, p. 30

Middle Grades

Instructional Objectives

1. Students will follow the visual guide while listening to the recording.
2. Students will discuss similarities and differences in the various sections of the composition.
3. Students will discuss the overall structure of the composition with particular emphasis on the differences between the bridge sections and the other parts of the composition.

Environment

An informal, teacher-centered environment is most effective. The visual guide should be prepared as a projection transparency and the room slightly darkened. An overhead projector will be needed. Ten to fifteen minutes should be adequate for this activity.

Initial Procedures

1. Say, "Imagine this music is from the soundtrack of a movie and that it describes someone. Listen to a little of the music. Do you think that person is a factory worker, a secretary, or a cowboy?"
2. Play about thirty seconds of the recording.
3. Give students the opportunity to respond, always asking, "What in the music made you think of a _____?" Return to the recording if necessary to develop the discussion.
4. Listen to the recording again, this time uncovering only the appropriate part of the visual guide. (Cover the transparency with a sheet of paper and slide it along, uncovering only the section that illustrates what students are hearing.)
5. Say, "This composition had seven sections." Ask, "In what ways were any of them the same? In what ways were they different? What does a bridge do? What did these musical bridges do? How did Copland make the bridges different from the other sections? What was especially different about the last section?"

Extended Procedures

1. Listen to the composition again with students uncovering the visual guide at appropriate times.
2. Have students add other illustrations, particularly in the bridge sections.

Modifications for Exceptional Learners

Begin the lesson by listening to the music and following the guide rather than with discussion.

Evaluation

1. Were students able to provide musical reasons for choosing an answer in the initial discussion? Do individual students seem to have particular problems describing the music? Do they have an adequate musical vocabulary?
2. To what extent did the students attend to the visuals while listening?
3. To what degree were students able to compare the sections of the music? To what extent did their discussion reflect critical listening? To what extent did their discussion reveal vocabulary development?

Call Chart for *Children's March*

1. INTRODUCTION
<u>LONDON BRIDGE</u> IDEAS

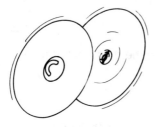

5. <u>THE FARMER IN THE DELL</u>
MELODY BY

LOW INSTRUMENTS

HIGH INSTRUMENTS

2. <u>MARY HAD A LITTLE LAMB</u>

DUPLE METER
COUNTER MELODY ON SECOND VERSE

6. INTERLUDE

3. <u>JINGLE BELLS</u>
BEGINS SOFTER *WOODWINDS*

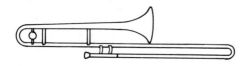

PLAY <u>FARMER IN THE DELL</u> AS A
COUNTER MELODY

7. <u>LAZY MARY</u>

4. <u>SING A SONG OF SIXPENCE</u>
• • •S•T•A•C•C•A•T•O • • •

OM–PAH

DUPLE
TRIPLE

8. <u>HICKERY DICKERY DOCK</u>

mp
ff

Call Chart for *Children's March*, continued

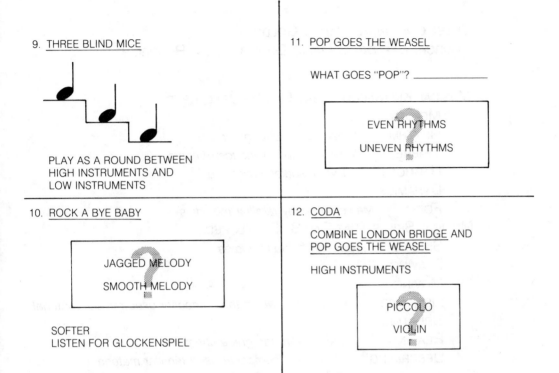

9. THREE BLIND MICE

PLAY AS A ROUND BETWEEN
HIGH INSTRUMENTS AND
LOW INSTRUMENTS

11. POP GOES THE WEASEL

WHAT GOES "POP"? _____

EVEN RHYTHMS

UNEVEN RHYTHMS

10. ROCK A BYE BABY

JAGGED MELODY

SMOOTH MELODY

SOFTER
LISTEN FOR GLOCKENSPIEL

12. CODA

COMBINE LONDON BRIDGE AND
POP GOES THE WEASEL

HIGH INSTRUMENTS

PICCOLO

VIOLIN

SOURCE: From Eunice Boardman and Beth Landis, *Exploring Music, Book 1* (New York: Holt, Rinehart and Winston, 1975), p. 26. Used with permission.

ANALYSIS OF MUSIC FOR LISTENING

TITLE: *CHILDREN'S MARCH*, GOLDMAN
SOURCE: *EXPLORING MUSIC*, BOOK 1, P. 94, RECORD 9

MUSICAL KNOWLEDGE THAT CAN BE DEVELOPED
    MELODY
    RHYTHM   *Steady beat, strong accents*
    TIMBRE   *Review of many wind instruments*
    HARMONY   *Two melodies combined*
    DYNAMICS
    FORM   *Medley of many familiar melodies*
MUSICAL SKILLS THAT CAN BE DEVELOPED
    SINGING   *Nursery-rhyme melodies*
    PLAYING
    MOVING
    LISTENING   *For ways in which the composer used familiar material*
    CREATING
    READING   *Notation from the guide sheet*
    DESCRIBING   *Ways the composer used familiar material*
GENERAL KNOWLEDGE THAT CAN BE DEVELOPED
    OF THE WORLD   *Many people enjoy recalling things from childhood.*
    OF RELATIONSHIPS   *Old things may be reworked into something new.*
    OF FEELINGS   *Feelings may change rapidly.*
GENERAL SKILLS THAT CAN BE DEVELOPED
    PERCEIVING
    COMMUNICATING   *Reading words and music from the guide sheet*
    SOCIAL SKILLS
    PHYSICAL SKILLS
    OTHER

Visual Guide

Children's March, Goldman
Exploring Music, Book 1, p. 94, Record 9

Middle Grades

Instructional Objectives

1. Students will identify familiar melodies used in this composition.
2. Students will follow the visual guide while listening.
3. When presented with choices, students will choose descriptive words, pictures, or notation that best represents the music.
4. Students will discuss the musical means employed by the composer to make each nursery-rhyme melody interesting to adults.

Environment

A formal, structured environment with students seated at desks is effective. Visual guides, pencils, and good-quality phonographs will be needed. You will direct initial discussion and the listening process. Following listening, students should discuss music freely with a minimum of teacher intervention.

Initial Procedures

1. Recall with students that composers sometimes use existing ideas to make interesting works of art.
2. Request that students listen to this composition and discover what Goldman used.
3. Play the recording in its entirety.
4. Let students identify nursery-rhyme melodies. Return to the recording if any are in question, playing only the excerpt being discussed.
5. Distribute guide sheets. Review procedures for following numbers. Notice in some places students are to make choices. Have students circle the correct choice.
6. Listen to the recording, following the guide.
7. Review sections in which questions were asked. If there is disagreement in any section, return to the portion of the recording that will enable students to verify answers.
8. Play the recording again, students following guides. You should not need to call the numbers this time.
9. Discuss the musical devices Goldman used to make the nursery-rhyme melodies interesting.

Extended Procedures

1. The guide sheet and recording should be placed in a listening center for students to review during independent study time.
2. Have students create their own medley of nursery rhymes, singing the melodies, changing tempo, rhythms, and accompaniments.

Modifications for Exceptional Learners

1. Students with learning disabilities may profit more from the visual guide provided in *Exploring Music*, Grade 1, Teacher's Book, page 94.

Evaluation

1. Which students were unable to identify at least three melodies?
2. Were students attending to the music and guide sheet during the listening time?
3. Which questions on the sheet did students have difficulty answering?
4. What musical devices did students identify in the discussion that followed the listening?
5. How frequently do students choose to listen to this composition in the listening center?

LISTENING GUIDES

At times it is desirable for students to listen to an entire composition and consider it as a whole in order to experience its cognitive and affective meanings. A *listening guide* is a series of general questions or statements about the entire composition or about large sections within it. This strategy is very much like discussion in that the questions or statements are introduced before listening and discussed in more detail after the listening experience. Notation, drawings of instruments, or other visual designs may also be a part of listening guides. Statements and questions of the following type are appropriate for listening guides:

1. The composition begins softly and gets continually louder.
2. The composition is in three parts. The first is slow and played by the woodwinds, the second very fast and played by the full orchestra. How would you describe the third?
3. What family of instruments is most important in this composition?
4. Do the feelings communicated through this music remain the same throughout the composition, or do they change?

5. What musical tools did the composer use to establish the festival mood of this composition?

6. Where did you find the greatest excitement in this music? How did the composer build this excitement?

In the discussion that follows the initial listening, it is important for you to frequently replay excerpts of the recording to verify the students' responses. We suggest that, after a brief discussion of the main points on the listening guide, you replay the entire composition so that students can synthesize knowledge developed through the discussion with their own emotional reactions to the music.

Pilot Lesson for *Little Fugue 355 in G Minor*

Subject

SOURCE: Pilot Lesson #61 for Fashions in Music from Bowmar Orchestral Library edited by Lucille Wood; copyright 1967 Bowmar/Noble Publishers, Inc., Los Angeles, California.

ANALYSIS OF MUSIC FOR LISTENING

TITLE: *LITTLE FUGUE IN G MINOR*, BACH
SOURCE: "FASHIONS IN MUSIC," *BOWMAR ORCHESTRAL LIBRARY, #86*

MUSICAL KNOWLEDGE THAT CAN BE DEVELOPED
     MELODY   *Melodies often outline chords.*
     RHYTHM   *Duple meter with strong accents*
     TIMBRE
     HARMONY   *Minor, polyphonic texture*
     DYNAMICS
     FORM   *Fugue*
MUSICAL SKILLS THAT CAN BE DEVELOPED
     SINGING   *Thematic melody*
     PLAYING
     MOVING
     LISTENING   *For overlapping ideas (fugue)*
     CREATING
     READING   *Notated theme*
     DESCRIBING
GENERAL KNOWLEDGE THAT CAN BE DEVELOPED
     OF THE WORLD   *J.S. Bach, an eighteenth-century German composer*
     OF RELATIONSHIPS   *Similar ideas may overlap one another.*
     OF FEELINGS   *Grandeur, majesty, growing in intensity*
GENERAL SKILLS THAT CAN BE DEVELOPED
     PERCEIVING
     COMMUNICATING   *Reading from the guide sheet*
     SOCIAL SKILLS
     PHYSICAL SKILLS
     OTHER

Listening Guide

Little Fugue in G Minor, Bach
"Fashions in Music," *Bowmar Orchestral Library, #86*

Instructional Objectives

1. Students will discuss the difference between *homophonic* and *polyphonic* texture.
2. Students will identify the texture of the fugue as polyphonic.
3. During a second and third listening, students will answer questions about the music on the listening guide.

Environment

Students should be comfortably seated at desks with pencils available for writing. You will direct the listening and the discussion. Copies of the guide should be provided for each student. Approximately fifteen minutes will be needed for this activity.

Initial Procedures

1. Begin the class by singing "Brother John" in unison with autoharp accompaniment.
2. Divide the class into two or three sections and sing the song as a round.
3. Discuss differences in the sound of the two versions. (In the first, everyone sang together; in the second, melodies over-lapped.)
4. Introduce or review the following:
   a) Homophonic—Similar sound (as in first version)
   b) Polyphonic—Many sounds (as in second version)
5. Instruct students to listen to the recording, identifying the texture. Ask, "Does it remain the same throughout?"
6. After identifying the texture as polyphonic, distribute listening guides and call students' attention to the notated theme by
   a) Having a student play it on the piano or a wind instrument
   b) Having the class sing the theme
   c) Playing the very beginning of the recording several times in order for students to hear the opening theme
7. Give students one or two minutes to read through the listening guide in order to determine the kinds of questions they will be answering.

8. Turn the listening guides over on the desks and listen to the recording again.
9. Return to the listening guides, giving students several minutes to respond to questions.
10. Play the recording again so that students can complete any additional items and check their answers.
11. Discuss items on the listening guide, returning to the recording to verify items on which the class did not agree.

Modifications for Exceptional Learners

1. Students studying piano may be playing other polyphonic compositions and/or compositions by J.S. Bach. Invite them to perform for your class.
2. Students with independent learning skills could complete this guide in a listening center without your help.
3. If there are students in your class lacking sufficient skills to read this guide, be certain to read all questions out loud or have students work in teams, assigning one reader and one nonreader to each team.

Evaluation

1. Were students able to identify the texture of the fugue on the initial hearing?
2. Which items on the listening guide presented problems?
3. Play another fugue—perhaps the fugal section from *Dance Macabre*. Do the students recognize the polyphonic texture?

NOTATION

Musical notation is the most precise method of symbolizing sound that has been developed. Musical notes can be used to guide the listener to a deeper awareness of the musical sounds. Notation can be used before the listening experience to acquaint students with musical ideas that they will hear; it can be presented on large charts, the chalkboard, on the overhead projector, or on individual handout sheets. It is important that students *hear* the themes as well as see them. It is also generally desirable to have the students directly experience the themes through performance. For example, some themes can be sung by the class on a neutral syllable. Or, students may play themes on recorders or other classroom instruments. Students in many upper-grade classes may be able to play themes on band or orchestral instruments, or the teacher or students may play them on piano. If the melodies are extremely jagged or cover a large range, having students merely clap the rhythms would provide them with some direct musical experience prior to listening.

It is also important to realize that some students may have difficulty recognizing similarities between a theme played on the piano or melody bells and that same theme played in the context of an instrumental ensemble. It is therefore important to play an excerpt from the recording that clearly illustrates the theme in context, thus helping students recognize the theme when it appears in the total composition.

Some discussion of notated themes is also appropriate. Questions such as the following may be utilized:

1. Does the melody cover a large or small range?
2. Does the melody move in steps or skips?
3. Will the tempo be fast or slow?
4. Will you hear mostly long tones or mostly short tones?
5. Will the rhythms be even or uneven?

When two or more thematic ideas occur in the same composition, the use of notation provides an excellent way to make comparisons. Notated themes can also be utilized to guide students' listening while a composition is being played. The teacher may point to each note of the theme as it is sounded, or he or she may simply point to the theme chart each time the theme is heard. This is particularly useful for compositions in which several themes are heard alternately. Pointing to the notation of a given theme helps students become more aware of which theme they are hearing.

While notation as a guide to listening is probably most helpful to students who have some music-reading skill, do not hesitate to use notation with young students. By watching notation as they listen to the musical sounds, they will begin to discover the relationships between what is seen and what is heard. Do remember that inexperienced readers will need larger notation, less complicated themes, and music that moves at a slower tempo. If properly chosen and presented, musical notation can serve as an effective guide to more perceptive listening.

Chester

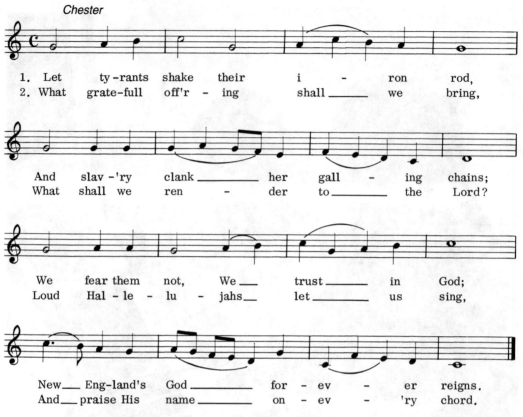

1. Let ty-rants shake their i - ron rod,
2. What grate-full off'r - ing shall we bring,

And slav -'ry clank her gall - ing chains;
What shall we ren - der to the Lord?

We fear them not, We trust in God;
Loud Hal - le - lu - jahs let us sing,

New Eng-land's God for - ev - er reigns.
And praise His name on - ev - 'ry chord.

Source: From Beatrice Landeck et. al., *Making Music Your Own*, Book 5 (Morristown, N.J.: Silver Burdett Co., 1971).

ANALYSIS OF MUSIC FOR LISTENING

TITLE: "CHESTER," FROM *NEW ENGLAND TRIPTYCH*, SCHUMAN
SOURCE: BOWMAR ORCHESTRAL LIBRARY #75

MUSICAL KNOWLEDGE THAT CAN BE DEVELOPED
    MELODY   *Use of a familiar melody in an orchestral composition*
    RHYTHM   *Use of melodic fragments, changing tempo—marchlike and*
        as a hymn
    TIMBRE   *Woodwind, brass, and percussion*
    HARMONY   *Use of dissonance*
    DYNAMICS
    FORM
MUSICAL SKILLS THAT CAN BE DEVELOPED
    SINGING   *An original hymn tune*
    PLAYING
    MOVING
    LISTENING   *For use of a familiar melody*
    CREATING
    READING   *Notation of the melody while listening*
    DESCRIBING   *Ways the composer changed the original melody*
GENERAL KNOWLEDGE THAT CAN BE DEVELOPED
    OF THE WORLD   *William Billings, a composer of Colonial America*
    OF RELATIONSHIPS   *Old ideas may be included in new things.*
    OF FEELINGS   *Different feelings may occur in one event; feelings*
        change rapidly.
        Stately, religious, energetic
GENERAL SKILLS THAT CAN BE DEVELOPED
    PERCEIVING   *Something familiar that has been transformed*
    COMMUNICATING
    SOCIAL SKILLS
    PHYSICAL SKILLS
    OTHER   *Historical research, locating "Chester" on New England map,*
        cultural life of the period

Reading Notation

"Chester," *New England Triptych*, Schuman
Bowmar Orchestral Library #75

Upper Grades

Instructional Objectives

1. Students will identify the number of times a notated melody occurs in a composition.
2. Students will discuss the means through which the composer transformed the notated melody.

Environment

A semiformal environment in which there can be free discussion between teacher and students is effective. The hymn-tune should be available in music books, on a song sheet, or on a projection transparency. It is assumed that students have learned the song in previous classes and can sing it with confidence.

Initial Procedures

1. Begin the class by singing the song, perhaps several times.
2. Discuss William Billings as a composer of the Colonial period, pointing out the importance of the church in community life and of music in the church. Hymns were often written for a particular church and took the name of the town. William Schuman, a composer living now, is interested in "musical antiques." He used "Chester" in a composition for orchestra.
3. Play the recording, asking students to follow their notation in order to determine how many times the hymn is heard.
4. Listen again to find out how Schuman changed the hymn. Ask, "How is it different from the way we sing it?"
5. Discuss various transformations, returning to the recording frequently to verify and clarify the discussion.
6. Sing the song using some of these techniques: very slow, very fast, different groups singing fragments of the melody.
7. Listen to the entire composition again, students still following the notation for the song.

Extended Procedures

1. Listen on several other occasions for more of the techniques used in transformation of the melody.

2. Construct a call chart or visual guide to show how the composer used the melody in each section of the composition.

Modifications for Exceptional Learners

1. Talented students may be able to create their own compositions based on a familiar melody using some of the techniques Schuman used in transforming this melody by Billings.
2. Pointing to each note of the melody as it is heard in the composition will help students with reading skills.

Evaluation

1. Were students able to follow notation as they heard the music?
2. Did students recognize specific places in the notation where changes in the melody occurred?
3. Play parts of the recording while students follow the notation. Suddenly "lift the needle." Can students point to the place on the notation where you stopped?

SELF-CHECK: LISTENING

Key

1. Listening to music is:
   a) A good activity for handicapped students who cannot perform
   b) A good activity for students without talent to create music
   c) A part of every music activity   c
   d) An activity that occurs only when listening to records

2. One of the more important reasons for including listening activities in the elementary classroom is
   a) Listening is a means for developing musical knowledge   a
   b) Listening to music helps children relax
   c) Listening to music motivates children to work harder to develop their own performing skills
   d) Listening activities provide an enjoyable break from more demanding activities

3. The reason that music is considered important within the total school curriculum is:
   a) Well-educated people can perform music
   b) Music provides a means for relaxation so that students learn more when working in other subject areas
   c) Music provides a general source of knowledge and a means for developing general skills   c
   d) Music provides a means for learning to appreciate life

4. The development of skill in listening to music
   a) Is unrelated to the development of musical knowledge
   b) Cannot be developed until a student has considerable performing experience
   c) Cannot be developed until a student has learned to read musical notation
   d) Is interdependent with the development of musical knowledge   d

5. Responsibility for listening activities
   a) Belongs to the classroom teacher
   b) Belongs to the music specialist
   c) Is shared by the classroom teacher and the music specialist   c
   d) Should be assigned to gifted students in the class

6. Competency in guiding listening activities is
   a) Dependent on the teacher's ability to read musical notation
   b) Dependent on the teacher's performing skills
   c) Dependent on the teacher's ability to share the delight and excitement found in music   c
   d) Dependent on the teacher's ability to discuss music in musical terms

7. Competencies in guiding listening activities
   a) Are a series of discrete behaviors that should occur in the prescribed order
   b) Are a series of discrete behaviors that may occur in random order
   c) Are a series of interrelated behaviors that may occur simultaneously   c
   d) Are the behaviors of performing, listening, and creating

8. Which of the following is *not* considered essential for effective guidance of classroom listening activities?
   a) Identification of goals
   b) Assessment of student needs
   c) Accurate and expressive performance of music by the teacher   c

d) Identification of instructional objectives
e) Analyzing musical materials
f) Designing and managing learning environments
g) Selection of teaching/learning strategies

9.. Goals for listening activities
a) Are the same as for performing activities
b) Should be based on assessment of student needs
c) Should be established by the teacher before planning a lesson
d) Should be based on the content of the music

b

10. The assessment of listening activities is primarily the process of
a) Determining what students hear and how they respond to music
b) Determining students' skills of performing, listening, and creating
c) Determining how well students read musical notation
d) Determining students' knowledge of the world, of relationships, and of feelings

a

11. Which of the following was *not* considered as a way to assess listening activities?
a) Noting verbal comments and questions about the music heard
b) Observing students' movements made to music while listening
c) Evaluating students' performance on test charts and written listening guides
d) Administering the *Listening to Great Music Test*, elementary form

d

12. An important criterion in making a selection for classroom listening is
a) Was this piece composed for children of this age?
b) Does this music tell a story the children will understand?
c) Does this music have a steady beat?
d) Do I enjoy listening to this composition?

d

13. In analyzing a selection for classroom listening activities, an important question for you to ask is
a) Have the students heard this before?
b) Was this piece composed for children of this age?
c) What can I help children hear in this music that they would not hear on their own?
d) In what key is this composition written?

c

14. For listening activities, the democratic environment
a) Is the most appropriate because it provides for student input
b) Is inappropriate since the teacher should direct students' attention to predetermined aspects of the music
c) Is one of several possible environments which the teacher could establish
d) Is appropriate if listening to music by American composers

c

15. The appropriate time for listening activities is
a) In special listening periods scheduled each week
b) As part of other classroom activities
c) When children need a break from other subjects
d) Special listening periods and as part of other classroom activities

d

16. The record player used for listening experiences should be
a) Of school quality so that it can be replaced if damaged by students
b) Of high quality to ensure accurate reproduction of sound
c) Inexpensive so that more money is available to purchase recordings
d) Of any quality since students should learn to listen to music under a wide variety of conditions

b

17. Which of the following was considered an effective management technique for listening activities?
    a) Speak loudly so that your voice can be heard over the recording.
    b) Play the recording softly so that students can think while they listen.
    c) Avoid playing short excerpts of a recording so as not to interrupt students' concentration on the music.
    d) Listen to music with the students modeling good listening behavior.

d

18. In utilizing the drawing-to-music strategy, the teacher should strive to have students' drawings represent
    a) Melodic or rhythmic patterns in the music
    b) Characters in the story told by the music
    c) Whatever the students think about as they listen to the music
    d) What the composer was thinking about as he created the music

a

19. An important advantage of moving-to-music strategies in guiding listening is
    a) They permit children to exercise while listening
    b) They provide a means for the teacher to assess what children are hearing since children translate what they hear into movements the teacher can observe
    c) They provide experiences in related arts since children learn how to dance as they learn how to listen
    d) They provide a means for classroom control by keeping children busy while they are listening

b

20. In listening to program music
    a) Emphasis should be placed on the feelings of the characters in the story
    b) Emphasis should be placed on creating an original story to go along with the music
    c) Emphasis should be placed on identifying and describing the musical patterns that the composer used to tell the story
    d) Emphasis should be placed on the country in which the composer lived or in which the story took place

c

21. Call charts provide a means to
    a) Point out specific musical events as they occur
    b) Call attention to the form of the composition before listening
    c) Assess the degree to which students remember what they heard
    d) Have the students chart the seating arrangement of the orchestra so that they know where to find each instrument

a

22. Test charts provide a means to
    a) Test students' knowledge of composers and instruments
    b) Test what students are hearing while they are listening
    c) Test the degree to which students remember what they hear
    d) Test students' ability to follow musical notation

b

23. In a listening experience, traditional notation
    a) Can be used to illustrate main ideas in listening selections
    b) Tends to confuse students since few can read music
    c) Should be used only if there are melodies that students can sing
    d) Should not be used in elementary grades since students at this level do not read notation

a

ENABLING ACTIVITIES: LISTENING

On your own

1. Develop a repertoire of five recorded selections that you know very well. Strive for a variety of popular, classical, and avant-garde music.
2. Attend a live concert in your community and read the newspaper review.
3. Read the record review section of your favorite magazine.
4. As you listen to your own records or to music on the radio, try to identify at least one aspect of melody, rhythm, harmony, timbre, and form.
5. After listening, discuss with your friends the aspects of music listed in the preceeding activity.
6. Develop a call chart or a listening guide for one of your favorite recordings.

In the schools

1. Observe a listening lesson and describe the learning environment, the teaching strategies, and materials used.
2. Identify several musical and general goals toward which the teacher may have been working.
3. Examine the records and listening equipment available in the classroom, in the music room, and in the learning resource center.
4. Observe students engaged in listening activities. Using the checklist on page 190, assess the involvement of individual students and of the class in general. Suggest future listening activities which will meet the identified needs of the students.
5. Plan and guide a listening experience for a large group of students that will lead to the development of at least one musical and one general learning goal.
6. Plan and prepare materials for a listening center that will lead to the attainment of at least one musical and one general learning goal.
7. With the help of the cooperating teacher, identify a student with special learning needs. Develop an IEP that will include listening activities as a means of meeting identified learning objectives.

In the library

1. Examine the elementary school record collections and teacher's guides that are listed on page 276.
2. Review the basic elementary music textbooks listed on page 182, noting the listening activities that have been included. Note also the different teaching strategies suggested in the teacher's editions of these textbooks.
3. Using the form found on page 195, complete an analysis of at least three recorded listening selections.
4. Examine the goals and objectives for listening activities found in state and local district music curriculum guides.

In the campus classroom

1. Listen to one musical selection on several different days, striving for deeper musical perception each time.
2. Plan a listening lesson using one of the strategies suggested in this chapter and present it to a group of your classmates. Invite the group to help you evaluate the listening experience.
3. Role-play a situation in which a teacher explains the importance of classroom listening experiences to a parent.

4. Role-play a situation in which a teacher justifies a request for quality listening equipment to a school superintendent.

LISTENING RESOURCES

Adventures in Music, Grades 1-6. RCA, 1962.

Bowmar Orchestral Library. Lucille Wood, ed. Glendale, Calif.: Bowmar Records, 1967.

Learning to Listen to Music, Bennett Reimer, consultant. Morristown, N.J.: Silver Burdett Co., 1969.

The Small Listener. Lucille Wood, ed. Glendale, Calif.: Bowmar Records, 1969.

Learning Through Creating

3

OBJECTIVES

- *State a rationale for creating music in the elementary classroom*
- *Identify goals and objectives for creating activities*
- *Assess the musical needs of students through creating activities*
- *Plan effective classroom environments for creating activities*
- *Demonstrate a number of strategies for guiding creating activities*

KINDS OF CREATING

Music is frequently called a creative activity, and so it is. Music, dance, poetry, sculpture, painting, and the other "fine arts" represent what are perhaps humanity's highest creative achievements. Each time we sing a song or play a musical instrument we create a new combination of sound elements. Since each performance is unique, it can be considered a creative experience. Because we respond in a different way each time we hear a composition, listening to music may be considered a creative experience. Moving in response to music can also be a creative experience. (Creating a dance, however, is something different from creating music.) It can easily be seen from these examples that there is indeed a creative element in all musical activities.

Because of its abstract qualities, however, music lends itself to a particular kind of creative activity in which students *select* particular sounds, *invent* sound patterns, and *organize* those patterns in a meaningful way, thus creating a composition that is a unique expression of ideas and feelings. We have found that children of all ages can find much enjoyment and satisfaction in creating their own music. This chapter will be concerned with helping you develop competence in guiding creative musical activities for children.

We would like to point out that in the language arts children begin to express themselves first with single words. Gradually, words are combined into phrases, then extended to sentences. It is a major accomplishment for an elementary-aged child to write a complete paragraph. The developmental process is quite similar in music. A young child's composition may be a three- or four-note pattern which is sung or played on an instrument. Gradually, patterns are extended and combined into phrases, then into short compositions. A child's musical creation may be a unique rhythmic accompaniment to a familiar song, or it may be a song describing a person or event that is invented as part of play activities. Indeed, children frequently *play* with sounds, an activity that may result in a musical creation. Children are aware that hands, feet, pencils, coins, keys, water glasses, soda bottles, newspapers, or almost any other object makes *sound* and thus has the potential for making music. Such sound sources can be used by children in musically creative experiences. The purpose of this chapter is to help you develop competence in guiding children as they work with sound—selecting sounds, inventing sound patterns, and organizing those patterns into expressive and original musical compositions.

WHY CREATE IN THE CLASSROOM?

Children play with many things—with toys, games, clay, and color in paint and crayons, with space and light and shadows. They can also play with sound. In fact we often talk of "playing music" because musical activities of all kinds can have elements of play. Play is an important part of a child's world, and children learn much from playing. The creative experiences that we will describe in this chapter may be considered "playing with sound," but they will also be activities through which much learning can take place.

The creative process in music provides children with the opportunity to develop knowledge about the basic components of music. Before you can select particular sounds to use in a composition, you must explore many sounds, determining how they are similar and how they are different. In the process, you will discover that sounds may be high or low, long or short, loud or soft and may have contrasting timbres. In exploring and selecting sounds, the child can develop knowledge about pitches, rhythms, timbres, and dynamics.

The process of inventing and organizing sound patterns provides children with an opportunity for further development of knowledge about sound. Sounds arranged in linear patterns form scales, intervals, meters, and ostinatos. Sounds arranged in vertical patterns form chords, textures, and harmonies. Creating and manipulating sound patterns provides the opportunity for children to extend and refine their knowledge about music. An important reason for including opportunities for elementary school children to create music is that *the creative process provides an excellent means to develop knowledge about music.*

The process of creating music requires the use of other musical skills. Creating music is working and playing with sound. In most cases, children's creations will be improvisations—played or sung—rather than written. In creating music, a child may find it necessary to play an instrument he or she has not played before, to play louder or softer than ever before, or to play faster than ever before. The creative experience thus provides a reason for the development and refinement of performing skills.

It is also necessary to listen in the creative process. Decisions made in the process of selecting sounds, inventing sound patterns, and organizing sounds are value judgments based on what is heard. Creating music requires critical and discriminating listening. A second reason for providing opportunities for elementary children to create music, then, is that *creative activities are a means for the development of musical skills*—of performing and listening.

Creative activities may also provide opportunities for children to gain general knowledge. Exploring the different sounds made by metal objects, wooden objects, or glass objects is a way to learn something of the different properties of these materials. If a composition is programmatic—that is, if it is to depict some specific object or event—the student will find it necessary to study and examine the object or event in great detail in order to select and organize sounds that best represent it. Through the process of creating music, children can gain knowledge of the people, places, and things in the world.

Because the creative process is the manipulation of the many properties of sound, it provides an excellent way to learn about relationships. Sound exists in time. Some sounds are longer than other sounds. Some can be extended while others cannot. Short sounds can be combined with longer sounds in an endless number of combinations. Similar relationships exist among pitches, timbres, and dynamic levels of sound. In creating music, students have the opportunity to explore unending relational possibilities and to make value judgments on the appropriateness of those relationships. The abstract qualities of sound make creative experiences in music an excellent source of knowledge about relationships.

Creative activities provide an opportunity to learn about feelings. To describe a character or event when creating music, it is necessary to consider the feelings of the character or the feelings of the people at the event. The feelings that are symbolized and expressed through the compositions of children may be feelings that are familiar to them; the creative experience provides a chance to share these feelings. Or, the feelings contained in a child's composition may be completely new. In these instances, the creative process provides the child with the opportunity to explore new possibilities in the realm of feeling. A third reason for ensuring that children in the elementary classroom have the opportunity to create their own music is that *such experiences are a way to develop general knowledge*—knowledge of the world, of relationships, and of feelings.

Musical compositions are a reflection of the world as it sounds to the composer. Creating music requires that children be perceptive of their world; the creative process is therefore a means for developing perceptive skills. Music is also a means of communicating both knowledge and feeling. We are convinced that there is a large body of knowledge and many feelings that cannot be communicated through traditional verbal channels. There are some children that find verbal communication extremely difficult. By creating music, these children may find a more effective means of communication. By developing skills in creating music, all children will develop a means to communicate those ideas and feelings that defy verbalization.

Although creating music can be an individual activity, the classroom strategies that we suggest will be group activities, many intended for small groups of children. They provide an excellent opportunity for students to develop essential social skills. Many of the children's compositions will be improvised on musical instruments, and some may be accompaniments for a movement/dance activity. Physical skills may therefore be developed through the creative process. A fourth reason for including opportunities for children to create their own music in the elementary classroom is that *such opportunities can lead to the development of many general skills.*

COMPETENCIES FOR GUIDING CREATIVE ACTIVITIES

Like performing and listening, creative activities provide an opportunity for the development of musical knowledge and skill and general knowledge and skill. Both music specialists and classroom teachers must be competent in guiding creative activities if these goals are to be achieved in the classroom. The competencies needed for guiding musically creative activities in the classroom are not unlike those needed for guiding performing and listening activities, and, similarly, they are not completely dependent on the teacher's own skill in creating musical compositions.

An error frequently made by teachers is to assume that their students cannot learn to do and enjoy things that the teacher cannot do. If this were the case, all learning would be limited to the knowledge and skills of the teacher. We have had many students progress far beyond what we know and do. This, indeed, is one of the great joys of teaching—to see students expand the boundaries of present knowledge and skill. It is particularly important in guiding creative activities that the teacher be able to establish a foundation and set parameters for the activities but, at the same time, not limit the final outcome of the experiences. The intent of this chapter is to help you develop competencies in designing and leading such learning experiences.

As in discussing competencies for guiding performing and listening activities, we have identified discrete behaviors in guiding creative activities. These will be discussed separately although they frequently must occur simultaneously in the classroom. The following is a listing of the specific competencies with which we will deal in this chapter.

The competent teacher can

- Identify musical and general goals that can be achieved through creative activities in music
- Assess students' musical knowledge and skill through creative experiences
- Identify instructional objectives for creative experiences
- Design and manage teaching/learning environments appropriate for creating activities
- Select and carry out specific strategies and procedures for guiding creating activities:

>   Creating accompaniments for songs
>   Creating songs
>   Creating with environmental sounds
>   Music for drama
>   Vocal improvisation
>   Instrumental improvisation
>   Composing with the tape recorder

IDENTIFYING GOALS FOR CREATING ACTIVITIES

In addition to the broad goals of developing knowledge and skill, there are some general goals for classroom creating activities. As a competent teacher, you will want to develop specific goals for creating activities, but these must be based on the identified needs of a particular group of students. Specific goals should also be formulated on the basis of developmental levels of students and should take other classroom activities into consideration. The following is a minimal list of musical goals for classroom creating activities. Classroom creating activities should provide students opportunities to

1. Experience the joy and satisfaction that comes from creating music

2. Develop an increasing understanding of melody, rhythm, harmony, dynamics, timbre, and form

3. Develop an increasing awareness of ideas and feelings expressed through music

4. Develop skill in selecting, inventing, and organizing patterns of sound

5. Develop skill in making aesthetic value judgments

6. Develop skill in performing and listening

7. Develop skill in using musical notation

ASSESSING MUSICAL NEEDS THROUGH CREATING ACTIVITIES

In Chapters 1 and 2 of this book, you learned that assessment is an ongoing process in all musical activities. The purpose of assessment is not to assign grades to students but rather to collect information for making decisions about the individual's or group's abilities, interests, and attitudes. Also, assessment is the process of comparing students' achievement with established criteria in order to determine the success of teaching and learning. Our experience has indicated that creating activities are an especially effective means for assessing musical growth. As students select, invent, and organize patterns of sound, they reveal much of their knowledge of melody, rhythm, harmony, dynamics, timbre, and form. By watching children as they manipulate sound, by listening as they talk about their work, and by listening to their original compositions, teachers can gain many insights into what students know about music, how they feel about music, and how they feel about themselves. When you combine the data gathered through the assessment of creating activities with data gathered from assessments of performing and listening activities, you will have fairly complete information about the musical knowledge and skills of individual students and of your entire class.

As in the assessment of performing and listening activities, there are essentially three questions that you will ask in assessing creating activities:

1. Do the students know this material (or have these skills) before I teach?

2. Did the students learn from what I taught?

3. Do they like what they learned?

Answers to these questions can be sought by observing students as they engage in any of the creating activities that we have suggested in the later section of this chapter. The checklist, which is on page 284, is intended to serve as an observational guide. If students appear to be concerned with pitch or rhythm as they explore sounds and invent sound patterns, you may assume that they have some knowledge of these aspects of music. We must point out that the failure of a student to be concerned with pitch difference in a given activity, for example, does not necessarily indicate a lack of knowledge about pitch. Lack of concern with differences of pitch in several activities, however, may indicate a need for the development of knowledge in this area. It is for this reason that assessment should not be considered a "one-time" task of the teacher but rather an ongoing part of the teaching process.

ASSESSMENT OF CREATING ACTIVITIES

Student (Class) _____ School _____ Date _____
Observer _____

During the process of creating, did the students' behavior indicate an awareness of
Melody
_____ different pitch levels
_____ different pitch movement—steps, skips, sliding, etc.
_____ repeated pitch patterns—sequences, etc.
_____ development and extension of melodic ideas
_____ use of fragments, inversion, adding tones, etc.

Rhythm
_____ long and short sounds
_____ steady beat
_____ metric organization
_____ repeated rhythm patterns—ostinato
_____ development of rhythmic ideas

Timbre
_____ use of several different sound sources
_____ classification by sound
_____ subtle variation of sound—rubber mallets contrasted with wood

Dynamics
_____ loud and soft contrasts
_____ sudden changes of volume
_____ gradual changes of volume

Harmony
_____ single sounds and combinations of sounds
_____ vertical (chordal) and horizontal (polyphonic) combinations
_____ building layers of sound

Form
_____ phrases
_____ sections
_____ contrast and repetition of sections
_____ an introduction
_____ an ending (coda)
_____ structural patterns—AB, ABA, rondo, etc.

Did the students' behavior indicate an awareness of the expressive potential of the composition?
_____ facial expressions
_____ nonverbal reactions
_____ verbal comments

Was the composition expressive?
Did the student enjoy the experience of creating?

ENVIRONMENTS FOR CREATING

What will be perhaps your most important role in providing experiences in which children create their own music will be establishing an environment for creativity. Concerns for the physical elements of time, space, and materials are important, but of even greater importance within an environment for creative experiences are the human elements. Students must feel sufficiently secure with physical elements, with themselves, and with other people to freely explore, invent, and organize elements of sound. There must be an acceptance of new and unusual sounds, and students must be aware that there is not a "right," "wrong," or "expected" solution to the questions asked or problems posed.

    At the same time, there must be sufficient structure to ensure some degree of success and a feeling of accomplishment. There is a difference between exploring sound and purposeless noise making. As a teacher, you must be able to recognize this difference. Any artist works within limits; the painter cannot paint beyond the edge of the canvas. Tomorrow he may have a larger canvas, but today he must work to create beautiful and meaningful art with the materials available. Both the artist and the child must respect the materials with which they work. Exploring sounds on the autoharp is one thing; destroying it is quite another. Discovering loud sounds that can be made with the voice can be an important part of the creative process, but no one can create with constant screaming. Limits must be established before children begin the experiences, not as constraints, but as boundaries within which to create.

The Human Environment

There are times when an autocratic environment can be most effective in a creative experience. This is particularly true when children are learning the skills of selecting, inventing, and organizing. Within such an environment, you would direct students through the learning process, being extremely careful not to direct the choices made within the process. The following might be some typical teacher behaviors for a creative activity found in an autocratic environment:

1. Giving students specific directions for selecting sound sources—"Find an object in this room that is made of wood that will make a sound."
2. Giving specific directions for exploring sound qualities—"Make short sounds, soft sounds, low-pitched sounds."
3. Giving specific directions for inventing sound patterns—"Invent a pattern that begins soft and gets louder and that will last for fifteen seconds."
4. Giving specific directions for organizing sound—"Create a composition, forty-five seconds in length, that uses two sound sources and has both long and short sounds, in ABA form."

As you may notice, in the preceding examples, the teacher is giving very specific directions, but the students still have the freedom to make many choices. Many decisions are open to the students, but the teacher is still very much in control. The way in which the teacher controls the *time* given to students to work is also extremely important in the autocratic environment.

The Democratic Environment

At times the less-structured democratic environment may be more suitable for creative experiences. The atmosphere in which the teacher and students are exploring, creating, and learning together reduces the need to find the "right" answer. Seeing the teacher engaged in a playful activity with sound may convince students to take part in the activity. Because children frequently imitate adult behaviors, however, you must be careful not to impose ideas on the creative experience by modeling. If it is necessary to give examples, give several so that students must choose from several alternatives. It is frequently more appropriate for you to listen to the sounds created by students and to imitate them rather than to initiate sound patterns yourself. The following might be some typical teacher behaviors found in a democratic environment:

1. Asking students to list sound sources that might be appropriate for the composition
2. Asking students to list sound qualities (pitch, rhythm, dynamics, etc.) that would be appropriate for the composition
3. Providing time, space, and materials for the exploration of sounds so that these choices can be made
4. Listening to patterns invented by students and making suggestions for extension and refinement where appropriate
5. Asking students to suggest a formal structure for the composition
6. Suggesting the students create a sound piece to introduce a puppet play (skit, story, etc.)
7. Helping students notate their composition
8. Helping students list criteria by which to evaluate composition

The difference between autocratic teacher behaviors and democratic teacher behaviors is not always distinct. A teacher frequently shifts from one role to another during a learning experience. The point that we wish to make is that a creative experience—indeed, any learning experience—may be highly structured by the teacher, or the students themselves may have a role in the development of the structure of the experience.

The student-centered open classroom environment may at times be the most appropriate for creative experiences. The child's natural interest in playing with sound will undoubtedly provide many opportunities for developing knowledge and skill by extending the sound-play. The teacher's role in the open environment is to watch, listen, and ask questions that will move the child deeper into the experience. Some typical teacher behaviors might be the following:

1. Noticing a child's playing with sound and asking questions such as:
   a) What do you like about that sound?
   b) How is this sound different from that sound?
   c) Why did you choose this sound rather than that sound?
   d) What could you do to make that pattern more interesting?
   e) What is the most exciting part of that pattern?
   f) Which two patterns are most similar?
   g) What is the greatest difference between these patterns?

2. Suggesting alternatives for the child:
   a) How would it sound if you played that pattern on something made of metal?
   b) Would it sound different if you played that pattern _____ (faster, slower, louder, higher, etc.)?
   c) What could you use to accompany that pattern?
   d) Could you find a sound that is contrasting to yours?

3. Helping the child find ways to organize sound patterns:
   a) What would make a good introduction to your piece?
   b) Can you find an interesting ending for your composition?
   c) Have you used both repetition and contrast in your music?

4. Helping the child notate the composition with either traditional or graphic notation

5. Helping the child evaluate the composition:
   a) What was the most interesting part?
   b) Was there enough variety to hold interest throughout?
   c) Did the introduction suggest something that was to come?
   d) Did the ending summarize the ideas and/or feelings of the composition?
   e) Did the composition express feelings?

In the open environment, the child is an actor, the teacher a reactor. True, the teacher must set the stage by carefully planning for space, time, and materials and by creating an atmosphere in which the child feels secure to freely explore within clearly established limits. Unlike the teacher-centered environments, in the open environment the ideas are initiated by the child. The teacher's role is to help the child extend and develop these ideas into meaningful experiences.

The Physical Environment

Time

Time is an important element in the creative process. Children need time to play with sounds in an exploratory way before they can select sounds for musical compositions. Too much time, on the other hand, can lead to purposeless activity and classroom disruption. Some creative activity can occur in large groups working together for specified periods of time. An entire class can, for example, work together for two to three minutes exploring high sounds and low sounds that can be made with the voice, or exploring the different kinds of sound that can be made with a sheet of paper. Other activities, such as exploring the sound that can be made with a water glass, are more individual activities, and time must be provided for individuals to work at their own pace.

Time for creative activities may be a part of "center time" or another less structured part of the school day. Creative experiences may grow out of other classroom activities, too. A group of students may decide to compose a song to describe something they saw on a field trip. Students may decide to create music to introduce a skit or a puppet play. A composition might evolve from a story read in language arts, or it may be a translation of a mathematical formula into sound. It may also grow out of a student's playing with the sounds of an object in the classroom.

We want to point out that creating music should be a thoughtful activity. Few works of art are spontaneous creations. Children should have the opportunity to work on a composition over a period of several days, creating, evaluating, revising, and refining. The competent teacher can provide appropriate periods of time for children to create music within the classroom.

Space

Flexible space is needed for creative activities. We have pointed out that children sometimes need a quiet space where they can explore a particular sound. Other creative activities are carried out by two or three students working together. They should also be working in a space where their sounds will not distract other children and where they can clearly hear the sounds with which they are working. The "Sound House" described in the Chapter 1 is a good space for creative activities.

Larger space may be necessary for creating music than for performance activities because children may need to explore a variety of instruments (sound sources) in choosing the ones with which to work. If they are notating their composition, they will also need space to work on large sheets of paper. There are, of course, some creative activities that can be carried out by an entire group in the regular classroom space. Unfortunately, most classrooms do not provide ideal space for individual and small groups to work in creative ways with sound. The competent teacher must find ways to adapt available space for these important activities.

Materials

Planning materials for creative activities is extremely important. We have pointed out that anything that makes a sound has the potential for becoming a musical sound source and could, therefore, be a material for a creative experience. Learning to create music is learning to make musical *choices*.

The teacher's role involves planning the alternatives from which a student may choose. A child may not be so likely to explore all sound possibilities on one instrument if many instruments are available. As a teacher, you must decide what choices the student is capable of making at a particular level of development and then provide materials that present those alternatives. As students gain skill in making musical decisions, you can provide them with more alternatives.

A variety of good-quality rhythmic and melodic instruments should be available for creative activities. Orff-type xylophones are especially desirable since they have a good tone and the removable bars enable you to limit the pitch choices available to students. All of the instruments that are used in performing activities are appropriate for creating activities as well.

Tape recorders are an especially valuable resource for creating activities. Recording sound is a way for students to remember particular patterns and organizational structures from one day to the next. It is sometimes desirable for students to devise systems for the notation of sound. Recording compositions on tape, however, provides a more accurate record and is less time consuming for the student than written notation. It is frequently possible for students to listen more objectively and to evaluate and refine their compositions when they hear them played back on the tape recorder. The tape recorder also provides a means for manipulating and organizing sound.

Managing the Environments

We have said before that a competent teacher is an effective manager. Management begins with knowledge of the students and the musical materials and includes careful planning of working procedures. Effective classroom management also requires knowledge of a number of alternative strategies and management techniques so that plans may be changed as classroom interactions progress. This is particularly the case in managing creating activities, in which the music itself grows out of the experience rather than being predetermined as in performing or listening activities. Instead of planning final outcomes for creating activities, you will find it necessary to plan the parameters within which the students will work and to determine procedures through which they will work. Meaningful creating activities do not result from an "anything goes" atmosphere, but instead they result from thoughtfully planned experiences. In most instances, the *process* of creating is far more important than the product that is created. You are teaching students the process and skills of creating; they must learn to make aesthetic value judgments in the process of selecting, inventing, and organizing patterns of sound. Competent teachers manage creating activities by thoughtfully planning the parameters within which students will work and the procedures through which they will work, and by clearly communicating these expectations to the students. Competent teachers also recognize the artistic value of the products of students' creations, helping students develop feelings of accomplishment and self-worth.

MANAGEMENT TECHNIQUES FOR CREATING ACTIVITIES

1. *Plan parameters within which students are to work.*
   a) Limit sounds from which students will select.
   b) Limit aspects of sound which students are to explore—pitch, duration, timbre, dynamics.
   c) Establish realistic time limitations on the length of the expected composition and the length of the activity.

2. *Plan working procedures for the students.*
   a) Plan procedures for getting out and returning instruments and other materials.
   b) Identify a hierarchy of activities, indicating what should be done first, second, third, and so on.
   c) Establish a "frame of silence" around each composition by beginning and ending with at least five seconds of silence.
   d) Predetermine which activities can be carried out in large groups and which will require smaller groupings.
   e) Plan procedures for dividing the class into groups and for moving to group work areas.
   f) Identify a leader for each group. Avoid putting two strong "leadership personalities" in the same group.
   g) Provide written instructions to group leaders when working in small groups.

3. *Communicate instructions and expectations clearly to students.*
   a) Be certain that students know what choices are available to them.
   b) Be certain that students know the limitations within which they are to work.
   c) Provide written instructions to group leaders when working in small groups.
   d) Use large graphic notation and/or conducting gestures when working with large groups.

4. *Help students develop skills of creating.*
   a) Use questioning techniques to help students explore, invent, and organize sounds.
   b) Help students develop criteria and procedures for evaluating their own compositions.
   c) Provide opportunities for students to work on one composition over an extended period of time (fifteen minutes each day for a week) to make numerous refinements.

5. *Recognize the artistic qualities of the student's compositions.*
   a) Reinforce the *process* rather than the product, giving verbal and nonverbal reinforcement to students who are efficiently working through the process of exploring, inventing, and organizing sound.

b) Help students develop criteria for evaluating their own compositions.
c) Help students revise and refine their compositions.
d) Provide opportunities for students to perform compositions in a concertlike atmosphere for other students and for adults.

IDENTIFYING OBJECTIVES FOR CREATING ACTIVITIES

Given the goals for creating activities and some notion of students' musical needs as identified through assessment procedures, it becomes your task as a teacher to identify specific activities through which those needs can be met and the goals achieved. As with performing and listening activities, instructional objectives for creating activities should be stated in terms of student behavior. Since the final product of a creating activity should be new and unique, it is important that instructional objectives describe the *process* through which students will work rather than the product or the outcome of the experience. The terms *select, explore, invent,* and *organize* frequently become the action verbs in instructional objectives for creating activities. Since the development of specific musical knowledge or musical skill is the ultimate goal, words describing specific musical concepts or skills are also frequently part of objective statements. In addition, we would like to remind you of the following goal for creating experiences: Experience the joy and satisfaction that comes from creating music. We therefore urge you not to overlook affective objectives for creating activities, even though the behavior of "enjoying" may not be as directly observable as playing, inventing, or organizing.

The following are some examples of objectives for creating activities:

1. Students will explore qualities of rhythm, dynamics, and timbre that can be produced by a sheet of paper.
2. Students will invent patterns that describe contrasting feelings.
3. Students will organize animal sounds into a ABA composition.
4. Students will invent patterns consisting of four different pitches.
5. Students will explore timbres of sounds possible from items found in the classroom.
6. Students will demonstrate an understanding of stepwise and skipwise melodic movement by creating a composition that contains these melodic contrasts.
7. Students will have the opportunity to continue working on their compositions until they demonstrate satisfaction in the product.
8. Students will demonstrate pride in their accomplishments by performing their compositions for another class in the school.
9. Students' facial expressions and verbal comments during the creating activity will demonstrate the degree to which they are enjoying the experience.

Additional examples of instructional objectives for creating activities can be found in the strategies that we have suggested in a later section of this chapter. We also point out that well-formulated objectives provide a basis for further assessment and for the planning of future musical activities.

STRATEGIES FOR GUIDING CREATING ACTIVITIES

As in selecting strategies for performing and listening activities, there is no one correct strategy for guiding creating activities. We have identified a number of strategies for guiding creating activities and categorized them primarily on the basis of the musical materials used in the creating process. Throughout this chapter, we have indicated our belief that the process of creating music is that of selecting sound, inventing sound patterns, and organizing sound patterns into expressive musical compositions. Most of the strategies that we suggest in the following pages reflect this three-part process.

We recognize that there are a number of common characteristics among these strategies and that many more examples of strategies could have been given. It is our belief, however, that a competent teacher is able to guide creating activities utilizing a number of different strategies in differing environments. We also believe that a creative teacher will be able to devise a limitless number of strategies to meet the ever-changing needs of students. It is our hope that the strategies that we have suggested will provide a basis from which you can work. We suggest that you work through each of these strategies, then combine ideas from several in inventing your own strategies to guide children in creating their own music.

CREATING ACCOMPANIMENTS FOR SONGS

One way children can create their own music is by creating accompaniments for the songs they sing. Creating accompaniments is more than merely "playing along" as the class sings the song. It should be a thoughtful process in which the student selects rhythmic and/or melodic patterns from the song, modifies them in the process of inventing new patterns, and organizes the new patterns in such a way as to fit with the song itself.

It is extremely important that students know a song well before attempting to create accompaniments for it. Accompaniment patterns may be as simple as the steady beat or the metric beat of the song, or they may be more sophisticated, using word rhythms or short melodic patterns from within the song.

In the initial stages of creating accompaniments, you may direct students to explore specific patterns from the song as possibilities, or students may discover patterns on their own. During the inventive stage, students may combine aspects of several patterns, forming new patterns, or they may invent new patterns that complement or contrast with patterns found in the song. Although the song itself provides an overall structure, the final phase of creating accompaniments involves organizing the invented patterns with the song. The newly created accompaniment may include an introduction and a coda, for example.

The most effective accompaniments are usually thin in texture (two to four parts), so we suggest using these strategies for small groups of students. Also, because a performance of the song itself is necessary, creating accompaniment strategies for small groups are most effectively combined with large-group performances.

The Angel Band

Accompanying A Song

"Angel Band"
Making Music Your Own, Book I, p. 12

Lower Grades

Instructional Objectives

1. Students will select instruments to use in accompaniment.
2. Students will explore long and short rhythmic relationships.
3. Students will select rhythm patterns to use in accompaniments.
4. Students will create and perform a rhythmic accompaniment to the song.

Environment

The entire class can work together in an autocratic environment for this activity. Students should be able to sing the song with confidence before attempting to create an accompaniment. Much of the initial work can be done through clapping; however, three or four percussion instruments with contrasting timbres should be available as well as a chalkboard or large sheets of paper for notating the word rhythms. Ten to fifteen minutes should be ample for this activity.

Initial Procedures

1. Sing the song with the class, all clapping on the first beat of each measure.
2. Sing the verse again, clapping on each number word.
3. Discuss the different ways of clapping. Ask, "When we clapped the number words, did we clap a steady beat, or did we stop sometimes?" (Repeat the song as necessary.)
4. Lead the class in singing the verse again, at the same time clapping the steady beat.
5. Ask, "Did we clap more that time? Was our clapping faster or slower? If I were to draw lines for clapping sounds, would they be long or short?"

First Beat: There was ‾one, there were ‾two, there were ‾three little

‾Angels,

Number Words: There was ‾one, there were ‾two, there were ‾three little

‾Angels,

Steady Beat: There was one, there were two, there were three little

Angels,

6. Invite students to select any one of these ways to clap or to think of new ways to clap while all sing the refrain of the song.

7. Invite two or three students who you noticed clapping in different ways to select instruments that "would sound good in the Angel Band."

8. Lead the class in singing the entire song, having students with instruments create their own accompaniment for the refrain.

Extended Procedures

1. Have students use different ways of playing for the verse and refrain.

2. Include the word rhythm

there was one

as a possibility.

3. Have students "think" the refrain as they listen to the instrumentalists create their accompaniments, all singing the verse together again to end the composition.

Modifications for Exceptional Learners

1. Select large, easy-to-hold instruments and set slow to moderate tempos that will assure success for students with poor motor coordination.

2. Use large cards with number pictures as well as number symbols to help slow learners recall the numerical sequence of the text.

3. Use the refrain of this song in a similar way to help students learn the sequence of days of the week. ("Wasn't that a band, Sunday morning . . . Monday morning," etc.)

Evaluation

1. Did the children's performance and their discussion reveal an awareness of the relationships between long and short sounds?

2. What criteria did students use to select instruments?

3. Did the accompaniment created by the students reflect an understanding of the relationship of long and short sounds?

Mary Ann

1. All day,— all night, Miss Mar-y Ann,———
2. If you— come to— this is-land fine,———

Down by— the sea - side,— sift-ing sand;———
You'll love— the sea and— bright sun-shine,———

All the lit - tle chil-dren— love Mar - y Ann,———
You will be— en - chant-ed — with this fair land,———

You, too— will love her,— Miss Mar -y Ann.———
You'll be— be - witched by— Miss Mar -y Ann.———

SOURCE: From Eunice Boardman and Beth Landis, *Exploring Music*, Book 5 (New York: Holt, Rinehart and Winston, 1975), pp. 190-191. Used with permission.

ANALYSIS OF MUSIC FOR PERFORMING

TITLE: "MARY ANN"
SOURCE: *EXPLORING MUSIC,* BOOK 5, pp. 190–191

MUSICAL KNOWLEDGE THAT CAN BE DEVELOPED
    MELODY
    RHYTHM   *Syncopated rhythm, calypso*
    TIMBRE
    HARMONY   *I–V^7 chord relationships*
    DYNAMICS
    FORM
MUSICAL SKILLS THAT CAN BE DEVELOPED
    SINGING   *Melody of song*
    PLAYING   *Calypso rhythms on percussion instruments*
    MOVING
    LISTENING   *To layers of accompaniment*
    CREATING   *Rhythmic accompaniment*
    READING   *Rhythmic notation*
    DESCRIBING
GENERAL KNOWLEDGE THAT CAN BE DEVELOPED
    OF THE WORLD   *West Indies*
    OF RELATIONSHIPS   *A complex whole is often made of relatively simple parts.*
    OF FEELINGS   *Self-satisfaction in creating accompaniments*
GENERAL SKILLS THAT CAN BE DEVELOPED
    PERCEIVING   *Relationships of parts to one another*
    COMMUNICATING
    SOCIAL SKILLS   *Working in a group*
    PHYSICAL SKILLS   *Small-muscle coordination in playing instruments*
    OTHER

Creating Accompaniments

"Mary Ann"
Exploring Music, Book 5, pp. 190–191

Upper Grades

Instructional Objectives

1. Students will read calypso pattern rhythm notation consisting of quarter and eighth notes.
2. Students will select patterns to be used in accompaniment of the song "Mary Ann."
3. Students will organize patterns, determining which will begin, which will be second, and so forth.

Environment

To begin this experience, the entire class should review the song. The creative experience will be most effective with a small group of students working in an open environment, returning to the large group for a final performance. Five or six percussion instruments should be available. If students do not know the song well, a recording might be helpful. Ten to fifteen minutes should be ample for the creating activity.

Initial Procedures

1. After the entire class sings the song, assign a small group of students to create a percussion accompaniment.
2. Observe the students as they work out the notation given on the printed page. The rests may present problems, especially in the last line. If so, suggest playing

   first, then omit the third eighth note, playing the patterns as written:

3. After students have explored all the patterns on the page, they must decide which to use as accompaniment. Suggest that some sing the song while others play one pattern at a time (or play along with the recording). Ask, "Which one sounds best?"
4. Suggest adding two accompaniment parts. Ask, "'Which will be the second part?"

5. Explore the sound of three and four parts together. Can students still hear individual parts?

6. Decide how many and which parts will be used as accompaniment today.

7. Decide how accompaniment will begin—will one part start as an introduction, adding one part at a time and then the melody, or will all parts start at once?

8. Decide how the composition will end—will all parts stop at the end of the song, or will some instruments continue as a coda?

9. Practice the accompaniment in the small group.

10. Return to the large group. Have the entire class sing the song while members of the small group play the accompaniment they have created.

Extended Procedures

1. Suggest to students that they create new rhythm patterns for the accompaniment by combining the given patterns in new ways— one measure from line three followed by one measure from line four, for example.

2. Suggest that students find word rhythms in the text of the song and develop accompaniments from them—"All day, all night," for example.

Modifications for Exceptional Learners

1. Talented students may be able to play the given rhythms on an autoharp, thus combining rhythmic and harmonic accompaniments.

2. Students unable to read notation or with poor coordination can play the steady beat (same as the first line) or play on the first beat of each measure.

Evaluation

1. Were students able to read rhythmic notation?
   a) Which patterns presented difficulties?
   b) Which students appeared to have particular difficulty?

2. Did the accompaniment created by the students reflect an understanding of the process of selecting and organizing patterns of sound?

CREATING SONGS

Children can gain much musical knowledge and skill from creating their own songs. Very young children often invent songs as part of their play. Perhaps it is only as they are taught "songs of others" that they begin to feel their own songs are inadequate and become inhibited in creating songs. Continued experiences in creating songs may help children realize the value of their own creations and develop a new sense of self-worth.

Songwriters usually begin with a text. The words of a song provide a basis for rhythm, thus limiting some of the choices which students must make when they write songs. Pitches for the word rhythms can be improvised by singing or by playing on a xylophone, tone bells, or a piano. If pitched instruments are used, we suggest setting further limits within which students are to work. For the first attempts at creating songs, two pitches may be adequate. As the students gain more experience, the choices may be expanded to three, four, or five pitches and later to the entire scale. Xylophones with removable bars or tone bells have an advantage in that you can make available to students only those pitches among which they are to choose. You can, however, indicate the pitches to be used on permanent-bar xylophones or the piano by placing a small piece of tape on the keys which students are to use. We remind you to be aware of children's singing ranges in selecting pitches for creating songs. Working from middle-C and A is generally appropriate for children in lower grades. This range can be expanded to the C octave for middle and upper grades.

Pet Songs

Lower Grades

Instructional Objectives

1. Students will write short statements about pets.
2. Students will invent pitch patterns for the word rhythms of the statements about pets.

Environment

A small group of six to eight students is preferable. Initial experiences will require much direction on your part, but after children become familiar with the procedures and comfortable with vocal improvisation they can create songs on their own. A xylophone, piano, or tone bells with E, G, and A clearly marked will be needed for this activity. Approximately two minutes for each child in the group should be allotted.

Initial Procedures

1. Play marked pitches (E, G, and A) as children sing syllables or nonsense words.
2. Invite a student to invent a pattern using these three tones. Discuss the pattern. Ask, "Did it go up? Down? Did any tones stay the same?"
3. Suggest that students make up songs about their pets. First, have them think of the words, considering the following questions. (You may need to help students write the words.)
   a) What is your pet?
   a) What is its name?
   c) What color is it?
   d) What does it eat?
   e) What special things does it do?
4. Help students write short sentences about their pets.
5. Have individual students first *say* the words, then play the words on the three marked tones. Provide time for students to explore several pitch patterns and select one that sounds best.
6. Have all students in the group sing the pet song.

Extended Procedures

1. Help students notate songs using either traditional notation or letter names. Place the songs in a book in the music center so that other students can play and sing.
2. Expand the text of the song to include more things about a pet.

Expand the choice of pitches from three to the five notes of a pentatonic (F, G, A, C, D) scale.

3. Using similar procedures, create songs about holidays, a field trip, or a story the children have read.

Modifications for Exceptional Learners

1. Identify a single tone within the students' pitch range and have students with tone-matching difficulties create pet songs as single tone chants.

2. Construct a sentence using words with problem sounds for children with speech difficulties and have them create melodies and sing their own songs.

Evaluation

1. Did students explore several pitch possibilities before finalizing a selection for their pet songs?

2. Did the process of creating a song reflect an understanding of high and low pitches? Of stepwise and skipwise movement?

3. Were students able to match pitches vocally?

4. Did students utilize word rhythms in their compositions?

Setting Poems to Music

Middle Grades

Instructional Objectives

1. Students will invent pitch patterns for the word rhythms of a poem.
2. Students will create a melody for the poem.
3. Students will sing the melody they create.
4. Students will devise notation for their composition.

Environment

This activity can be successful in either a democratic or open environment. In a large group, most students will be performers rather than creators, but there will be sufficient activity for all. Melodic instruments, preferably Orff-type instruments set to play C, D, E, G, A, will be needed as well as some space for physical movement. A poem should be selected before the activity. The poem should be in regular meter and may be one from the literature or one created by a student. Students should know the poem from memory or have printed copies for this activity. Large sheets of art paper and colored markers will be needed for the notational activity.

Initial Procedures

1. Read or recite the poem together, clapping the steady beat.
2. Repeat the poem, stepping to the steady beat.
3. Recite the poem, clapping the word rhythms.
4. Repeat the poem, stepping to the word rhythms.
5. Discuss the meaning of the words. Are there any that suggest specific aspects of melody—upward or downward motion? Small steps or large leaps? Repeated tones?
6. Working with small sections of the poem (one or two lines), have the entire group recite and clap word rhythms while students with instruments explore possible melodic patterns.
7. Listen to each melodic pattern. Ask, "Which seems to fit these words best? Is it an interesting melody?"
8. Repeat the melody several times, students listening to the melodic movement.
9. All sing the melody.
10. Using traditional notation, letter names, or numbers, notate the melody.
11. Continue working in this manner until a melody has been created for the entire poem.

12. Evaluate the musical composition. Ask, "Is there some repetition? Is there musical contrast? Does the most exciting part of the music occur at the same place as the most exciting part of the text?"

Extended Procedures

1. On another day, create accompaniment patterns for the song based on the steady beat, the metric beat, or repeated word patterns.
2. Create a book of songs composed by the class. Perform some of them for a parent group.

Modifications for Exceptional Learners

1. Students taking piano lessons may be able to improvise a piano accompaniment for the song.
2. An outstanding student may be able to create a descant or countermelody for the song.
3. Students with short attention spans may need to work with single-line proverbs rather than with an entire poem. If students have difficulty choosing from five pitches, limit their choices to three.

Evaluation

1. Were students able to differentiate between the steady beat and the word rhythms of the poem?
2. Did students' exploration of melodic possibilities reflect an understanding of high and low pitches? Of stepwise and skipwise movement?
3. Were students able to sing the melodies that they created?
4. Did the notation devised by the students accurately symbolize the sounds of their compositions?

CREATING WITH ENVIRONMENTAL SOUNDS

We pointed out earlier that any sound has the potential for becoming music. Many contemporary composers are using everyday sounds from the environment as sources for musical compositions. Working with environmental sounds helps children become more keenly aware of the sounds around them and of the qualities of those sounds. The performing skills needed for working with environmental sounds are usually quite different than those needed to play traditional instruments, making these strategies appealing to those students who do not feel successful when working with traditional music. It is important, however, to approach creating with environmental sounds as music making rather than as noise making. Listening to recorded compositions that have been created with environmental sounds may help students develop a more serious attitude toward the activity.

The source of environmental sounds is endless. It is therefore important that you establish clear limitations on those with which children are to work. We have suggested a strategy for working with "paper sounds" as an example of an activity in which children will explore, invent, and organize the sounds that can be made with a single sheet of paper. Similar experiences can be provided in working with other materials. A battery-operated tape recorder can be an important tool in working with environmental sounds. Students can collect sounds from around the school, the playground, or at home and organize these sounds by physically manipulating the tape. (See p. 335.)

In most cases, traditional notation will not be useful for encoding environmental sound compositions. Students will need to create their own form of notation. We have found colors, geometric shapes, and other graphic designs to be especially helpful. We have also found that creating notation for musical compositions provides an opportunity for students to integrate experiences in the visual arts.

Paper Sounds

Middle Grades

Instructional Objectives

1. Students will explore the qualities of rhythm, dynamics, and timbre that can be produced by a sheet of paper.
2. Students will invent patterns that describe contrasting feelings.
3. Students will arrange patterns into a musical composition.

Environment

An autocratic environment in which you lead the entire class in a creative activity is effective. This strategy could easily be adopted for small groups or individual activity; however, students should be seated in chairs with sufficient "arm room" to manipulate a large sheet of paper. A number of discarded newspapers (several full pages for each student) will be needed. Five to ten minutes is sufficient for this activity.

Initial Procedures

1. Distribute one sheet of newspaper to each student while discussing the sheets as musical instruments. Discuss ways of making sound with paper: shaking, crumpling, tearing, rubbing over a smooth surface, and other ways the children may suggest. Musicians know how to control instruments so that they make sounds only when the players want them to. (Replace paper as necessary for individual children.)
2. Lead students in exploring sound possibilities, giving the following instructions:
   a) Make the softest sound you can on your paper instrument.
   b) Let the sound get a little louder.
   c) Make a very loud sound.
   d) Make a sound so short that it lasts only as long as it takes you to wink your eye.
   e) Make three short sounds in a row.
   f) Make a sound that lasts as long as it takes me to count to ten.
   g) Make sleepy sounds.
   h) Make happy sounds.
   i) Make angry sounds.
3. Accept suggestions from students for an organization for a composition. Find a way to notate the sequence using words, numbers, or other symbols. Use the following questions to elicit students' ideas about organization:
   a) What sounds should we have first?
   b) How long (in seconds) should this section be?

c) What kind of sounds should come next?

d) Will that be the end of the composition?

Extended Procedures

1. Tape-record the composition for further evaluation and refinement.

2. Explore a greater variety of paper sounds by using different kinds of paper—heavy art paper, tissue paper, wrapping paper, foil paper, and so on.

3. Invite individuals and/or small groups to create paper compositions and perform them for the rest of the class.

4. Hold the paper so that it touches a microphone of a tape recorder while performing. Listen to the amplified sounds of the paper.

Evaluation

1. Did students' exploration of environmental sounds reflect an awareness of rhythm, dynamics, and timbre?

2. Did patterns invented by students describe contrasting feelings?

3. Did the compositions of the students reflect an understanding of the principles of repetition and contrast?

4. Did individual students appear to have particular weaknesses in any of the above areas?

Animal Sounds

Lower Grades

Instructional Objectives

1. Students will explore the sounds made by three different animals.
2. Students will demonstrate an awareness of high and low pitches.
3. Students will organize animal sounds into a musical composition.

Environment

This activity is designed for an autocratic environment in which either you or a student may be the leader. Any number of students may be the creators/ performers, but this activity will be most effective with a large group of students. Two pictures of each of three different animals will be needed. Students should be informally seated so that they can easily see the pictures. Five minutes is ample time for this activity.

Initial Procedures

1. Show the class one of the animal pictures. Ask students to make the sound this animal might make. "Could you make that sound at a very low pitch? At a very high pitch? Can you make that sound start low and get higher? Can you make that sound start high and get lower?"
2. After giving students the opportunity to explore the sound possibilities, repeat the above procedures with the other two animal pictures.
3. Arrange the animal pictures so that at least one sound occurs twice. Instruct students to decide if they like the sounds best at high pitches, low pitches, or moving up and down. They should perform the sound in the way they decide is best when you point to the picture.
4. Lead the class in a performance of the composition by pointing to the pictures.
5. Invite a student to rearrange the pictures and to lead the class in a performance of the new composition.

Extended Procedures

1. Add dynamic variation to the composition by placing, under each animal picture, cards marked musical symbols for loud or soft.
2. Add contrasts of duration to the composition by placing, under the animal pictures, cards marked with the words *fast* and *slow*.

3. Add the element of harmony by placing pictures above one another and dividing the class so that two sounds are performed at the same time.

Modifications for Exceptional Learners

Beginning the experience with contrasts of loud and soft may be more appropriate than contrasts of high and low for children with perceptual difficulties.

Evaluation

1. Did students' exploration of animal sounds demonstrate an awareness of different timbres?

2. Did students' exploration of animal sounds demonstrate an awareness of pitch levels?

3. Did students' composition demonstrate an awareness of the principles of contrast and repetition? Of musical form?

Creating with Environmental Sounds: Waste Can Sounds

Upper Grades

Instructional Objectives

1. Students will explore some qualities of metal.
2. Students will explore pitch, duration, and timbre of sounds that can be made on a metal waste can.
3. Students will invent patterns of sound from those made on the waste can.
4. Students will organize the sounds made on the waste can into a musical composition.

Environment

Ideally, this experience would be initiated by a small group of students "playing with sounds" in an informal environment. We are suggesting, however, that you first use an autocratic environment in leading exploration and then give students freedom to invent and organize their own compositions. A large metal waste can and an assortment of items to use as "mallets" will be needed. Fifteen minutes should be provided for this activity.

Initial Procedures

1. Ask students what different sounds can be made on the waste can. Give them about five minutes to work, returning to listen to the sounds.
2. Lead a discussion classifying the sounds. Ask, "Are there sounds with different pitches? Can sounds of different timbres be made? Are all sounds the same length? Are different dynamic levels possible?"
3. Suggest that students select three sounds and then decide on a sequence and a way to connect the sounds.
4. Suggest students find ways to vary the pattern:
   a) Reverse the order of the sounds.
   b) Play the sounds faster or slower.
   c) Play the sounds on another part of the can or with another "mallet" to change the timbre.
   d) Find new ways to connect the sounds.
5. Have students select several patterns and combine them into a composition. Which will be first, second, and so on?
6. Perform the composition for the class.

Extended Procedures

1. Prescribe a traditional musical form such as ABA or rondo for a composition.
2. Create compositions using similar procedures on other materials— water glasses, a wooden box, and so forth.
3. Tape-record the composition, playing it back on another day while creating a second part on another sound source.

Evaluation

1. Did students' exploration of sounds produced on the metal waste can demonstrate an awareness of pitch, of duration, and of timbre?
2. Did the patterns invented by the students contain contrasts of pitch, of duration, and of timbre?
3. Did the students' composition demonstrate an awareness of musical form?

MUSIC FOR DRAMA

Creating music for drama can be a meaningful classroom activity. Children experience much dramatic music on television and in films. At times it may be useful to analyze "sound tracks," employing some of the listening strategies, prior to creating music for drama; this will help students become more aware of the importance of music in drama.

It is important to point out to students the difference between music for drama and mere sound effects. Sound effects reinforce the drama, but music helps carry the action forward. Sound effects have little interest or meaning in themselves, while dramatic music frequently can stand on its own. (This is the case with many sound-track albums.) Music for drama may begin with a sound effect, but students should explore a broadening range of possibilities for that sound. Patterns that use the sound in interesting ways can be invented. Those patterns can then be organized so that they express the feelings of a character or carry forward the action of the drama through an overture, song, or music for a dance.

Creating An Overture

Upper Grades

Instructional Objectives

1. Students will research geographical features of a particular location.
2. Students will identify sound qualities that establish the location and general mood of a drama.
3. Students will select sound sources that describe the location and general mood of a drama.
4. Students will invent musical patterns that describe the setting and general mood of a drama.
5. Students will organize musical patterns into an overture for a drama.

Environment

A small group of students, working in a democratic environment, can carry out this activity. The drama may be one from the literature or one that has been created by the students. In either case, students must be generally familiar with the setting, the characters, and the plot. A variety of rhythmic and melodic instruments should be available. Fifteen to twenty minutes may be as long as students can productively work on this task. If necessary, the activity may be carried out over several days.

Initial Procedures

1. Review the drama, listing the location, characters, and main action.
2. Suggest that students research the location, developing a list of facts about the setting of the play—in the city or in the forest? Long ago, right now, or sometime in the future? In the United States or in Spain?
3. Develop a list of sound qualities that would describe the location. Ask, "What sounds might you expect to hear there? What kinds of pitches, rhythms, timbres, and dynamics?
4. Select instruments or other sound sources to represent those sounds.
5. Invent several sound patterns that describe the location, characters, and action of the drama.
6. Determine a sequence for the patterns so that they give a hint of the drama that is to follow.
7. Find a way to connect the patterns.
8. Practice the entire composition several times, then tape record it.

9. Play the recording and evaluate it. Does it introduce the drama by suggesting something about the location, characters, and actions?

Extended Procedures

1. Create music for each character and/or event in the drama. Afterwards, create an overture that includes some musical ideas from each of the other musical selections created for the drama.

2. Compare the overture with "title music" from a film or a TV program. Ask, "In what ways are the two compositions similar? In what ways are they different?"

Modifications for Exceptional Learners

1. Since there are many tasks to be performed even within a small group, be certain each student has a task that is within his or her ability. Some may perform rather simple parts, others more difficult parts.

Evaluation

1. Were the students able to describe geographical and other physical characteristics of the setting of the story?

2. Did the sound sources selected by the students symbolize aspects of the setting appropriately?

3. Did the students use the setting and mood of the story as criteria in selecting sounds and in inventing patterns?

4. Did the overture created by the students demonstrate an awareness of musical form?

5. Did the overture created by the students successfully establish the mood and/or location of the drama?

Music for a Character

Instructional Objectives

1. Students will select sounds to represent a character in a story or drama.
2. Students will invent patterns to describe that character.
3. Students will organize patterns into a composition that expresses an event from the story.

Environment

Students should be working individually or in small groups in a democratic environment. A variety of classroom instruments and other sound sources should be available as well as a tape recorder. A fifteen- to thirty-minute time block will usually be necessary, but it may be spread over several days. Students should be familiar with the story to be used.

Initial Procedures

1. Guide individuals or groups to each select a character with which to work.
2. Assist students as they list important features of each character: Age? Size? How would he move? How does she feel about herself? About others? What is happening?
3. Encourage students to explore available sound sources in order to find sound that best describes the features listed.
4. Invent short patterns that describe some action of the character— walking, running, laughing, and so on.
5. Expand patterns by thinking of the actions of the character. Consider questions like these: How would he walk when happy? When sad? How would she sound when she met another character?
6. Organize patterns in sequence to describe a portion of the story. Encourage students to repeat patterns to emphasize a particular action or to vary a pattern—get faster or louder, for example—to illustrate changes in the feelings of the character.

Extended Procedures

1. Tape-record the "compositions" for future evaluation and refinement.
2. Play the tape as students act out the drama. Ask, "Does the music fit the action of the story? Does the music suggest the movement of the character?"

Modification for Exceptional Learners

1. Students with outstanding language skills may be able to write poems that express the ideas of a character. The poems may then be set to music and sung by the character in the drama.

2. Students with limited ability may be able to work with only one characteristic of a character—size, weight, or a feeling.

3. Students lacking skills necessary to create patterns on instruments may be able to improvise vocal sounds to express features of a character.

Evaluation

1. Did the students thoroughly consider the character in selecting a sound source and in inventing sound patterns?

2. Did each composition communicate some essential idea or feeling from the drama?

3. Did students gain confidence in working with sound in this experience?

INSTRUMENTAL IMPROVISATION

Children enjoy playing instruments. At almost every opportunity they will play with the sounds of instruments, exploring possibilities and inventing sound patterns. All too frequently we as teachers prescribe exactly what patterns are to be played, denying children the joy of creating their own music.

Many of the other strategies that we have suggested call for the use of classroom instruments or could be easily adapted for instrumental playing. In this section, we will suggest a few additional strategies in which children can select, invent, and organize sounds produced on instruments commonly found in the elementary classroom.

When planning experiences in which children will create music for instruments, you should carefully consider which instruments will be available. At times you may need to preselect particular kinds of instruments. If students are to explore high and low pitches, for example, they should use only those instruments that have clearly identifiable pitches—the pitch of a drum or claves is difficult to determine. Similarly, if one of your goals is to have students learn about long and short sounds, you must be certain the instruments available are capable of producing a sustained sound.

It is also important that students remember that they are working with *musical instruments* and not noise makers as they explore sound possibilities. You can do much to establish an attitude of respect by the way you handle and store the instruments. Treat the tambourine as you would a fine violin, and you will greatly increase the possibility that your students will do likewise.

Instrumental improvisation is generally most effective when students can work individually or in small groups. There are seldom enough instruments available for an entire class to play at once, and the level of sound produced by many instruments playing would prevent individuals from hearing, selecting, and inventing subtle variations of sound patterns. We suggest that you provide a music center in your classroom in which you place a few carefully selected instruments and provide the opportunity for students to work through these and other strategies for instrumental improvisation.

Fast Sounds—Slow Sounds

FAST SOUNDS—SLOW SOUNDS

Sometimes you run.
Sometimes you walk.

How do you move in your classroom?
How do you move to win a race?
How do you move when you are happy and excited?
How do you move when you are tired and sleepy?

Music moves too—sometimes FAST and sometimes SLOW.

Make a drum sound happy and excited.
Does it sound FAST or SLOW?

Make a drum sound tired and sleepy.
Does it sound FAST or SLOW?

Make a triangle sound happy and excited.
Does it sound FAST or SLOW?

Make a triangle sound tired and sleepy.
Does it sound FAST or SLOW?

You and several classmates use these instruments to compose
music that sounds like this:

FAST
SLOW—FAST
FAST—SLOW—FAST

SOURCE: From Robert Choate et al., *Enjoying Music*, New Dimensions in Music (New York: American Book Co., 1976), p. 33. Used with permission.

Fast and Slow

Enjoying Music, New Dimensions in Music, p. 33

Lower Grades

Instructional Objectives

1. Students will explore the speed of sounds.
2. Students will explore the timbres of sounds.
3. Students will organize sounds in a "fast-slow" composition.

Environment

The initial experience should be teacher-directed. The movement activities should take place in a large open space which will permit free movement. The creating activity can take place with either the entire class working in a formal classroom setting or with small groups working in an informal learning center. A drum and a triangle will be needed. Five to ten minutes should be sufficient for this experience.

Initial Procedures

1. Ask students to walk around the room. Select the walking tempo of one student and play the walking beat on the drum.
2. Select one student to run across the room. Play drumbeats to match the running tempo of the student.
3. Play the running tempo on the drum, inviting all students to run in time with the drum.
4. Alternate walking and running tempos on the drum, with the students moving appropriately.
5. Invite a student to play the drum while the other students move to the appropriate beat.
6. Repeat the above sequence with happy movements, tired movements, excited movements, sad movements, and so on.
7. Provide the opportunity for students to explore fast and slow sounds on both the triangle and the drum.
8. You or a student can lead the group in performing the composition on page 319 by pointing to the word *fast* or *slow*, indicating the way in which the performers should respond. The performance may be on one timbre (drum) or on both drum and triangle combined.

Extended Procedures

1. Make a tape recording of the composition and have students move to their own music.
2. Write the words *fast* and *slow* on several large cards. Have students develop their own organizational patterns of fast and slow sequences for the composition.

Modifications for Exceptional Learners

1. Use a large drum (perhaps a bass drum) and a large cymbal (instead of a triangle) for students with poorly developed motor skills.
2. Orthopedically handicapped students may not be able to engage in the suggested movement activities, but they may be able to make shadows move fast and slow to the beat of music. Colored cellophane on the stage of an overhead projector will provide an excellent light source.

Evaluation

1. Did students' movements reflect an awareness of fast and slow tempos?
2. Were students able to adjust movements to the tempo of the drum? Which students were not?
3. Did students' exploration of instruments demonstrate an awareness of fast and slow tempos?
4. Did students' explorations reveal an awareness of different timbres?
5. Were students able to organize compositions that demonstrated awareness of fast and slow tempos?

Sound and Silence

SOUND AND SILENCE

All music is SOUND and SILENCE

A person who uses sounds and silences to create musical ideas is a COMPOSER. A composer uses many different kinds of sounds.

What kinds of sounds can you make?

. . . sounds with your mouth,

. . . sounds with your hands,

. . . sounds with your feet,

. . . sounds with a drum,

. . . sounds with a triangle,

. . . sounds with a piano.

Some sounds are LOUD sounds. Some sounds are SOFT sounds.

Can you make loud sounds with your mouth? Soft sounds?
Can you make loud sounds with your hands? Soft sounds?
Can you make loud sounds with your feet? Soft sounds?
Can you make loud and soft sounds with a drum? A triangle? A piano?

YOU are a composer when you arrange sounds and silences to create musical ideas. With five classmates, select three LOUD sounds and three SOFT sounds. Assign one sound to each classmate. Working together, compose a musical idea that sounds:

LOUD— SOFT
SOFT—LOUD
LOUD—SOFT—LOUD

SOURCE: From Robert Choate et al., *Enjoying Music*, New Dimensions in Music (New York: American Book Co., 1976), p. 27. Used with permission.

Loud and Soft

Enjoying Music, New Dimensions in Music, p. 27

Lower Grades

Instructional Objectives

1. Students will explore the timbres of sounds.
2. Students will explore the dynamic variations of sounds.
3. Students will organize sounds in a "loud-soft" composition.

Environment

The initial experience should be teacher-directed; however, students may be able to work in small groups in an open-environment music center, following the instructions given on page 322. A drum, triangle, and piano should be available, but other instruments may be substituted if necessary. Five to ten minutes should be sufficient for this experience.

Initial Experiences

1. Invite students to explore, one at a time, possible sounds that can be made by the mouth, hands, feet, and so on.
2. Request that students explore, one at a time, the loud sounds and soft sounds that are possible from each sound source.
3. Discuss the role of a composer in arranging sounds in an order that makes a composition.
4. Have each student select a sound source for use in the composition.
5. You or a student can lead the group in performing the composition on page 322 by pointing to the word *loud* or *soft* indicating the dynamic level for the performers.

Extended Procedures

1. Make cards with pictures of the sound sources, such as those on page 322, to place above the words *loud* and *soft*, thus organizing the composition by timbre as well as by dynamic level.
2. After working with extreme contrasts of dynamics, create a composition with subtle dynamic shadings—very soft to soft, medium loud to loud.

Modifications for Exceptional Learners

For children having difficulty reading the words *loud* and *soft*, rewrite them on cards using large letters for *LOUD*, smaller letters for *soft*.

Evaluation

1. Did the students' composition demonstrate an awareness of differences in timbre and dynamics?
2. Did the students' composition demonstrate emerging performing skill?
3. Did the students enjoy the experience?
4. Did the students feel pride in their composition?

Echo Patterns

Middle Grades

Instructional Objectives

Given eight-beat rhythm patterns, students will invent melodic patterns for the rhythms.

Environment

An autocratic environment is effective. Ideally, each student should have a melodic instrument set to play the pentatonic scale. If only a few melodic instruments are available, however, other students can play rhythm instruments or clap. Three of four minutes is sufficient for this activity. It is an effective introduction to other *playing* activities.

Initial Procedures

1. Begin with a very brief period of echo clapping.
2. Lead to echo clapping of eight-beat patterns such as the following:

3. Continue to lead the echo clapping and invite students to echo responses by inventing pentatonic melodies for rhythms.

Extended Procedures

1. Remove the rhythm restrictions. Students' response should still be eight beats long, but they may also invent the rhythm pattern to fit within the eight beats. (The leader plays eight even beats.)
2. Invite a student to be the leader.
3. Divide the class, perhaps on the basis of sound classification—wooden sounds, metal sounds, high sounds, and low sounds, for example. Have one group be the leader, the second group the "echo."
4. Select students to perform as soloists. Have the entire group play eight beats. Soloists should then respond, the entire group should play eight beats, the second soloist should invent an eight-beat response, and so forth.
5. On other days, use different length patterns—eleven beats, fifteen beats, and so on.

Modifications for Exceptional Learners

1. Advanced students should be encouraged to notate the patterns they invent.

2. Students with poor coordination should have the largest tone bells and mallets.

3. Generally slower tempos will be needed for students with poor muscular control.

Evaluation

1. Were students able to echo the rhythms that you clapped?
   a) What rhythms presented problems?
   b) What students had problems?

2. Were students able to invent new rhythm patterns to fit within the eight-beat limitation?

3. Did the solos of the students contain a variety of rhythms?

Prepared Autoharp

Middle Grades

Instructional Objectives

1. Students will explore pitch, timbre, and duration of sounds on a modified autoharp.
2. Students will invent patterns and organize a composition for a prepared autoharp.

Environment

This activity is best suited for individuals or groups of two to three students working in an open environment. An autoharp and a variety of objects, such as paper, a plastic ruler, paper clips, and so forth, should be available. Ten to fifteen minutes should be sufficient for this activity.

Initial Procedures

1. Demonstrate ways to change the sound of the autoharp by placing various objects on the strings.
2. Suggest that students explore a variety of sound possibilities by strumming chords and playing individual strings when
   a) Paper has been placed on the strings
   b) Metal has been placed on the strings
   c) Plastic has been placed on the strings
3. Suggest that students select three sounds they like best and organize them in a composition. Ask, "Which will be first? Which will be second? How will the sounds be connected? Will there be an introduction?"
4. Provide time for students to work on the composition and perform it for the class.

Extended Procedures

1. Experience a composition made from similar sounds by listening to Henry Cowell's *Banshee*.
2. Suggest that students create their own ghost story which can be told through the sound patterns performed on a prepared autoharp.

Evaluation

1. Did students' exploration of the autoharp demonstrate an awareness of pitch, timbre, and duration? Which students seemed to lack an understanding of many of these concepts?
2. Did the composition contain patterns and reflect an awareness of musical form?
3. Did the students enjoy the experience?
4. Did the students feel pride in their composition?
5. Did the students work well together?

An Event for Six Players

AN EVENT FOR SIX PLAYERS

What would happen if . . .
                you played the events in this circle?

Choose any order. Try going **faster** when the staff goes **up** and **slower** when it goes **down**.

Think about which instruments you will choose.
Will you play with *legato* or *staccato* sounds?
Will all the instruments play all the time?
Will they start and stop at different times?

SOURCE: From Eunice Boardman and Beth Landis, *Exploring Music*, Book 5 (New York: Holt, Rinehart and Winston, 1975), p. 37. Used with permission.

An Event for Six Players

Exploring Music, Book 5, p. 37

Upper Grades

Instructional Objectives

1. Students will explore timbres, pitches, dynamics, and rhythms.
2. Given notational and graphic patterns, students will translate patterns into sound patterns

Environment

An open environment in which students work in small groups is most desirable. Some traditional pitched instruments, as well as several nontraditional sound sources, should be available. Ten minutes should be ample for the initial procedures.

Initial Procedures

1. Present students with the printed page, then suggest they read and follow directions.
2. Observe and listen to the students' discussion. Do they seem to understand what to do?
3. Help students select parts to play. Can they find six different parts (designs) on the page?
4. Students may need help in identifying pitch names of musical notation. Suggest they write note names on another piece of paper.
5. Encourage students to explore sound possibilities considering the questions at the bottom of the handout.
6. Encourage students to tape-record their composition and then listen to and evaluate the performance. Ask, "Can you hear patterns of pitch, dynamics, and rhythm? Can you hear contrasts of pitch?"

Extended Procedures

1. On another day, encourage students to extend their composition by
   a) Repeating their original parts
   b) Exchanging parts (playing a different line on the same instrument) for a contrasting section
   c) Playing the pattern backwards

2. Suggest that students find other visual patterns to "perform":
    a) Perform the lines, colors, and shapes of painting.
    b) Perform the patterns found on a shirt or blouse.
    c) Perform a graph found in a math book.
3. Suggest that students create their own notation using paint or cut paper, then perform the composition.

Modifications for Exceptional Learners

1. Invite students who play band or orchestral instruments to perform the composition on their instruments.

2. Students with perception problems may have difficulty identifying and following just one pattern on this page. Reproduce each part on a separate large sheet of paper, simplifying where necessary. We suggest using different geometric shapes in various sizes and colors (similar to the ovals in this notation) rather than any of the traditional notational patterns.

Evaluation

1. Did students' explorations demonstrate an understanding of pitch, timbre, dynamics and rhythms?

2. Were students able to translate printed symbols to sound? Which students had difficulty with the note names of the printed notation?

3. Did students' composition reflect musical decision making (rather than chance noise making)?

VOCAL IMPROVISATION

The voice is a sound source accessible to almost everyone. Very young children play with vocal sounds when they are learning to talk. Much of the current popular music contains vocal sounds which, if taken out of context, are meaningless, but they are integral parts of these musical compositions and may be considered a kind of "playing with vocal sounds." Children, particularly in early grades, frequently invent word-rhythm patterns to accompany their play. For these reasons, creating music with the voice can be a natural experience for children.

There is, indeed, a subtle distinction between creating songs and vocal improvisation. We have arbitrarily classified *songs* as compositions in which the words are meant to be heard and understood. *Vocal improvisations* are compositions in which vocal sounds are used, but it is not necessarily expected that these sounds will be words or that the listener will identify words or word meanings.

In most vocal improvisation activities, students should be given an opportunity to explore a limited number of vocal sounds, to select some sounds with which to work, to invent patterns (which may be classified and symbolized with graphic notation), and to organize the patterns into a musical composition. Vocal improvisation activities are especially effective for large groups since everyone can take part. However, small groups or individual students can also create vocal improvisations. With large groups, it is usually necessary to have a "conductor" who makes some of the musical decisions, such as when to begin, when to change from one sound to another, and how loud or how soft the sounds should be. Individual performers still make decisions as to the exact pitches, rhythms, and kinds of sounds to be used in the composition.

After a melody has been created, it can be written down either in traditional notation or with letter names, color codes, or other forms of graphic notation that the students may devise. It is important that children's songs be preserved so that they can be performed on other days and by other students in the classroom. We have seen classrooms in which a notebook of children's original songs is placed in the music center for all children to play and sing.

Name Composition

Middle Grades

Instructional Objectives

1. Students will explore the sound qualities of their own names.
2. Students will invent patterns of pitch, duration, and dynamics using word sounds.
3. Students will organize patterns into a musical composition.

Environment

This activity is designed for a democratic environment. You can work with an entire class, but each student will be creating his or her own composition. Some time will be needed for individual work. No special equipment or materials are necessary. Ten to fifteen minutes should be sufficient for this activity.

Initial Procedures

1. Direct students to say their names out loud three times.
2. Have students repeat their names very softly, then very loudly.
3. Have students say their names very slowly, then as fast as they can.
4. Ask students to repeat their names four times, starting on a low pitch and moving to a higher pitch each time.
5. Ask students to repeat the first sound or syllable of their names three times, then the last sound or syllable three times.
6. Say, "Find a vowel sound in your name and prolong it while I count to ten."
7. Say, "Find a consonant in your name and repeat it five times in rapid succession."
8. Using some of the ideas given above, invite each student to create a composition using his or her name. The composition should
   1. Be about thirty seconds in length
   2. Use both high and low pitches
   3. Use fast and slow sounds
9. Give students about five minutes to work on their compositions and then invite some to perform them for the class.

Extended Procedures

1. Suggest that students notate compositions using the letters that form each sound as well as other graphics that they may devise.

2. Suggest that students reverse the order of sounds in their name for the composition.

3. Create another section based on last names. Combine the two to create a composition in AB form.

Modifications for Exceptional Learners

1. Students with poorly developed language skills or poorly developed work habits may be unable to work alone on this composition. Select one name and work together as a class with either yourself or a student being the "conductor" for the composition.

Evaluation

1. Did students' exploration reflect an understanding of the musical qualities of sound?

2. Did students' exploration reflect an understanding of the sound qualities of words?

3. Did the students' composition contain repetition and variety of timbre, pitch, and duration?

4. Did the students' work demonstrate an understanding of the process of selecting, inventing, and organizing sound?

5. Did the students' work demonstrate confidence in performing with their voice?

Creating an Ensemble for Voices

Upper Grades

Instructional Objectives

1. Students will select words and analyze their sound qualitites.
2. Students will invent a steady beat, a metric beat, and rhythmic patterns from the sounds of words.
3. Students will organize patterns in order to create a three-part composition for voices.

Environment

This experience will begin with your taking an autocratic role, but the environment will become an open one as the students, working in groups of six to nine, explore, invent, and organize their own compositions. Students' familiarity with the concepts of beat, meter, and rhythm of the melody is assumed. No special materials are needed for this activity. Fifteen to twenty minutes should be adequate time.

Initial Experiences

1. Lead the entire class in exploring the sound qualities of several words, perhaps from this week's vocabulary list. Ask, "Which sounds can be sustained? What sounds are explosive? Which sounds are soft? Which sounds can be repeated in rapid succession?"
2. Using a one-syllable word or one sound from a word, establish a steady beat by having several students repeat the sound over and over.

   Pop, Pop, Pop, Pop, Pop, Pop, Pop, Pop, Pop, Pop,

3. Establish a metric accent by having another group of students add another word or sound on every second or third beat.

   Corn   Corn   Corn   Corn
   Pop, Pop, Pop, Pop, Pop, Pop, Pop, Pop, Pop, Pop,

4. Combine several words to form a rhythmic phrase and have still another group of students add it to the other two patterns.

   In the movies munching . . .
   Corn   Corn   Corn
   Pop, Pop, Pop, Pop, Pop, Pop, Pop, Pop, Pop, Pop,

5. Divide the class into groups of six to nine students, having each group work through the process of selecting word sounds, inventing patterns, and organizing them into a composition.
6. Have each group perform their composition for the class.

Extended Procedures

1. Using ideas from the composition itself or contrasting ideas, create an introduction and coda.
2. Change words to nonsense syllables for a more abstract composition.
3. Work toward dynamic contrast within the compositions. Ask, "Where should the sounds get louder? Where should they be very soft?"
4. Using words with contrasting sounds and/or contrasting meanings, create another section. Combine the two making a composition in ABA form.

Modifications for Exceptional Learners

1. Talented students could create a melody using strategies from "Creating a Song" and could sing each part.
2. Select words containing problem sounds in order to provide extended drill for students with speech difficulties.
3. If students are having language difficulties, use their names or other familiar words and analyze them in written form.

Evaluation

1. Did the students' explorations reflect an understanding of the sound qualities of words?
2. Did the composition demonstrate an understanding of steady beat, metric beat, and rhythmic patterns?
3. Were the students able to work together to create the composition and to perform together in ensemble?

COMPOSING WITH TAPE RECORDERS

Until rather recently it was necessary to either remember sound patterns or to learn a rather complicated system of notation in order to manipulate and refine sounds in the compositional process. The tape recorder, however, provides a means for storing sound so that it can be repeated whenever desired. In addition, the tape recorder provides a means for the mechanical manipulation and transformation of sound. By physically cutting, arranging, and splicing sections of tape, students can manipulate the abstract qualities of sound in a concrete way.

We strongly suggest using reel-to-reel tape recorders for most compositional activities. Battery-operated cassettes do have the advantage of being portable, but reel-to-reel recorders usually can be operated at several different speeds. Also, the reel-to-reel tape can be cut and spliced, and the quality of sound reproduction on reel-to-reel is generally better.

It is important that children have skill in operating tape recorders before attempting the compositional activities that we have suggested. Most tape recorders are easy to use and, if operating instructions are followed, are not easily damaged. We suggest that you provide group instruction on the operation of the tape recorder and also fasten a card with operating instructions on each recorder as a reminder to the students.

Because of the potential to amplify sound and change the speed of sound, tape recorders offer the opportunity to explore aspects of sound that cannot be discovered in other ways. An exciting variety of new sound patterns can be invented by combining and manipulating familiar musical and/or environmental sounds. Tape compositions can be organized by either transferring sound from one tape to another or by physically cutting and splicing the tape.

We have pointed out the value of tape recording *all* student compositions as a means for evaluation and refinement. In this section, we will suggest a different use for the tape recorder. In these strategies, the tape recorder becomes a performing instrument, a source of sound for exploration, invention, and organization.

A Sound Collage

Middle Grades

Instructional Objectives

1. Students will select and record three to five sounds from the school environment.
2. Students will analyze the sounds as to timbre, pitch, and duration.
3. Students will organize sounds into a musical composition.

Environment

Although this activity begins with an autocratic environment, most of the activity is carried out in an open environment. Students should work in groups of two or three in collecting and organizing sounds. Battery-operated tape recorders should be available for each group. Twenty to thirty minutes will be needed for this activity; however, the sound organizing could take place on a day following the selection and recording of the sounds.

Initial Procedures

1. Discuss sound and silence as raw materials of music.
2. Sit quietly for forty-five seconds. List and describe the sounds that are heard in terms of timbre, pitch, and duration.
3. Assign groups and distribute tape recorders. Each group is to select and record three to five sounds heard around the school. Each sound excerpt should be fifteen to twenty seconds in length.
4. Provide ten to fifteen minutes for students to collect sounds.
5. Discuss the role of the composer in selecting and organizing sounds. As composers, students need not use all of the sounds they have collected. They may decide to use one sound several times in a composition, and they may also decide to include silence in the composition. A good composition is one with variety and repetition.
6. Provide ten to twelve minutes for students to listen to sounds, select sounds, and decide on an organization for the final composition.
7. Provide an additional tape recorder so that sounds may be transferred to tape in the decided order.
8. Play the final compositions for the entire class.

Extended Procedures

1. Replay the compositions and evaluate them in terms of contrast and variety of timbre, pitch, and duration.

2. Repeat the experience, this time limiting each group to particular classes of sound—sounds of machines, sounds of people, or sounds of glass, for example.

3. Obtain a contact microphone and repeat the experience using "lost sounds," or those that are too soft to hear without amplification.

Modifications for Exceptional Learners

1. Students with experience in working with tape recorders may be able to create interesting effects using "sound-on-sound" echo and reversal recording techniques.

2. Students unable to operate tape recorders should be assigned to teams in which there is a competent "technician."

Evaluation

1. Did students thoughtfully select sounds from the environment?
2. Did students' discussions reveal an understanding of timbre, pitch, and duration?
3. Did students' compositions demonstrate an understanding of musical form?
4. Did students demonstrate a feeling of pride in their compositions?

Tape Loops

Upper Grades

Instructional Objectives

1. Students will explore possibilities for pitch and speed manipulation of sound on the tape recorder.
2. Students will create a two-layer composition using tape loops.

Environment

After receiving initial instructions, students can work in groups of six to eight in an open environment. A reel-to-reel tape recorder and tape splicing materials will be needed. A short poem from the literature or one written by students will form the basis for the composition. Twenty to twenty-five minutes will be necessary for this activity.

Initial Procedures

1. You should demonstrate the process of making tape loops. (See *Music*, Book 5, p. 105.)
2. Review specific instructions and provide task cards for groups working in the music center:
   a) Read the poem several times.
   b) Select one word from the poem that you think is the most important.
   c) Explore different ways of saying that word.
   d) Make a tape loop.
   e) Record the word, saying it several different ways on the loop.
   f) Play the loop at different speeds. Decide which will sound best as an accompaniment to the poem.
3. Replay the loop while one student reads the poem.
4. Repeat the performance, trying the loop at other speeds. Select the one that sounds best and perform the composition for the class.

Extended Procedures

1. Using a second tape recorder, create another loop from either another word phrase or from an instrumental accompaniment in order to add another layer of sound.
2. Turn the loop inside out (shiny side of the tape next to the recording head). With the loop played this way, the sounds will be backwards.

Modifications for Exceptional Learners

1. Students with experience in working with tape recorders may be able to create interesting effects using sound-on-sound or echo techniques.
2. Prepare the loops beforehand for students that may have difficulty splicing tape themselves.

Evaluation

1. Did students' exploration of sound on the tape recorder demonstrate an awareness of pitch changes?
2. Were students able to make tape loops?
3. Did students' composition demonstrate an awareness of simultaneous sounds?

SELF-CHECK: CREATING

1. A creating activity in the classroom implies
   - a) Any musical activity
   - b) Writing notation for new songs
   - c) Selecting, inventing, and organizing patterns of sound
   - d) Playing with objects that make sound

2. Creating activities provide an opportunity for students to develop
   - a) Skills of abstract thinking
   - b) Musical knowledge and skills and general knowledge and skills
   - c) Greater appreciation of all art
   - d) Skills of performing, listening, and writing music

3. The development of skill in creating music
   - a) Is dependent on the students' ability to read musical notation
   - b) Is dependent on the students' musical knowledge
   - c) Is interrelated with the development of musical knowledge
   - d) Is dependent on the students' musical talent

4. A unique contribution of music to human development is
   - a) The development of knowledge of pitch and rhythm
   - b) The development of performing skills
   - c) The development of knowledge about people and events in the world
   - d) The development of knowledge about human feelings

5. Creating activities in the classroom
   - a) Are the responsibility of the classroom teacher
   - b) Are the responsibility of the music specialist
   - c) Are the responsibility of the creative art teacher
   - d) Are shared by the classroom teacher and music specialist

6. To effectively guide creating activities in the classroom
   - a) The teacher must have highly developed skill in creating music
   - b) The teacher must be able to read and write musical notation
   - c) The teacher must be able to play compositions on the piano
   - d) The teacher must establish foundations and set parameters

7. Which of the following was *not* considered to be an important goal for creating activities in the elementary classroom?
   - a) Developing an increasing understanding of melody, rhythm, harmony, dynamics, timbre, and form
   - b) Developing skill in making aesthetic value judgments
   - c) Preparing some students for careers as composers
   - d) Developing the skills of performing, listening, and using musical notation

8. Goals for creating activities in the classroom should be
   - a) Based on an assessment of students' musical needs
   - b) Based on an analysis of musical materials
   - c) Based on the interests and skills of the teacher
   - d) Based on the requirements for becoming a professional composer

9. Assessment of students' musical needs should be made
   - a) Primarily on the basis of observed performance skills
   - b) Primarily on the basis of observed listening skills
   - c) Primarily on the basis of observed creating skills
   - d) On the basis of observed musical behavior in a variety of activities

Key
c
b
c
d
d
d
c
a
d

10. An autocratic environment for creating activities
    a) Would not be effective because the teacher would dominate those activities
    b) Is essential if the teacher is to remain in control of the class
    c) Is acceptable if the teacher directs the process but not the choices that students make
    d) Is acceptable if the teacher directs the choices but not the creative process itself

11. Establishing limits for creating activities
    a) Provides boundaries within which children can create
    b) Will stifle original thinking
    c) May be necessary for younger children but not for older ones
    d) Is the best way for the teacher to maintain classroom control
    e) All of the above

12. Listed below are some teacher behaviors. Indicate the type of environment in which each might be found with A—autocratic; D—democratic; O—open, informal:
    _____ Giving specific directions for inventing sound patterns
    _____ Suggesting alternatives such as "How would it sound played in a lower pitch range?"
    _____ Assisting students in listing sound sources that might be appropriate for a particular composition
    _____ Asking students what could be added to create more tension near the end of the composition
    _____ Asking students to create a composition for water glasses in rondo form
    _____ Listening to students' compositions and asking which part they found to be most exciting

13. Effective classroom management requires
    a) A strong, autocratic teacher
    b) Knowledge of those strategies that give the teacher most control
    c) Knowledge of management techniques used in business and industry
    d) Knowledge of alternative strategies and management techniques

14. Which of the following was *not* considered an effective management technique for creating activities?
    a) Planning parameters within which students are to work
    b) Planning working procedures for the students
    c) Planning for specific aspects of the final product
    d) Recognizing the artistic quality of the students' composition

15. Early experiences in creating melodies should
    a) Use pitches of the major scale
    b) Use pitches of the minor scale
    c) Use nonpitched instruments
    d) Use a limited number (two or three) pitches

16. When creating songs, students should
    a) Begin by exploring word rhythms of the text
    b) Begin by exploring melodic patterns, then add words
    c) Begin by writing notes on staff paper, then play them on the piano to see how they sound
    d) Begin by selecting instruments on which to play accompaniments

17. In creating accompaniments for songs, students should
    a) Play anything they want as the class sings the song
    b) Play patterns given by the teacher but on instruments that they select
    c) Select melodic or rhythmic patterns from the song and organize them to fit with the song
    d) Invent new patterns in a different key or meter than the song

18. Working with environmental sounds such as dripping water
    a) Is more noise making than music making
    b) Is a way to study science of sound but not music
    c) Can be a musical experience if students manipulate and organize sound patterns in an expressive way
    d) Can be a musical experience if students can find a way to notate the sound

19. When planning for instrumental improvisations the teacher should
    a) Provide as many different kinds of instruments as possible
    b) Provide at least one melodic and one rhythmic instrument
    c) Provide at least three different timbres so that students can make some choices
    d) Limit the choices available to those that will enable students to meet the stated objectives of the lesson

20. Vocal improvisation strategies
    a) Can be used with large groups as well as individual students
    b) Generally are more effective with individual students
    c) Are primarily for young students since they enjoy playing with vocal sounds
    d) Are primarily for older students who have well-developed language skills

Key
c
c
d
a

ENABLING ACTIVITIES: CREATING

On your own

1. Spend five minutes each day for a week listening to environmental sounds in your room, in a shopping center, or on campus. Can you identify patterns of pitch, rhythm, timbre, and dynamics?

2. Using strategies suggested in this chapter, create (a) a song, (b) a vocal improvisation, (c) a composition using environmental sounds. Record your composition, listen to it, and analyze it, using the form for analyzing music for listening found on page 258. Play the recording of your composition for a friend and discuss the musical aspects.

3. Listen to recordings of contemporary art music by composers such as Karl Stockhausen, John Cage, and Harry Partch.

4. Attend an art exhibit or study reproductions of modern art.

5. Observe children on a playground or in a shopping center, noting the ways in which they play with sound.

In the schools

1. Observe a creating activity and describe the management techniques used by the teacher.

2. Identify several musical and general goals that were accomplished in the lesson you observed.

3. Observe students engaged in creating activities. Using the checklist on page 284 assess the present level of musical development for two individual students and for the group in general. Suggest future creating activities that may help students develop greater knowledge and skill.

4. Plan and guide a creating activity for a small group of students that will lead to the development of at least one musical and one general learning goal.

5. Plan and guide a creating activity for a large group of students that will lead to the development of at least one musical and one general learning goal.

6. With the help of the cooperating teacher, identify a student with special learning needs. Develop an IEP that will include creating activities as a means for meeting identified learning objectives.

In the library

1. Review the basic elementary music textbooks listed on page 182, noting the teaching strategies and the kinds of notation that have been included for creating activities.

2. Examine the goals for creating activities found in the teachers' editions of basic music textbooks and in state and local music curriculum guides.

3. Examine three or more of the references listed at the end of this chapter in order to gain further competency in guiding creating activities.

In the campus classroom

1. Using strategies suggested in this chapter, create several group compositions. Record, listen to, and evaluate your composition using the form on page 195.

2. Plan and conduct a series of minilessons in which you will guide a small group of your peers in creating activities. In planning your minilessons, use a variety of teaching strategies and several different learning environments.

3. Role-play a situation in which you attempt to convince another teacher that creating experiences should be part of the elementary school curriculum.

4. View one or more of the films suggested at the end of this chapter and discuss the process of selecting, inventing, and organizing sound patterns as demonstrated in the films.

REFERENCES

Benson, Warren. "The Creative Child Could Be Any Child." *Music Educators Journal*, April 1973, p. 38.

Biasini, Americole; Thomas, Ronald; and Pogonowski, Lenore. *MMCP Interaction.* Bardonia, N.Y.: Media Materials, 1972.

Drake, Russell; Herder, Ronald; and Modugno, Anne D. *How to Make Electronic Music.* Pleasantville, N.Y.: Educational Audio Visual, 1975.

Dwyer, Terence. *Composing with Tape Recorders.* London: Oxford University Press, 1971.

Konowitz, Bert. *Music Improvisation as a Classroom Method.* Port Washington, N.Y.: Alfred Publishing Company, 1973.

Paynter, John, and Perter, Aston. *Sound and Silence: Classroom Projects in Creative Music.* Cambridge, Mass.: Cambridge University Press, 1970.

Schafer, R. Murray. *Creative Music Education.* New York: Schirmer Books, 1976.

Thompson, Keith P. "Electronic Music at the Elementary Level." *Music Educators Journal,* March 1978, p. 42.

Vaughan, Margery M. "Cultivating Creative Behavior." *Music Educators Journal,* April 1973, p. 34.

FILMS

"Creating," *Children Are Musicians.* University Park, Pa.: The Pennsylvania State University, 1978 (video cassette).

Discovering Electronic Music. Los Angeles: Bernad Wilets, 1970.

New Sounds in Music. Los Angeles: Churchill Films, 1970.

Song Index